$60 4/16

The

RED GUARD
GENERATION

and

POLITICAL
ACTIVISM
in **CHINA**

Studies of the Weatherhead East Asian Institute, Columbia University

STUDIES OF THE WEATHERHEAD EAST ASIAN INSTITUTE, COLUMBIA UNIVERSITY

The Studies of the Weatherhead East Asian Institute of Columbia University were inaugurated in 1962 to bring to a wider public the results of significant new research on modern and contemporary East Asia.

For a list of titles in this series, see page 263.

The

RED GUARD
GENERATION

and

POLITICAL
ACTIVISM
in **CHINA**

Guobin Yang

COLUMBIA UNIVERSITY PRESS
NEW YORK

Columbia University Press
Publishers Since 1893
New York   Chichester, West Sussex
cup.columbia.edu
Copyright © 2016 Columbia University Press
All rights reserved

Library of Congress Cataloging-in-Publication Data
Names: Yang, Guobin.
Title: The Red Guard generation and political activism in China / Guobin Yang.
Description: New York : Columbia University Press, 2016. | Series: Studies of the
    Weatherhead East Asian Institute, Columbia University | Includes bibliographical
    references and index.
Identifiers: LCCN 2015039845 | ISBN 9780231149648 (cloth : acid-free paper) |
    ISBN 9780231520485 (e-book)
Subjects: LCSH: Chongqing (China)—Politics and government—20th century. | Hong
    wei bing—History—20th century. | Hong wei bing—Biography. | Political activists—
    China—Chongqing—Interviews. | Social movements—China—Chongqing—History—
    20th century. | Youth—Political activity—China—Chongqing—History—20th century. |
    Political violence—China—Chongqing—History—20th century. | Interviews—China—
    Chongqing. | Urban-rural migration—Political aspects—China—History—20th
    century. | China—History—Cultural Revolution, 1966–1976.
Classification: LCC DS796.C59257 Y36 | DDC 951/.38—dc23
LC record available at http://lccn.loc.gov/2015039845

To Lan and Jeff

CONTENTS

NOTES ON DATA

THIS BOOK IS BASED on the analysis of three types of primary data collected over a period of almost twenty years. These are historical documents, retrospective documents, and interviews and life histories. Most of the interviews were conducted in 1998 and 1999 for my doctoral dissertation at New York University, which was completed in 2000. Since then, large volumes of new collections of Red Guard publications, memoirs, and scholarly monographs have become available, which I have made full use of. I also made new research trips to China, especially a trip to Chongqing in the winter of 2009 for archival research. Additional interviews were also conducted.

HISTORICAL DOCUMENTS

My analysis of the Red Guard movement is based on Red Guard publications produced during the movement and official newspapers of that period. I examined all 148 volumes of Red Guard newspaper reprints now available. These are:

- *Hong wei bing zi liao* [Red Guard publications]. 20 vols. Oakton, VA: Center for Chinese Research Materials, 1975.
- *Hong wei bing zi liao xu bian yi* [Red Guard publications supplement 1]. 8 vols. Oakton, VA: Center for Chinese Research Materials, 1980.
- *Hong wei bing zi liao xu bian* er [Red Guard publications supplement 2]. 8 vols. Oakton, VA: Center for Chinese Research Materials, 1992.

- *Xin bian hong wei bing zi liao* [A new collection of Red Guard publications]. 20 vols., ed. Zhou Yuan. Oakton, VA: Center for Chinese Research Materials, 1999.
- *Xin bian hong wei bing zi liao II* [A new collection of Red Guard publications, part 2: a special compilation of newspapers in Beijing area]. 40 vols., ed. Yongyi Song. Oakton, VA: Center for Chinese Research Materials, 2001.
- *Xin bian hong wei bing zi liao III* [A new collection of Red Guard publications, part 3: a comprehensive compilation of tabloids in the provinces]. 52 vols., ed. Yongyi Song. Oakton, VA: Center for Chinese Research Materials, 2005.

In addition, I also made use of the Cultural Revolution electronic database edited by Yongyi Song in 2002.

For the Red Guard movement in Chongqing, I studied local archives in the fabulous Chongqing Library, which had gazettes of each district of the city and some factories, schools, and universities. Although many of these archives were not open to the public at the time of my visit in 2009, I was fortunate enough to gain access through the introduction of friends in Chongqing.

In addition, I consulted several hundred unpublished diaries and notebooks from the 1950s and 1960s among the Cultural Revolution Diaries, part of the East Asian Collection of the University of Melbourne Library, and the *Yang Zhichao: Chinese Bible* collection of the Sherman Contemporary Art Foundation in Sydney curated by Dr. Claire Roberts.

Historical materials for the sent-down experiences include letters, diaries, poems, songs, and other works produced by sent-down youth during the period. Many of these were published in the decades since the end of the sent-down campaign. They are not listed in the bibliography unless they are cited.

The April Fifth movement, the Democracy Wall movement, and the democratic elections in universities in 1980 yielded many movement documents. The most comprehensive document collection of the Democracy Wall movement was the *Ta lu ti hsia k'an wu hui pien* (Collection of mainland underground publications), published in Taipei between 1980 and 1984 in twenty volumes. Documents for the democratic elections in 1980 have been collected in *Kaituo—Beida xueyun wenxian*, edited by Hu Ping and Wang Juntao and published in 1990.

RETROSPECTIVE DOCUMENTS

These include book-length memoirs and short essays in collected volumes. Numerous memoirs about the Cultural Revolution are published in English and Chinese. I have mainly used Chinese-language rather than English-language memoirs, because English memoirs target specific kinds of audiences and have been subject to much critique. See, for example, Kong, "Swan and Spider Eater in Problematic Memoirs of Cultural Revolution" and Zarrow, "Meanings of China's Cultural Revolution: Memoirs of Exile."

The study of factionalism in Chongqing is greatly facilitated by the many memoirs written by former rebel leaders and published in recent years outside of China. These include memoirs by Huang Lian, Huang Ronghua, Huang Zhaoyan, Li Musen, Li Zhengquan, Yang Zengtai, and Zhou Ziren. I have also read many of the memoirs by former rebels and Red Guards in other parts of the country, such as Beijing, Shanghai, and Hunan. These are not listed in the bibliography unless they are cited.

The sent-down experiences are the subject of numerous volumes of retrospective essays published in collected volumes. I have a personal collection of over fifty volumes that were published in 1998 alone on the thirtieth anniversary of the beginning of the sent-down movement.[1] Many more volumes have been published since 1998.

Since 2008, two online journals, *Remembrance* and *Yesterday*, have generated large volumes of both historical and retrospective documents about the Maoist era—well over ten thousand pages as of March 2015—which I have made use of.

INTERVIEWS AND LIFE HISTORIES

In 1998 and 1999 I conducted thirty-five interviews with former Red Guards and sent-down youth for this project, mostly in Beijing, a few in New York with exiled activists. Since 2009, when I started revising and rewriting this book, I have conducted nine more individual interviews and one focus group interview. These interviews were used to gain insights into the subjective experience of the social actors; they are supplementary to primary historical documents.

Finally, I compiled many life histories based on published materials. These include the life histories of 248 sent-down youth and 122 activists in the Democracy Wall movement. Information for these life histories is not always complete. For example, for the 122 Democracy Wall activists, I have age information for only 47 of them. Nonetheless, these life histories provide useful supplementary information to the historical documents I have used for this study.

ACKNOWLEDGMENTS

MANY PEOPLE HELPED TO bring this long overdue book to completion. I want to thank Craig Calhoun for his mentorship and support from the very beginning. Without his vision, guidance, and inspiration, this book would not have been written. And thank you to Pam DeLargy for your kindness and care for me and my family.

Judith Blau, Judith Farquhar, Jeff Goodwin, Guang Guo, Doug Guthrie, Hyun Ok Park, Steven Pfaff, and Gang Yue helped from early on. Over the years I have benefited from the works on the Chinese Cultural Revolution by many scholars, including Joel Andreas, Michel Bonnin, Anita Chan, Arif Dirlik, Roderick MacFarquhar, Barbara Mittler, Elizabeth Perry, Stanley Rosen, Michael Schoenhals, Tang Shaojie, Jonathan Unger, Andrew Walder, Shaoguang Wang, Lynn White III, Xu Youyu, and Yin Hongbiao.

Many others are vital sources of support and inspiration through their work or friendship. They are Xiaomei Chen, Deborah Davis, Presenjit Duara, Tom Gold, Michael Hechter, Jiang Hong (Beijing), Ching Kwan Lee, Lianjiang Li, Daniel Little, Xinmin Liu, Michael McQuarrie, Kelly Moore, Kevin O'Brien, Ban Wang, Gungwu Wang, Jeffrey Wasserstrom, Lanjun Xu, Enhua Zhang, Zhang Kangkang, and Gilda Zwerman.

Some of the ideas in chapter 1 of the book were first explored in a paper written for a conference organized by Alexander Cook at the University of California-Berkeley and later published in *Mao's Little Red Book: A Global History* (Cambridge University Press, 2014), which Alex edited. I thank Alex and Cambridge University Press for permission to use this material. Chapter 2 was presented at a conference organized by Chris Berry, Sun Peidong, and

Patricia Thornton for the *China Quarterly* and then at the University of New South Wales in Australia at the invitation of Professors Wanning Sun and Haiqing Yu. My 2015 trip to Australia was also greatly facilitated by Gerry Groot, who made me the keynote speaker at the fourteenth convention of the Chinese Studies Association of Australia. Of course, my dear friends Nick Jose and Claire Roberts made that trip more than about conferences and research. Chapter 3 was presented in a talk I gave at the International Center for Studies of Chinese Civilization in Fudan University. Chapter 5 was presented at the University Seminar on Modern China at Columbia University and later at the Department of Sociology of the New School in New York. I thank the organizers of all these events for their invitations and the participants for sharing their responses and insights. Some of the material in chapter 7 first appears in my article, "China's Zhiqing Generation: Nostalgia, Identity, and Cultural Resistance in the 1990s," published in *Modern China* 29, no. 3 (July 2003): 267–96. I would like to acknowledge my indebtedness to the journal and its editor Kathryn Bernhardt.

I have been fortunate enough to have had the support of wonderful colleagues in multiple institutions while I worked on parts of this book. At the University of Hawaii at Manoa, I want to especially thank Kiyoshi Ikeda, David Johnson, Hagen Koo, Fred Lau, Patricia Steinhoff, Eldon Wegner, and Ming-bao Yue. At Barnard College and Columbia University, I was most deeply indebted to Rachel McDermott and to Myron Cohen, Eyal Gil, Carol Gluck, Robert Hymes, Dorothy Ko, Eugenia Lean, Lydia Liu, Xiaobo Lü, Debra Minkoff, Andrew Nathan, David Weiman, and Madeline Zelin. The students in my seminars on the Chinese Cultural Revolution were a great inspiration. One of them, Rime Shuangyun Sun, kindly gave me permission to use her long interview with her parents.

At the University of Pennsylvania, I would like to mention especially the support from Charles Bosk, Michael delli Carpini, Randall Collins, Jacques deLisle, Avery Goldstein, David Grazian, Emily Hannum, Grace Kao, Marwan Kraidy, Klaus Krippendorff, Annette Lareau, Carolyn Marvin, Emilio Parrado, Monroe Price, Barbie Zelizer, and Tukufu Zuberi. Special thanks are due to the many talented doctoral students at Penn, but especially to Rosemary Clark, Jasmine Erdener, Elisabetta Ferrari, Leslie Jones, and Bo Mai for offering comments on parts of this book, assisting with the formatting of notes and bibliography, or simply sharing their passion and energy.

Numerous individuals in China helped me with my research by accepting my interviews or providing crucial contacts or research resources. My research in Beijing was greatly facilitated by sociologists Shen Yuan and Dai Jianzhong and former sent-down youth Wang Dawen, Wang Si, and Yan Yushuang. My research in Chongqing would not have been possible without He Shu's help, about whom I will have more to say in chapter 7. In Shanghai I was fortunate to find support from such superb Cultural Revolution scholars as Jin Dalu in the Shanghai Academy of Social Sciences and Jin Guangyao and Sun Peidong at Fudan University.

I am deeply indebted to scholars and librarians in the archives, libraries, and museums around the world. Yongyi Song not only makes available numerous volumes of Red Guard newspapers to researchers through his editorial work but is always responsive to my queries about sources. Sincere thanks are due to Chengzhi Wang at the C. V. Starr East Asian Library of Columbia University, Nancy Hearst at the H. C. Fung Library of the Fairbank Center for Chinese Studies, Gao Qi at the University Services Center of the Chinese University of Hong Kong, and Sharon Black and Min Zhong at the library of the Annenberg School of Communication at the University of Pennsylvania. Chen Chen and Susan Millard at the University of Melbourne kindly opened their special collection of Cultural Revolution diaries to me, even when their reading room was closed for renovation. Claire Roberts made special arrangements with Sherman Contemporary Art Foundation in Sydney for me to study the diaries in the stunning "China Bible" exhibition she curated.

Anne Routon, my editor at Columbia University Press, deserves my profound thanks for regularly, but always ever so gently, nudging me to finish the book. I cannot say how grateful I am to Anne for her faith in this project. And to Susan Pensak, my manuscript and production editor at the press, I am indebted for her superb editing work and for keeping the production on schedule.

My parents and siblings gave me unfailing long-distance moral support, as well as practical help when I did my field research in China. When he was in college, Jeff once wandered into the middle of my Cultural Revolution seminar to my pleasant surprise. I hope he will find in this book something to surprise him as well. Despite my routine absent-mindedness over the many years in writing this book, Lan has been my strongest champion and supporter. This book is dedicated to Jeff and Lan.

The
RED GUARD GENERATION

and

POLITICAL ACTIVISM

in CHINA

INTRODUCTION

TUCKED AWAY IN A hidden corner of Shapingba Park in the city of Chongqing is a little-known cemetery, which buried about 400 young people who were killed in the armed battles of the Red Guard movement in 1967 and 1968. Among the 196 dead with available age information, 69 were below twenty and 66 of them were between twenty-one and thirty. The youngest was a fourteen-year-old girl. On their tombstones were inscriptions such as "Born great, died in glory" or "Long live revolutionary martyrs!"[1]

In 1980, the twenty-four year-old poet Gu Cheng published a poem dedicated to those buried in this Cultural Revolution graveyard. The poem captures in a touching personal tone the tragedy of the political idealism of an entire generation. It has the following lines:

Everyone knows
it was the Sun who led you
off
to the tunes of a few marching songs,
in search of Paradise.
Later, halfway there
you got tired,
tripped over a bed
whose frame was inlaid with bullet holes and stars
It seemed as if
you had just played a game
and everything could start all over again.[2]

For those buried there, the game would never start over. For the vast majority who survived, the same game would not start again either. History had other things—other games—in store for them.

What made these young people, who could have been classmates, schoolmates, lovers, neighbors, or fellow factory workers, willingly engage in deadly factional warfare at the cost of their own lives? Decades of painstaking scholarship have illuminated the political and sociological conditions of these factional battles, yet scholarly views continue to be divided.

My first goal in writing this book is to bring a new perspective to the understanding of Red Guard radicalism in the 1960s. Yet instead of ending my account with Red Guard radicalism, my second goal is to use it as the starting point for tracing the longer-term biography of the Red Guard generation from the 1960s to the present. In the course of my research, it became clear to me that the biography of the Red Guard generation is also a history of political culture and political protest in modern China. History and biography are so deeply intertwined that an analysis of one cannot be separated from the other. Thus, my third goal is to offer an account of the transformation of the political culture and political protest in the People's Republic of China. An exhaustive treatment of these three questions is beyond the scope of a single book. I have therefore adopted some analytical strategies to translate my three central concerns into manageable questions while trying to strike some balance between breadth and detail, generality and texture.

First, to understand factional violence in the Red Guard movement, chapter 1 offers a case study of Chongqing, which witnessed some of the most violent factional fighting in the country in the rambunctious 1967–68 period. The Chongqing case shows most starkly that a political culture that had consecrated the Chinese communist revolutionary tradition significantly influenced factionalism and the escalation of violence. It did so by making revolution a sacred script for youth of the Cultural Revolution to follow and enact. Despite significant regional differences, the central features of the Chongqing case may be found in other cities, suggesting that the causes of factional violence in Chongqing were not unique to the city, but had to do with the influences of forces in Chinese society at large.[3]

Chapter 2 broadens the scope of the analysis to examine how and why the political culture of the 1950s and early 1960s could have had such powerful influences on the Red Guard generation. While multiple factors combined to produce the effects, the central condition was the sacralization of the Chinese communist revolutionary tradition and the deliberate and sustained media campaigns to cultivate Chinese youth into revolutionary successors. This political culture worked, and could only have worked, under specific historical circumstances. These circumstances constituted the social world of the Red Guards and rebels, a world, as I will show, of enchantment and danger in the cold war context. Methodologically, as I move beyond factional violence to analyze political culture, dissent, and the sent-down and other movements that followed, this and the subsequent chapters also move beyond Chongqing.

Chapter 3 surveys the broad landscape of Red Guard dissent from 1966 to 1968 and argues that besides a commitment to revolutionary practice, a small minority of Red Guards and rebels were actively performing revolutionary theorizing. Just as factional violence was the result of practical revolutionary action, so dissent was ironically the outcome of theoretical revolutionary action. This chapter shows that the same myth of revolution that fired Red Guard passions for revolutionary practice, and led to violence, also drove their passion for revolutionary theory. And it was in the pursuit of revolutionary theory and in attempting to apply this theory to the analysis of Chinese reality that some young people began to entertain and express ideas of dissent. The proliferation of Red Guard newspapers, wall posters, leaflets, and other publications inadvertently provided the media spaces for expressing dissent, just as factional rivalry called for, and were intensified by, a war of words.

One of the key ideas of Red Guard dissent centered on the privileges of family origin. Not surprisingly, the supporters of theories of family origin were children of cadres (*gan bu zi di*) while their critics were children of ordinary families (*ping min zi di*). This chapter shows that a wide divide between the offspring of these two different types of families (*gan bu zi di* versus *ping min zi di*) surfaced in 1966–1968 in the starkest of ways and that the most sophisticated political dissent was a systematic attack against the caste system implicit in the class policies of the Chinese communist party. This was the same divide that would emerge today between ordinary Chinese and the offspring of Chinese communist leaders, now often called the "princelings" (*tai zi dang*) or "second-generation reds" (*hong er dai*), a question I will return to in the conclusion of this book.

Chapters 4 and 5 cover a longer time span, from about 1968 to about 1979, and follow the trajectories of the Red Guard generation through their years as sent-down youth. Historical circumstances decisively taught youth of the Red Guard generation that their role as characters in the grand historical drama of an imagined revolution had come to a close. With the end of that drama, the script that had guided their thinking and actions lost much of its magic. Thrust into changing circumstances, they would have to learn new life scripts—new outlooks, new values, and new moral frameworks. Chapter 4 reviews the history of the sent-down campaign and shows that the new scripts they gradually learned in their daily labor as sent-down youth contradicted and further eroded the scripts that had guided them in the Red Guard movement. In contrast to the values of the "good life" of revolution, they came to affirm the values of ordinary life and developed new understandings of "personal interest," "class enemy," and "the people" – indeed, of the meaning of life.

Chapter 5 shows that, during the sent-down period, members of the Red Guard generation were engaged in an underground cultural movement, which consisted of an amalgam of semiopen, underground, or surreptitious cultural activities. On the production side, there was the writing of letters, diary, poems, songs, political essays, short stories, and novels. On the reception side, the movement was about the reading, copying, and circulation of forbidden books and unpublished manuscripts, about singing, storytelling, and listening to foreign radio stations. I argue that the meaning of the underground cultural movement lies in its practices of transgression and self-cultivation. In contrast to the "high" political culture of the Red Guard period, the underground culture desacralized the revolutionary culture of the earlier period and articulated a new sense of self and society through miscellaneous forms of self-writing.

Chapter 6 studies the wave of protest activities toward the end of the Cultural Revolution era, starting with the April Fifth movement in 1976 and ending with the democratic campus elections (xiao yuan xuan ju) unrest in 1980. It argues that this new protest wave was both a radical reversal of the Red Guard movement and a precursor to the student protests in 1989. As such, it represented a crucial new turning point both in the trajectory of the Red Guard generation and in the history of modern China. Insofar as the 1976–1980 protest wave marked an emergence from a historical nonage and a farewell to idolatry, it inaugurated a new era of enlightenment in modern Chinese history.

Chapter 7 studies the memories of the Cultural Revolution from the beginning of the reform era to the present. It shows that the Cultural Revolution is remembered selectively, its history broken and fragmented. A decisive factor in shaping the memories of the Cultural Revolution is the same class line, albeit sometimes in different masks, that was the locus of political struggle between "old Red Guards" (*lao bing*) and rebels in 1966. Post-CR memories are a field of contestation between the same forces that were at war in the Cultural Revolution, suggesting that the history of contemporary China may be read as a continuation of the history of the Cultural Revolution.

Throughout this book, I use such terms as *trajectories, journey,* and *life course* to talk about the history of the Red Guard generation. These words may convey a sense of linear progress, as if, from the time of birth, members of the Red Guard generation were destined to march toward a clear, fixed, and grand goal. For much of their youth, that was indeed the horizon and limit of their imagination. But this book is not an exercise in teleology. On the contrary, I hope it will demonstrate fully the tragic consequences of such teleologies for the protagonists of my book. By analyzing the longer history of the Red Guard generation, which will highlight the many ups and downs of the generation, I hope this book will show the futility of grand teleological perspectives for understanding history. There is neither linearity nor teleology to the trajectory of the Red Guard generation, or perhaps other political generations in other times and places.

Ultimately, as I will argue in the conclusion, the historical transformation of the Red Guard generation was full of paradoxes. For the protagonists of my story, the history of a generation was nothing less than a history of perpetual disruption of personal lives. Yet remarkably, amidst these endless disruptions, they retain a sense of optimism and hope up to the present day.

In what follows I will first discuss why I use the term the *Red Guard generation* and who belongs to it. Then I will review the state of art in the study of the Chinese Cultural Revolution and outline my theoretical approach.

DEFINING THE RED GUARD GENERATION

According to Karl Mannheim's sociology of generations, a sociological generation comes into being through shared historical experiences. Among members of a generation, as Mannheim puts it, "a concrete bond is created . . . by their being exposed to the social and intellectual symptoms of a process of dynamic de-stabilization."[4] Thus the same age cohort may produce different sociological generations if it is exposed to different historical experiences. Within a generation, different "generational units" may be differentiated due to differences in social location.[5]

The Red Guard generation refers to members of the age cohort born around 1949 who experienced the Red Guard movement. This was the first age cohort raised and educated after the founding of the People's Republic of China. Its most significant formative experiences were the Red Guard movement. The core of this generation, totaling about 10 million, was in middle school in 1965 on the eve of the Cultural Revolution. If we count the elementary school population in 1965, which was less likely to be directly involved in Red Guard activities, but not unlikely to be sent down, then the number reaches 120 million.[6] The Red Guard generation also included students in colleges and universities in 1966–1968, which numbered at 674,000 in 1965. Xu Youyu estimates that the total size of the Red Guard generation was between 10 and 30 million.[7]

At least two generational units may be identified within this generation—those that experienced only the Red Guard movement and those that experienced both the Red Guard movement and the sent-down movement. Most students in colleges in 1966–1968 did not experience the sent-down movement. Students in junior and senior high schools (or middle schools) in 1966–1968, however, experienced both. This second demographic group was by far the larger of the two generational units in sheer numbers. Often called the "old three classes" (lao san jie), it also has a more distinct generational identity than the first group. For the most part, however, my study of the Red Guard generation comprises both groups without treating them separately. Many youth who were sent down in the second part of the 1970s were too young to have experienced the Red Guard movement; strictly speaking, they do not belong to the Red Guard generation.

The Red Guard generation has variously been called the lost generation,[8] the thinking generation,[9] the disillusioned generation,[10] the zhiqing generation,[11] the lao san jie,[12] the Red Guard generation,[13] and the Cultural Revolution generation. I use Red Guard generation, because this term captures the first major transformative event of this generation, the Red Guard movement. To be sure, the same generation also experienced the sent-down movement and is often called the "educated-youth" or sent-down generation. Yet, as a formative experience, the Red Guard movement was the first and decisive watershed in its history. I have chosen not to use the term Cultural Revolution generation because there is no consensus among scholars as to the exact periodization of the Cultural Revolution. Chinese official historiography considers the Cultural Revolution a ten-year disaster lasting from 1966 to 1976.[14] While many scholars follow this convention, others contend that the Cultural Revolution lasted only from 1966 to 1969, a periodization that coincides with the Red Guard movement.[15]

The term *Red Guard movement* is used here by convention more than with precision. I use it to refer to the three years from May 1966 to July 1968, even though it may be more precise to speak of the period from May to October in 1966 as the Red Guard movement and the later stage as the *zaofanpai*, or rebel, movement. When the children from elite cadre families in Beijing first launched the Red Guard movement, they expressed a clear sense of ownership—that the movement was theirs and that only students who met their criteria could join Red Guard organizations. Those who did not meet their criteria were not only excluded but could also become the target of their attacks. In this sense, the Red Guard movement was their way of showing that they were the true heirs of the Chinese communist revolution. In contrast, the rebels who gradually dominated the Red Guard movement after October 1966 often identified themselves as zaofanpai rather than "red guards," a distinction that former rebels still maintain today.

In a broad sense, China's Red Guard generation may be viewed as part of a global 1960s generation. Almost everywhere, from France to the United States to Brazil,[16] this generation found itself in the middle of radical social movements. There was mutual awareness among youth revolutionaries in different nations, and to all of them, Mao and the Chinese Cultural Revolution offered new ways of imagining the world. Although my book focuses exclusively on the trajectories of the Chinese Red Guard generation, I hope that a recognition of the global context of youth agitation in the 1960s will help to avert making China's Red Guard generation appear too exceptional, however extraordinary the generation's trajectory might be. Even their violent performances of a revolution, studied in chapter 1, are not so unique as to be without international parallels. As Richard Wolin notes, Italy's Red Brigades and Germany's Red Army both "embraced the (erroneous) Marxist view that bourgeois democracy and fascism were natural political bedfellows" in their strategy of using violence to "unmask" the fascist character of the state, whereas, in France, "from the outset the Maoists had *emulated* [my emphasis] the comportment of the disciplined, professional revolutionaries vaunted in Lenin's *What Is to Be Done?*"[17]

TWO LEVELS OF ANALYSIS

The long-term trajectory of the Red Guard generation presents several analytical difficulties. Theories for explaining the Red Guard movement, for example, may not be as applicable to the sent-down campaign. And studying these major historical events is different from studying the memories of the generation in the twenty-first century. My analysis is thus conducted at two levels.

First, at the general level, this book studies the transformation of the first political generation that came of age in the People's Republic. I conceptualize the trajectories of the Red Guard generation as a ritual process lasting from birth around 1949 all the way to the present. In this process, the Red Guard movement was a decisive liminal event, and what came later were different forms of reaggregation and routinization, as well as varieties of new beginnings and new liminal events.

In Victor Turner's anthropology of the ritual process, the liminal is the second phase of a three-stage ritual process. The first stage separates the ritual subject from previous structural conditions. The second stage, the liminal, is antistructural, where the ritual subject redefines his or her identity under conditions that have "few or none of the attributes of the past or coming state."[18] The final stage of aggregation marks the subject's settling back into society. The process of reaggregation may also be considered as one of routinization according to Max Weber's sociology of charisma and routinization. The transformation of China's Red Guard generation thus has two central analytical components. One is the "ritual" practices in the liminal stage, the other is the stage of routinization.

Second, and at the more concrete level, I identify and analyze specific events within the protracted ritual process. The analysis in the individual chapters takes place at this concrete level (but without neglecting the broader framework) and draws on theories and concepts about the specific issues dealt with in the individual chapters. Thus the study of factional violence in chapter 1 is informed less by theories of the ritual process and more directly by theories of social movements and collective violence, especially theories of performance for explaining collective action. Similarly, the analysis in chapter 2 draws on theories of embodied memory and the invented tradition in explaining how political culture shaped Red Guard behavior, while later chapters introduce still other concepts appropriate for my analysis.

The Red Guard movement being the most crucial event in the shaping of the Red Guard generation, I use most of the remaining space in this introduction to discuss the scholarship in this area and outline my own analytical perspective. At the end of this introduction, I return to the notion of routinization and briefly outline the trajectories of the Red Guard generation in the decades after the Red Guard movement.

STUDIES OF THE RED GUARD MOVEMENT

The Red Guard movement occupies a central place both in the life course of the Red Guard generation and in the history of popular protest in modern China. Since studies of it are often mixed with studies of the Cultural Revolution, my review will include both types of works.

An earlier tradition studies the Cultural Revolution from the perspective of political culture,[19] but, as Lowell Dittmer points out, these studies tend to conceive of political culture as a conservative force resistant to change, "functioning to reinforce the persistence and equilibrium of the system."[20] Reconceptualizing political culture as a system of symbols rather than values, Dittmer examines how participants in the Cultural Revolution used symbols to inform and guide their action. He argues that the bipolar structure of political symbolism, of good versus evil and light versus darkness, both legitimated the expression of popular grievances *and* unleashed tendencies toward polarization and anarchy. His analysis, however, focuses on the interactions between elites and the masses without differentiating either or showing how political symbolism affected factionalism.

Mao's role in the Cultural Revolution was an elephant in the room. While some scholars continue to emphasize Mao's role,[21] others turn to the social origins of factionalism. Studies of factionalism in Guangzhou middle schools find that Red Guards and rebels were divided along the lines of class interests formed prior to the Cultural Revolution.[22] Perry's and Li's study of labor factionalism in Shanghai finds three different modes of activism (rebellion, conservatism, and economism) and explains each mode by emphasizing one of three factors—psychocultural, social network, and social interest.[23] The linguistic and rhetorical dimensions of the Cultural Revolution have also attracted some attention, although these aspects are seldom tied directly to factional violence.[24]

In his study of the Cultural Revolution at Tsinghua University, Andreas shifts attention from factionalism to unity by asking what united a rebel movement consisting of individuals with weak organizational ties such that it could overturn the entrenched power of local party organizations. His answer is that the rebel movement derived its power from charismatic mobilization. Andreas's insightful study, however, may have overestimated the unity of the rebel movement and the clarity and coherence of the charismatic mobilization efforts. In fact, in most provinces, after overthrowing local authorities in the "power seizure" in early 1967, the rebel movement split from within itself. Two rival factions grew out of the same rebel faction, and the most violent phase of the Red Guard movement was between these new rivalries.[25] This factional violence is similarly not the focus of Yiching Wu's recent book. Focusing on bottom-up grievances and discontent, Wu views the protests in the Red Guard movement as expressions of a longing for equality and democracy, without considering the causes of rampant violence between rebel factions.[26]

Rejecting social explanations, Andrew Walder proposes a political explanation. In his prolific studies of factionalism in universities in Beijing and Nanjing, Walder argues that what mattered was not class interest or family origins, but the choices people made under the uncertain conditions of the initial period in June 1966. He finds that individuals in similar structural positions often made opposed choices because of the ambiguity of the contexts and the political signals from above, and the different choices they made bound them to antagonistic factions.[27]

Together, these theories have significantly contributed to our understanding of the complexities of the Red Guard movement and the Cultural Revolution. The question of faith and belief, as well as their associated passion, however, is understudied. Yet, as Michael Dutton writes of the violence inflicted on the "enemy within" in Chinese revolutionary history, "the excesses are, in the main, not the result of nonbelief—the cynical deployment of smoke screens to hide true egoistic intentions which usually relate to the gaining or maintaining of power—but are produced as an effect of believing in the cause too much. In this way moral zealousness expresses itself in a semiotics of tyranny."[28] In the conceptual language I will adopt in this book, as I will explain, this amounts to saying that the moral zealousness of the Red Guards and rebels performed itself in a drama of revolutionary violence.

THEORIES OF COLLECTIVE VIOLENCE

Collective violence encompasses a great variety, from brawls and duels to looting, riots, and violence in revolutionary situations. In the field of social movements and contentious politics, collective violence refers to "those repertoires of collective action that involve great physical force and cause damage to an adversary to impose political aims"[29] Collective violence has a distinctly political character and is therefore sometimes referred to as political violence.[30] Patricia Steinhoff and Gilda Zwerman define political violence as "deeply contested actions, events, and situations that have political aims and involve some degree of physical force."[31]

Charles Tilly outlines a relational approach to collective violence, arguing that the combination of a small number of relational mechanisms such
as brokerage and boundary activation can explain all the main types of collective violence from violent rituals to brawls and duels.[32] The relational
approach, however, underestimates the role of ideas, emotions, and ideology in collective violence. As Jeff Goodwin puts it, a preference for relations
over ideas is problematic, because "the possibility that social interactions
might themselves be structured and shaped by cultural beliefs, habits, and
'structures of feeling' is largely ignored."[33] Donatella della Porta similarly di-
rects attention to the "mediating processes through which people attribute
meaning to events and interpret situations," although she also stresses the
role of state repression.[34]

While Tilly opts for a relational approach, he did not reject the role of
ideas. In fact, Tilly acknowledged his teacher Barrington Moore's insights
about how religious ideas of purity led to violence. The centrality of ideas
and ideology is evident in studies of a broad spectrum of historical phenomena, from revolutions and nationalism to religious and ethnic violence, student radicalism, and terrorism.[35]

Richard Drake's study of left- and right-wing terrorism in the Italy of the
1970s shows the power of ideological beliefs behind those radical movements
and traces their roots to the 1960s. Drake writes about one of the founders of
the Red Brigades in Italy, Alberto Franceschini, who, in his memoir, *Mara, Re-
nato e io,* emphasizes his ideological itinerary, beginning with the communist
indoctrination he had received as a young boy:

> The fabled exploits of Gramsci, Togliatti, Lenin, and Stalin took the place of
> fairy tales in the Franceschini home. His grandfather, one of the first in Reggio
> Emilia to join the PCI, had fought as a partisan in World War II and never forgave
> Khrushchev for de-Stalinizing Communism. Alberto took his political bearings
> from this adored grandfather. As a young man in the 1960s, he moved from the in-
> creasingly mainstream Communist party to the outer fringes of the extraparlia-
> mentary left. Franceschini believed he was keeping faith with communism's true
> Bolshevik traditions by modernizing them to meet the needs of contemporary
> Italy's revolutionary situation. In helping to found the Red Brigades, Franceschini
> hoped to participate in a new Resistance, one that would finish the work of re-
> generating Italy left undone by the partisans of 1943–1945. All the Red Brigadists,
> he wrote, were "drug addicts of a particular type, of ideology. A murderous drug,
> worse than heroin."[36]

Works on nationalism show that sacred categories like the nation could inspire collective violence. Benedict Anderson argues that nationalism arose at a time when religion was on the decline. Thus the nation took the place of the divine in the imagination of the people. The willingness to kill and die for the nation was a willingness to sacrifice for the sake of the divine.[37] Carolyn Marvin and David Ingle argue that American patriotism is a civil religion organized around a sacred flag, whose followers engage in periodic blood sacrifice of their own children to unify the group.[38] The violent side of modern nationalism is thus inseparable from its sacred character. Indeed, in René Girard's work on violence and early religions, violence is identical with the sacred. It is through violence that the sacred is engendered. The category of the sacred demands sacrifice.[39] The relationship between the sacred and violence is also examined in John Hall's comprehensive study of apocalyptic violence. He finds that both religious and secular movements had an apocalyptic character. Puritans and Jacobins alike treated violence as a sacred vehicle in their fervor to build a kingdom of God on earth. Although Hall finds a great variety of the apocalyptic from the ancient world to the present, his book suggests that the apocalyptic imagination, and the violence that comes from it, is a universal category.[40]

Also affirming the centrality of the sacred in collective violence, Mark Juergensmeyer's study of terrorism emphasizes the symbolic and performance character of violence. He argues that religious terrorism is not just tactics, but rather, "like religious ritual or street theater, they are dramas designed to have an impact on the several audiences that they affect."[41] The scripts for this performative violence are none other than sacred religious texts about cosmic war.

Stuart Kaufman develops a theory of symbolic politics to explain ethnic violence. By symbolic politics, he refers to "any sort of political activity focused on arousing emotions rather than addressing interests."[42] The core assumption of symbolic politics is that "people choose by responding to the most emotionally potent symbol evoked."[43] The most potent symbols, such as national flags, sacred temples, and certain social values, have a mythic and sacred quality. Although Kaufman analyzes the role of elites and opportunities, ultimately he maintains that mythic hatreds and fears are sufficient to produce violence.

The divide between what Tilly calls the "relation people" and the "idea people" is a variation of the objectivism and subjectivism dichotomy much critiqued in social theory.[44] A cluster of theoretical articulations hinging on the notions of performance, practice, ritual, and cultural pragmatics in developments in cultural sociology offers promising ways of bridging the divide.[45] A theory of performance built on the assumption of social action as meaningful action oriented to an audience integrates relations and ideas into one coherent model, which I will outline in the following section.

A PERFORMANCE THEORY OF COLLECTIVE VIOLENCE

The dramaturgical approach in sociological analysis comes from a simple idea, captured in a Shakespearean monologue beginning with the lines "All the world's a stage, / And all the men and women merely players." By comparing social activities to dramaturgical action and people to dramatic personae, sociologists focus their analysis on actors performing to an audience.[46]

The idea of people performing for an audience raises questions about the authenticity of the performance and the gap between performance and reality. Some may argue that performances are inauthentic by their very nature, that they are mere appearances. Although Goffman's work rejects such a gap by denying there is a reality beyond performance, his analysis of the management of self-presentation conveys a strong sense of strategic motivation.[47] Recent sociological work on performance, however, underscores the fusion, or inseparability, of performance and reality by analyzing performances as rituals. In this view, performance, like rituals, is constitutive of reality.[48] In my analysis of Red Guard performances, I will make no claims about their authenticity or inauthenticity. What matters are the causes and effects of their performances. Red Guards proclaiming their resolve to die for the revolution may be doing so out of a deep and sincere commitment to the revolution, or it may be completely phony. What matters is why such utterances seemed to have gained such powerful influence over both the people who uttered them and their audience. An analysis of the origins of this symbolic power is essential for understanding their impact on the radicalization of collective violence.

A basic element of performance is the script. For Robert Benford and Scott Hunt, "Scripts are not rigid texts that movement participants are required to follow. Rather, they are interactionally emerging guides for collective consciousness and action, guides that are circumspect enough to provide behavioral cues when unanticipated events arise yet sufficiently flexible to allow for improvisation."[49] Scripts do not preclude possibilities for improvisation and creativity. Thus Bernhard Giesen argues that "as detailed as the script may be, there is always space for varying interpretations and creativity—no theatrical performance will exhaust the meaning of a dramatic text completely and no theatrical performance can entirely be reduced to the script. Like constitutive rituals theatrical performances, too, allow for contingencies."[50] Similarly, David Apter argues that political theatre "is not mimetic of the world around it but an aspect of the world itself." It may be theatrical and entertaining, as is often the case with political campaigns, but it may also be deadly, especially when words, symbols, and scripts become sacred and are "blown up to virtually biblical proportions." Apter continues:

> In the past the most disjunctive and theatrical political events involved ideologies of nationalism, socialism, or other doctrinal alternatives. Today the emphasis is on ethnic and religious or sectarian forms of nationalism and identity. Incorporated into narratives and texts, the language itself is revelatory. Reconstructed in the form of a drama engaging in mythological exercises, political theatre in this sense can lay claim to embodied truths that become more true the more they transcend ordinary reason, to become at the extreme the justification of self-immolation and martyrdom.[51]

Later we will see how for Red Guards and rebels in Chongqing, performance was their reality.

The performance of a script takes place in concrete contexts and in often fluid processes. The contexts, such as a theater or a public square, give reality and meaning to the show. The processes of a performance involve multiple characters, including audiences, in interaction. Although they may be more or less predictable, there are always contingencies. Improvisation is an essential part of acting.

When applied to political performances such as political violence, the script may be interpreted broadly as political culture or narrowly as political symbols and myths (as in Kaufman's symbolic politics). Contexts may be structural or cultural and may include class relations, organizational affiliation, regional histories, national politics, and even international relations. Process is interactive and relational and may include political opportunities and the mutual influences of different types of actors. With the notions of context and process, therefore, a performance theory of collective violence integrates the social and political explanations of Red Guard factionalism with key elements in cultural theories of nationalism, ethnic violence, and political violence such as Kaufman's theory of symbolic politics.

In the first three chapters, a performance theory is used to explain the causes and consequences of Red Guard violence. But what about the trajectories of the Red Guard generation *after* the Red Guard movement? As chapter 3 shows, the sacred script that had led to violence had paradoxically also led to dissent. The holy script of revolution achieved its pinnacle in the Red Guard movement, but it also reached its point of exhaustion. What happened in the years after the Red Guard movement was a process of desacralization of the holy script and the emergence of new values and practices.

THE ROUTINIZATION OF LIMINALITY

To conceptualize what happened to the Red Guard generation after the Red Guard movement, I return to Turner's notion of the ritual process. What happened to the violent political passions after the Red Guard movement was brought to an end in July 1968? The "drama" of the Red Guard movement had ended, but history would thrust the Red Guard generation through one new drama after another.

Presumably, the stronger the liminal effects of the Red Guard movement, the more difficult it will be for the participants to forget about those experiences and move on to new lives. We will see that this is true to the extent that members of the Red Guard generation never seem to have left their past behind. Their memories of it have accompanied them all the way to the present.

Nevertheless, in the long run, personal biographies inevitably confront new historical forces, and new conditions will complicate the impact of an early experience. Thus to understand the long-term biographical impact of the Red Guard movement requires an extension of the concept of liminality.[52]

In the reaggregation stage of the ritual process, the ritual subjects settle back to society. But Turner stops short of showing exactly how this process happens, essentially assuming that it is a natural, unproblematic process. Weber's analysis of the routinization of charisma becomes useful here. With the routinization of charisma, he argues, "Only the members of the small group of enthusiastic disciples and followers are prepared to devote their lives purely idealistically to their call. The great majority of disciples and followers will in the long run 'make their living' out of their 'calling' in a material sense as well."[53] Combining Turner's concept of the liminal process with Weber's concept of routinization, I will use the notion of the routinization of liminality to conceptualize the history of the Red Guard generation in the decades after the Red Guard movement.

Weber emphasizes the centrality of economic interests in routine life in the process of routinization: "The process of routinization of charisma is in very important respects identical with adaptation to the conditions of economic life, since this is one of the principal continually operating forces in everyday life."[54] Adapting to the conditions of economic life is an "affirmation of ordinary life." Weber pointed out that the rational achievements of Occidental monasticism were seemingly irreconcilable with its charismatic, antieconomic foundations, although in fact it followed the same logic of the routinization of charisma.

This logic of the routinization of charisma was evident among China's Red Guard generation. The difference was one of content. The Red Guard movement partly resulted from an idealism underwritten by sacred beliefs in charismatic endowments.[55] This idealism was linked culturally to the Confucian vision of an autonomous moral self and historically to the nationalistic aspirations of China's twentieth-century revolutionary youth.[56] It affirmed ideals similar to those embodied in the Aristotelian concept of "good life" and held in contempt, if only implicitly, the values of ordinary life. A major development in the life course of the Red Guard generation is the transformation of political idealism into an affirmation of ordinary life, although, as I will show in later chapters, a sense of idealism has persisted.

THE SENT-DOWN EXPERIENCE AS A NEW BEGINNING

Coming after the Red Guard movement, the sent-down period was a process of routinization. The radicalism of the Red Guard movement had receded; everyday life became more of a routine. Yet the everyday life of the sent-down period had its own radical meaning for sent-down youth, because it turned out to be more of an ordeal than they had ever dreamed of. In that sense, the sent-down experience was the beginning of a new ritual process with profound new influences.

Within the framework of the performance of a sacred revolutionary tradition, the sent-down period proved to be a process of desacralization. The revolutionary romanticism that fired Red Guard radicalism hit the reality of rural labor. Subsistence struggles on a daily basis brought new interests, values, and human relations to the fore. The more intellectually bent sent-down youth turned to books, reading, note-taking, and other cultural pursuits for mental nourishment, doing so in an environment of cultural and material impoverishment. Chapters 4 and 5 offer an account of these activities, revealing a profound albeit quiet shift in the way the generation imagined the world and their own role in it. Without such a shift, the new wave of protest in 1976–1980 would barely be imaginable. Representing the Red Guard generation's emergence from a historical nonage and a farewell to idolatry, that new wave of protest may rightly be called China's new enlightenment, the "old" enlightenment being associated with the May Fourth movement.[57]

The significance of the sent-down experience as another defining moment in the trajectory of the Red Guard generation may also be seen from another angle. Although full of pain and hardship, that experience became a fountainhead of nostalgia and memory ever since sent-down youth returned to the cities. It became a part of their self-identity as much as, if not more than, the Red Guard experience.

For many people, the Red Guard experience remains a powerful memory, so much so that, beginning in the early reform period, the party-state instituted a whole system aimed at controlling the history and memory of the Cultural Revolution and the Red Guard movement. Leaders of zaofanpai, after enjoying fleeting moments of glory in 1966–68, lost out in the political struggles of the Cultural Revolution. When the Cultural Revolution came to an end, they were thrown into prison and never given an opportunity to defend themselves or tell their side of the story until after they had served their prison time or retired. Chapter 7 analyzes the context in which these former zaofanpai make a comeback in their collective efforts to narrate their own history. The chapter also traces the reconstruction of a "red culture" and the role of "second-generation reds" in it. The analysis shows that contemporary memories of the Cultural Revolution are factionalized along the lines of the divisions in the Red Guard movement, suggesting that the politics of the Cultural Revolution has persisted to the present day.

1
VIOLENCE IN CHONGQING

ON MAY 28, 1967, as rebel factions in Chongqing were entering the most violent period of factional warfare in the Cultural Revolution, a radical middle-school group called "September 1 Column" (*jiu yi zong dui*) published a widely known testament. Quoting a line of Mao's poetry as its title—"Death only strengthens the bold resolve"—this document expressed a strong yearning to die for the cause of the revolution. It described Mao as an object of boundless love and loyalty and the revolutionary cause as noble, awe-inspiring, and yet dangerous because of the existence of murderous enemies.[1]

This two-thousand-odd-character document was just one of numerous that appeared in the Red Guard press in the heydays of the Cultural Revolution. Its pronounced passion for Mao and the revolution was nothing extraordinary in the political milieu of the time and may easily be dismissed as rhetoric. Yet its effects were real. Several members of this group would later die in battles with their factional rivals. By the end of 1968, over twelve hundred would die in the fierce factional warfare in Chongqing alone.[2] Thousands died around the country.

What was extraordinary was that barely half a year earlier, they and their rivals had belonged to the same faction fighting common conservative opponents, *conservative* here meaning Red Guard organizations sponsored by local party authorities. After their conservative rival was defeated, however, a process of intrafactional splitting ensued. From within the same faction, a minority splintered off to form a more radical wing. Thereafter, the moderate and radical wings were to engage in a spiraling cycle of violence for over a year until it was stopped by the deus ex machina of Mao himself. "September 1 Column" belonged to the more radical wing.

To understand this historical document and the violence with which it was associated requires an analysis of the whole history of the Red Guard movement in Chongqing. This history will show that violence did not happen overnight, but appeared in a gradual process of escalation. In this process, municipal and provincial party authorities followed the scripts of political campaigns familiar to them, conservative organizations sponsored by party authorities rose and fell, and rebel organizations triumphed over the conservative groups, only to split again into two opposing factions locked in a battle of life and death till the end.

It will become clear from my analysis that this process was characterized more than anything else by revolutionary competition. Individuals and groups fought one another to show and prove that they, and not others, were the true revolutionaries. The logic resembled that of a political marketplace, where the most valuable currency was the idea of the sacredness of Mao and revolution. Because it was an idea, it was up to the individuals to prove that they possessed revolutionary credentials. They had to do so through revolutionary performances. When the majority of the society was engaged in such competitive performances, the bar for the proof had to be constantly raised to show that one had more of it than others. As death was the ultimate proof, violence at the risk of one's life became an attractive option. The escalation of violence happened as a result of this competition.[3] This logic was made possible by the conjoining of several conditions: a political culture that apotheosized revolution, a political context of domestic fears and external threats, and a political process of ambiguity and uncertainty that compelled public displays and performances of revolutionary faith. This chapter focuses on the political process of factional violence in Chongqing. Political culture and context will be the subject of the next chapter.

WORK TEAMS IN CHONGQING

Municipal and provincial party authorities played a decisive role in the first stage of the Cultural Revolution in Chongqing. They were the interpreters, transmitters, and executors of central party policies. As such, they scripted and staged performances that directly influenced the unfolding of the drama. The most important of their actions was the dispatching of work teams and the sponsorship of conservative organizations. In these actions they followed the Chinese communists' long-standing practice of political campaigns. Under the sponsorship of party authorities, conservative Red Guard organizations carried out a cultural revolution against familiar targets from before the Cultural Revolution, but without challenging party authorities. It was in this process that rebel groups appeared, clashed with the conservatives, and then were bolstered by encouraging messages from Beijing that called for national support of rebels "in the minority." For authorities and conservatives, the script of the revolution was equivalent to the suppression of counterrevolutionaries.

The first work team in Chongqing was sent to Chongqing University on June 8, 1966. The work team announced that "Chongqing University is not the same as Peking University. In the main, the party committee at Chongqing University is good."[4] This policy aimed to divert attacks away from the leadership down to students and faculty. Consequently, "Mutual attacks happened among both students and faculty and staff. The campus was in chaos. As a result, many cadres and faculty inside and outside the party, especially some senior scholars and people with historical problems, became particularly frightened, nervous, and insecure."[5]

In taking this line of action, the Chongqing municipal leadership followed instructions from the leaders in Sichuan Province and the Southwest Regional Bureau.[6] On May 26 and June 7, 1966, the Southwest Regional Bureau and the Sichuan provincial party committees issued policy guidelines about how to implement the "May 16 Notification." The "May 16 Notification" made "capitalist-roaders" the target of the Cultural Revolution. Yet the policy guidelines issued by Sichuan party authorities did not mention capitalist-roaders as the target, but instead called for criticisms of persons with "incorrect thought" in the fields of culture and ideology.[7] In effect, they shifted the targets from party leaders downward to the masses and a few known cases of "problem" intellectuals.

In directing the target of the Cultural Revolution toward the masses rather than party leaders, Sichuan party leaders justified their policies with long-standing practices in mass political campaigns. They performed the revolution according to the script familiar to the party authorities. They compared student rebellions to the "Hungarian incident" and viewed the activists as rightists.[8] Ma Li, a deputy mayor of Chongqing, confessed the following in March 1967:

> I rarely exposed my own problems, exposed some of the problems of some other leaders, while mainly directing my target at the masses. This created a tense

atmosphere among the masses. . . . The reason why I was a conservative was because I had a wrong understanding [of the situation]. For example, I confused the Cultural Revolution aimed at digging out capitalist-roaders within the party with the anti-rightist campaign in 1957 which was a counter-attack against rightists who had attacked the party. I exaggerated the impurity of some revolutionary organizations and did not believe that the masses could solve this impurity problem on their own.[9]

In other work units in Chongqing, the initial work teams also took this approach of targeting the grassroots rather than the leadership. At No. 6 Middle School, a work team dispatched by the party committee of the Chongqing Center-City District (*shi zhong qu*) arrived at the end of June. Upon arrival, the work team made an announcement that was almost identical to the one made by the work team sent to Chongqing University on June 8: "The Chongqing party committee is not the same as the Beijing party committee. The party committee at Chongqing No.6 Middle School is not the same as the party committee at Peking University. There are no signs of rottenness so far."[10]

At an iron mining factory, 13,789 posters were put up during the work team stage. These posters reportedly exposed 449 antiparty, antisocialism personnel. The number breaks down into the following:[11]

Leading cadres: 7
Middle-level cadres: 42
Ordinary cadres: 72
Teachers: 26
Technical and medical personnel: 29
Workers: 273

Although the targets included some cadres, the majority of the persons under attack were ordinary workers. Li Musen, a factory worker who later became a leader of the Smashers (*za pai*) in Chongqing, explained that he became a rebel because a friend of his accidently discovered that the party leadership in his factory had classified workers into different categories, a standard practice of investigation in the "Four Cleans" campaign prior to the Cultural Revolution. Li's friend was put in the fourth category, which was considered the worst. Even though Li himself was listed as a second category, he was upset because he thought he deserved to be in the first and best category.[12]

THE RISE OF CONSERVATIVE ORGANIZATIONS

While work teams were busy mobilizing attacks against "cow ghosts and snake spirits," municipal and provincial party leaders actively sponsored the establishment of Red Guard organizations. In Beijing the earliest Red Guard groups were organized by students in elite high schools without party sponsorship. In fact, many of them were denounced by work teams and labeled as counterrevolutionary. In Chongqing, however, the launching of the earliest Red Guard organizations was orchestrated by municipal and provincial party leaders.

The organizing work was done behind closed doors. For example, in late August 1966, before the inauguration of the major conservative organization Maoism Red Guard Headquarters, Li Jingquan, the party secretary of the Southwest Regional Bureau and Sichuan Province, traveled from Chengdu to Chongqing to give on-site instructions. On September 7, 1966, he convened two secret meetings with student representatives in Chongqing. At the meetings he instructed students to set up Maoism Red Guard Headquarters immediately to counter rebel students, noting that the organization should recruit students from "five red" categories. When a student responded that there were not so many students from "five red" families, Li instructed that in that case they should recruit workers and peasants.[13]

In a self-criticism published on March 13, 1967, Chongqing party secretary Xin Yizhi named eight ways in which the municipal party committee supported the conservative organization Maoism Red Guard Headquarters, listing the following: 1. The municipal party committee let its secretary deliver a speech at the inaugural meeting of the organization; 2. invited local army leaders to serve as political instructors of the organization; 3. sent liaison personnel; 4. mobilized workers and peasants to enter their children in the organization; 5. promoted the organization in its newspapers; 6. sent Chairman Mao's works to the organization; 7. gave prominence to this organization during National Day parade; and 8. provided logistical support.[14]

These activities encompassed the staging and performing of revolution on the part of party authorities and conservative Red Guards organizations. Giving media visibility to the conservative organizations was especially important, because it legitimized the organizations. The inauguration of the organization was held on September 8, 1966. The following day, the official *Chongqing Daily* covered the event on its first page and editorialized that the organization was a revolutionary organization comprising of the children of "five red" categories ("Salute the Heroic Red Guards!"). On September 10, 1966, also on its front page, *Chongqing Daily* published an open letter by thirty-six workers and peasants calling on fellow workers and peasants to join the Maoism Red Guard Headquarters. For the next few days, *Chongqing Daily* reported the enthusiastic responses to the thirty-six parents' open letter, claiming that many parents had brought their children to register at the recruitment station of the Maoism Red Guard Headquarters. On September 15, 1966, the paper reported that the previous day, the Maoism Red Guard Headquarters had conducted a mass meeting of its thirty thousand members, together with ten thousand supporters from worker and peasant organizations, to pledge loyalty to Chairman Mao and determination to carry out the Cultural Revolution. All major party and military leaders of the city spoke at the meeting.[15]

Besides public performances like these, party authorities staged smear campaigns to undermine rebel organizations. On August 28, 1966, students of the August Fifteenth group at Chongqing University, which had just been founded on August 26, went to Jiangbei District to mobilize residents. In the downtown area they put up many slogans and posters, one of which was titled "Concentrate battle fire, bombard the municipal party committee." It happened that over two hundred school teachers were being subject to criticisms and investigations by the work team at the Xiahengjie Elementary School in the neighborhood. They were in a state of insecurity and anxiety, fearing that they might become victims of a new "antirightist" campaign. Seeing posters attacking the municipal party committee, they took this as an opportunity to show their loyalty to the party. They denounced the activities of the August Fifteenth students as another "Hungarian incident" and covered the August Fifteenth posters with their own. This led to fist fights with the students from Chongqing University. Afterward, municipal party leaders orchestrated a smear campaign to denounce August Fifteenth for their "atrocities." Public exhibitions were held and leaflets were distributed which falsely accused August Fifteenth of injuring over one hundred teachers and even stripping a female work team member of her clothing and parading her naked in public.[16] It was in the middle of these events that rebel organizations walked onto the historical stage.

THE FIRST INSURGENCE OF REBEL ORGANIZATIONS

Although the first rebel organization, August Fifteenth, was officially launched only on August 26, 1966, acts of rebellion had happened earlier.

The work team sent to Chongqing University announced soon after its arrival that "practice has shown that the Chongqing University Party committee is a correct, Marxist-Leninist committee."[17] This was an attempt to channel student activism away from university leaders toward "dead targets," namely, cadres or intellectuals already labeled as rightists before the Cultural Revolution and during the "Four Cleans." This approach backfired, however, provoking students to question why the work team tried to suppress student activism. Under student pressure, the work team arranged for the university's party secretary, Zheng Siqun, to make a self-criticism to faculty and students. Departmental meetings were called, at which department-level party secretaries were also supposed to make self-criticisms to students and faculty. The meeting in the Department of Radio was called off in the middle as students began to fire questions at party and work team leaders.

On June 18 deputy work team leader Zhang Haiting remarked at a cadre meeting that party and youth members must firmly follow the instructions of the party committee, "even if [the instructions] are wrong." Zhang's remarks further angered students. On the night of June 18, students in the Department of Radio held a meeting to denounce the work team and Zhang's report. The meeting attracted students from other departments as well and lasted until 2 AM. At the end of the meeting, the students held a demonstration on campus. The next day the Chongqing municipal party authorities declared this to be a "counterrevolutionary incident." Students who participated in these activities were subject to mass criticism at mass meetings on campus.[18]

The "June 18" incident marked the beginning of student rebellion against party authorities at Chongqing University. On June 21, 1966, at a campuswide meeting, Chongqing municipal party secretary Xin Yizhi announced that university president Zheng Siqun had been suspended from work and put under investigation and that a new work team under vice mayor Yu Yueze would be running the university. For the duration of its stay at Chongqing University, the work term tried to focus the attention of the campus on denouncing Zheng Siqun. At a meeting on July 29 it declared that Zheng Siqun was guilty of opposing the party. Zheng committed suicide on August 2 while under detention by the work team.[19] Zheng's suicide shocked the students and provoked strong reaction against the work team. The work team withdrew on August 5.

About the same time when students rebelled against the work team at Chongqing University, similar activities happened at the neighboring

Chongqing Teachers Junior College (CTJC). In a poster put up on June 23, students at CTJC denounced the work team and the college's party committee for repressing the student movement and being "royalist." At a campuswide mass meeting on July 19, Gong Qinting, head of the work team at CTJC, ordered the disbanding of two small rebel groups. On August 12 the party committee at CTJC made another attempt to disband the rebels by announcing a plan to send them to the countryside to do agricultural work.[20] On August 13, rebel students from CTJC pleaded for help from fellow rebels in Chongqing University. Their plea met with immediate response, and students in Chongqing University decided to go to CTJC to show their support.

Upon learning that students from Chongqing University were coming, CTJC reinforced security guards at the college's entrance to prevent the unwelcome visitors from entering the campus. Students from Chongqing University arrived at around 9 AM on August 15 and burst open the locked gate. Once inside the campus, these students were joined by CTJC rebels and began to hold a mass meeting on the sports ground. The gathering was four thousand strong.[21] The meeting went on in the heat of the sun amidst power cuts, quarrels, and debates between the rebels and CTJC authorities and supporters. Angry with the opposition they met, some rebel students went to the municipal party committee to request that municipal leaders attend the meeting. Chongqing municipal party secretary Xin Yizhi reluctantly arrived at the scene at CTJC in the evening. Students questioned why the work team was still operating at CTJC when the central party committee had ordered the withdrawal of work teams and why the party authorities wanted to disband the rebel groups in CTJC. Seeing that his answers did not satisfy the students, Xin left the meeting. The students declared victory and concluded the meeting with parades in the streets. Because this was the first major confrontation between the rebels and conservatives in Chongqing, when rebel students in Chongqing University formally launched an organization on August 26, they adopted August Fifteenth as its name.[22]

A period of rivalry and clashes between conservatives and rebels followed. As the August Fifteenth rebel faction met with such organized resistance, new rebel groups appeared. August Thirty-First Combat Corp (8·31 *zhan dou zong dui*) was founded at Southwestern Teachers College on September 3 (so named because it had a major clash with the campus royalists on August 31). August Thirty-First also gave its name to a workers' rebel organization at Red Crag Machinery Factory (*hong yan ji xie chang*). On that day the rebels at the factory, ignoring orders from the municipal party authorities, left their jobs and went to city center to study wall posters. This public demonstration of their rebel position turned Red Crag August Thirty-First into the firm allies of August Fifteenth.[23]

On September 5, faced with organized opposition from the party-supported conservative groups, rebels left for Beijing to plead their case directly to higher authorities, where they attended Mao's second review of Red Guards on September 15. At this point, it is necessary to discuss the role of central party leaders in Beijing.

CENTRAL LEADERS AS DISTAL DIRECTORS

Rebels' interactions with central leaders in Beijing were crucial for rebels' rise to dominance. If municipal authorities treated rebels as counterrevolutionaries, central elites under Mao and the Cultural Revolution Small Group (CRSG) praised them as heroes and true revolutionaries. From the central leaders, local rebels received support and encouragement to continue their revolutionary struggles and prove themselves in the revolutionary process.

In early September 1966, faced with attacks from party-sponsored conservatives, August Fifteenth decided to travel to Beijing to *gaozhuang*, i.e., to petition the highest authorities. In late September, a delegation of middle school rebels did the same. And then, in mid-October 1966, a delegation of worker rebels made their way to Beijing as well. *Gaozhuang* literally means submitting a written petition to a higher authority. The tradition goes back to imperial history, when imperial subjects would travel to the capital city to submit their grievances to the emperor. Petitioners took this action when they felt there was no way of seeking redress for the wrongs they had suffered from the local authorities. Rarely, however, had gaozhuang involved as many people as these cases in the Cultural Revolution. Even more important, the organizers of these trips all announced that they would travel to Beijing *on foot* as a way of showing their determination to undergo hardships and ordeals.[24] These gaozhuang trips thus clearly had a performative function. They were to demonstrate to both local opponents and central elites the revolutionary credentials of the participants.

Once in Beijing, petitioners visited university campuses to read wall posters and sought to meet with central leaders. If there happened to be a public review of Red Guards on Tiananmen by Mao, they would try to make it to the reviews. For example, on their first gaozhuang trip to Beijing in early September, members of the August Fifteenth not only attended Mao's review of Red Guards on September 15, but their delegates, including their leader Zhou Jiayu, were selected and invited onto the Tiananmen rostrum to meet with the party leaders.

Among the most important morale boosters for the petitioners were the speeches delivered to them by central party leaders. Gaozhuang petitions were not limited to rebels from Chongqing. Rebels everywhere made it to Beijing to petition their cases. Central leaders from Zhou Enlai to members of the Cultural Revolution Small Group met numerous times with these petitioners to hear their complaints, give instructions and advice, and explain central policies. Transcripts of their speeches given on these occasions were quickly printed on leaflets or in Red Guard newspapers and became guidelines for local activists.

A main goal of the petitioners at these meetings was to seek affirmation from central leaders that their actions were revolutionary, not counterrevolutionary. At the earlier stage they invariably received affirmative answers. For example, on November 12, CRSG members Wang Li and Qi Benyu met with the Chongqing middle school delegates. Wang Li started his speech by saying: "You asked whether your gaozhuang trip to Beijing was a revolutionary action. We believe it is. You submitted that some people said that your act of bombarding the Chongqing municipal party committee was a counterrevolutionary act. Was it a counterrevolutionary act? We don't think so." Wang's responses won loud applause from the students.[25]

Central leaders rarely just used their power to give directives to Red Guard petitioners. More often than not, they resorted to persuasion and sometimes goading. Like dramatic directors, their approach was not simply to tell the actors how to put on a particular act, but to help the actors "enter their role" so that the actors themselves could put on a performance successfully. They did so by invoking the already familiar myth of the revolutionary struggles of the CCP, by adding their reinterpretations, and by offering tips about methods of acting.

In their speeches, central leaders often talked about the meaning and nature of revolution during the Cultural Revolution. In these, they both invoked the familiar myth of the revolutionary struggles of the CCP and added their re-interpretations. They emphasized that the Great Cultural Revolution was an unprecedented world-shaking revolution, that it had to be made by people themselves rather than being directed from above, and that the best test of a true revolutionary was through revolutionary practice. At the meeting with students from Chongqing on November 12, 1966, when asked whether the central party leadership should intervene in the struggles in Chongqing by removing local party leaders from their official positions, Wang Li said:

> It is better not to remove them yet. Why? Because that should come as a result of your own struggle. In my view, you haven't struggled enough. Under such circumstances, before effective struggles are carried out, removing them [from their positions], reshuffling power—that would be too easy for them. They would no longer be responsible for anything. . . . Usually we do not use the method of removing people from top down. This would not solve the problem. Problems in the revolution should be resolved by Chongqing people themselves.[26]

At the same meeting, Qi Benyu talked about the necessity of revolution and dangers of capitalist revision by citing the history of class exploitation in Sichuan. Referring to a work of sculpture about the exploitation of peasants by landlords, which inspired a documentary film called *Rent Collection Courtyard,* Qi said: "One thing I want to say is that we support your rebellion. Your rebellion was well done, but has not yet done enough. You should have bigger rebellions. I have seen Sichuan's *Rent Collection Courtyard.* Have you seen it? It is a living textbook for class education. If we do not carry the Cultural Revolution thoroughly, then it is possible that capitalism and feudalism will have a comeback. Our country will change color."[27] When answering questions about who was revolutionary and who was not, central leaders called on the young people to prove themselves by going through the trials of the revolutionary process. A speech given by Tao Zhu, one-time head of the Cultural Revolution Small Group, included the following remarks:

> What is counterrevolutionary? Earlier, it refers to people from Taiwan, or people with radio transmitters.[28] Now, the masses want to do revolution. If you suppress revolution you are counterrevolutionary. True revolutionaries, false revolutionaries, half-revolutionaries, 1/3 revolutionaries, 1/4 revolutionaries—they all must be tested in this movement. "Good people" in the past may not necessarily still be good people. . . . At present, there is more than one Red Guard organization in Beijing's schools. You can compare one with another to see who is red and who can be red all the way to the end. You cannot allow yourselves to organize but forbid others to do it. You cannot say you are true revolutionaries and they are fake. This is mass organizing. Their organizations may also be revolutionary. Maybe hold a revolutionary competition. Good ones will grow, bad ones will

collapse. . . . True or fake revolutionaries will be distinguished in revolutionary practice.[29]

Tao Zhu's remarks inadvertently captured the hidden logic of the Cultural Revolution. During the revolution, nothing could be taken for granted; individuals had to prove whether they were "fake" or true revolutionaries. The proof had to come from people's observable behavior—their performances. Thus while there was push for people to perform from the bottom up, there was also a pull for them to do the same from party leaders at the top.

PERFORMING MARTYRDOM: THE "DECEMBER 4 INCIDENT"

As in other parts of the nation, with the launching of the "criticizing bourgeois reactionary line" campaign in October 1966, conservative organizations in Chongqing headed for their demise. Orchestrated by the Cultural Revolution Small Group with Mao's support, the campaign supported rebel organizations as true revolutionaries and attacked conservative factions for taking the "bourgeois reactionary line." This campaign strengthened the rebels, who had been under attack by royalist organizations. The fatal blow to conservatives in Chongqing was the "December 4 Incident."

On December 4, 1966, the four conservative organizations, under the leadership of Workers Fighting Troops (*gong ren zhan dou jun*), held a rally in the Datianwan Stadium as a last attempt to demonstrate their revolutionary credentials and rejuvenate their weakening power. In accordance with the common practice of the time, they announced that the rally would be open to the public. August Fifteenth made careful plans to disrupt the rally, another common practice of the time. In the morning of December 4, members of August Fifteenth showed up at the rally. As soon as the mass meeting began, Zhou Jiayu, leader of August Fifteenth and an invited guest with a seat on the podium, seized the microphone in an attempt to make a speech.[30] Members of August Fifteenth began shouting slogans in praise of "their own organization" while more of its supporters entered the stadium. Amidst the chaos, the two opposing factions got embroiled in fist fights. Bricks, stones, and shoes were hurled. There were injuries and bloodshed. The August Fifteenth faction lost no time in launching a publicity campaign, charging the conservative groups with murder and bloodshed. Street rallies were immediately held to protest conservatives' cruelty. Alleging that several of its members were killed by conservatives in the "December 4 incident," August Fifteenth held a memorial service the following day. Zhou Ziren's diary contains detailed descriptions of the demonstration on December 4 and the memorial service the following day, revealing their highly dramatic quality. The performative nature of the memorial service, however, was little known to the participants.[31] Rumors had already spread that the "December 4 incident" caused the death of dozens of members of August Fifteenth. To those who wanted to use bloodshed as a battle cry, rumors were easily taken as truth, because, as Zhou Ziren puts it, "if somebody is killed, then it becomes easy to spin a story" (死了人，文章就好做了").[32] Later it turned out that the corpses used for the memorial service were not people killed in the December 4 incident, but had been seized from the crematorium. Yet at that point truth no longer mattered because August Fifteenth had achieved its purpose of defeating its conservative opponents. The corpses from the crematorium had been used effectively to stage the power of martyrdom.

To condemn the alleged bloodshed and death caused by conservative organizations, August Fifteenth took their case to Beijing. On December 17, 1966, in Beijing, the leading rebel organization in Beijing, the Third Headquarters, held a high-profile mass rally in celebration of the victories of rebel organizations. Central leaders including Zhou Enlai and Jiang Qing attended the meeting. The only speaker from outside Beijing was Luo Guangbin, a main figure of August Fifteenth and author of the famous revolutionary novel *Red Crag,* who spoke as an eyewitness to the "bloody case" of December 4 in Chongqing. As a result, August Fifteenth gained national fame for its purported heroic struggle against "bourgeois road takers."

It was also in this period that August Fifteenth launched its newspaper *August Fifteenth Battle News.* Its first issue, published on December 9, 1966, devoted most space to the "bloody case" on December 4. These attacks from both local rebels and national rebel organizations sealed the fate of Chongqing's conservative organizations.

In a way, the rise of rebel Red Guards was a response to the political strategy of the municipal and provincial party leaders described earlier. The leaders' plan to divert attacks away from themselves down to the grassroots and to sponsor conservative organizations alienated those who were eager to join the Cultural Revolution. They drove them into the ranks of rebels by labeling and treating them as rightists and counterrevolutionaries. The far-reaching consequences of such labels on one's life and career were well understood by everyone, and it was not surprising that those who were so labeled would fight hard to remove them.[33] The only way to do this was to show that they were the true revolutionaries. They had to perform a revolution.

THE SPLIT OF THE REBELS

The second stage of the Red Guard movement in Chongqing, from December 4, 1966 to May 16, 1967, was one of uncertainty and internal division. In this period, the August Fifteenth split into two factions and began to engage in open and fierce factional warfare that would last to the end of the Red Guard movement.

The dynamics of conflict in the second stage differed from the first stage. In the first stage, municipal and provincial leaders played a key role in the rise of both conservative and rebel Red Guards. In the second stage, however, they became mere props of shows enacted by the rebels. Rebel factions held numerous mass meetings at which they put "capitalist roaders" on the stage for mass criticism. Sometimes, rebel factions fought over the "ownership" of an individual cadre qua "capitalist roader," and the higher ranking the official was, the more intensely they fought, because, as one interviewee puts it, "the bigger the capitalist roader, the stronger the sense of accomplishment. It was a way of showing one's own status" (走资派越大，成就感越大，表明自己的身份).[34] The No. 1 "capitalist roader" in Sichuan being Li Jingquan, Li was subject to many mass criticism sessions. One piece of sensational news in 1967 was that Li Jingquan went to Shanghai to hide from criticism sessions, but was abducted back to Chongqing by rebels.

A turning point in the history of the Cultural Revolution in Chongqing and nationally was the January Revolution in Shanghai. On January 4, rebels in Shanghai took over power at *Wen Hui Daily*. The next day, power seizure took place at *Jiefang Daily* (or, *Liberation Daily*). Then, on January 6, the leading rebel organization in Shanghai held a mass meeting and announced that they no longer recognized the leadership of the Shanghai mayor and party secretary, thus effectively declaring a municipal power seizure. On the night of January 21, the Central People's Radio broadcast a *People's Daily* editorial. Titled "Proletarian Revolutionaries Unite, Seize Power from Those Powerholders Who Take the Capitalist Road," the editorial praised the seizure of power by Shanghai rebels as a revolutionary action. On February 5 the

Shanghai Commune was established as the new organ of power in Shanghai, but the name was changed to Shanghai Revolutionary Committee on February 23. This "January Revolution" in Shanghai became a national model for rebels to seize power from the existing authorities.

Chongqing's version of January Revolution followed the national model closely. On January 16, 1967, the August Fifteenth at Chongqing University took over power of the university.[35] On January 22, the day *People's Daily* published its editorial, major rebel organizations in Chongqing met to discuss and coordinate their power seizure plans. On January 24, under the auspices of the Chongqing Garrison Command, aka the Fifty-fourth Army, about fifty rebel organizations formed a Preparatory Committee for the United Committee of Proletarian Revolutionary Rebels of Chongqing City (United Committee, 重庆市无产阶级革命造反联合委员会筹备会) and proclaimed control over all municipal party and government agencies.

The seeds of division were sown at the same time. On February 1 dozens of rebel groups led by the Chongqing Workers Rebel Troops (工人造反军), "August Thirty-first Fighting Column" of Southwest Teachers College, and the Chongqing Liaison Office of the Capital Third Headquarters sent a telegraph to the Party Central in Beijing, accusing the January 24 power seizure by the "United Committee" of being a mere show orchestrated by the power establishment and the military. From then on, the rebels openly split into two factions. The moderate and majority faction was called the United Committee (*ge lian hui*), with August Fifteenth of Chongqing University as the leading organization. The radical and minority faction was initially called the Smashers, because its slogan was to smash the United Committee. Later, its name was changed to Rebel to the End (*fan dao di*). The August Thirty-first of Southwest Teachers College led this faction.

Throughout February and March 1967, the two rebel factions fought each other verbally and physically. Backed by the Chongqing Garrison, August Fifteenth emerged as the victor. By mid-March, many groups on the Smashers' side had been disbanded, and some of their members arrested by public security authorities after being branded as counterrevolutionaries. The August Fifteenth faction in the municipal public security department estimated that 36 "reactionary" organizations were disbanded by the public security bureau (*gong an ju*), while 82 organizations were "smashed" by mass organizations and 146 organizations voluntarily disbanded.[36] The crackdown on radical rebels happened nationwide and was later dubbed the "February adverse currents" or "February repression of counterrevolutionaries."

On April 1, 1967, Mao approved the release of Zhongfa (67) Document No. 117 to curb this crackdown. The document stated that mass organizations must not be randomly disbanded or accused of be counterrevolutionary. With the issuing of this document, the United Committee faction came under attack for its role in repressing rebels. The organizations previously branded as counterrevolutionary were rehabilitated, and imprisoned rebels released. Reenergized by policies from the center and full of pent-up anger at the United Committee, the Smashers reassembled their organizations and went on the offensive. The conflicts between United Committee and the Smashers soon escalated into armed conflict. On April 23, 1967, for example, the Smashers held a three-hundred-thousand-strong "Down with Liu Shaoqi, Smash United Committee" rally in the city stadium. In the street parades following the rally, the Smashers clashed with August Fifteenth. More clashes took place in the days following.

The intensifying conflicts between the two factions led to the issuing of Circular No. 159 (Zhongfa 67) on May 16, 1967. Titled "CCP Suggestions About Resolving the Chongqing Problem," and known as the "five red articles" for short,[37] it approved establishment of the Preparatory Group of Chongqing Municipal Revolutionary Committee (重庆市革命委员会筹备小组), to be headed by the deputy political commissar of the Fifty-fourth Army, Lan Yinong. The circular demanded the rehabilitation of organizations and individuals who had been wronged in the "February counterrevolutionary campaign," but was reticent on the status of either the United Committee or the Smashers. The ambiguity of this document catapulted the two rival sides into a more deadly period of warfare.

SOURCES OF REBEL SPLIT

The crucial development in the second stage of the Cultural Revolution in Chongqing was the irreparable split of August Fifteenth into two opposing factions. In some parts of the country, factional conflicts were between conservative and rebel factions.[38] In other provinces, conservative factions were defeated by the end of 1966 while rebels split into two opposing factions. These included Shandong, Jilin, Henan, Hunan, Hubei, Yunnan, Shanxi, and Sichuan.

It is puzzling that after the defeat of the conservatives, rebel groups that had fought against conservative organizations shoulder to shoulder would split into rival camps and fight each other to death. In current scholarship, one view holds that the January power seizure created the condition for the split inside rebel ranks, and it was hunger for power that drove the same faction to split. Yet, although the power seizure was a galvanizing event, the split had already begun before it.

Xu Youyu documents the beginning of the split in Chengdu in an event on November 13, 1966.[39] In Chongqing the split began in December 1966, also before the power seizure.[40] Thus the cause of the split was not only or even mainly a hunger for power triggered by the January power seizure. Xu Youyu finds the following differences between moderate and radical rebel factions at the national level:

1. Members in moderate factions had better family backgrounds, whereas many of those in radical factions came from "black families." Radicals were less "pure" in family background.

2. Assessments of persons in power were different. Moderates believed that most of those in power were "good" or "relatively good," whereas radicals believed they were all bourgeoisie and should be removed.

3. Moderates were less hostile to the military than radicals. Conversely, the military tended to support the moderate faction.

4. Radicals accused moderates of being "right-leaning opportunists" who were reformist and half-hearted about a real revolution.

5. Moderates were proud followers of Mao's grand strategy, whereas radicals gave Mao's policies more radical interpretations and took them further.

6. Moderates and radicals had different views about cadres. Moderates used the same political standards that they had employed for the past seventeen years, while radicals argued that only those who were persecuted by the work teams in the initial period of the CR were true revolutionary cadres.

7. Radicals were critical of Zhou Enlai, who seemed to favor moderates.[41]

The differences between the moderate and radical divisions in Chongqing were more or less similar to Xu Youyu's list. From today's vantage point, these differences might appear unremarkable, and certainly not so gravely consequential as to lead to sustained factional violence. The central issues of contention between the August Fifteenth and the Smashers, for example, concerned the political character of the January power seizure and the question of cadres. The United Committee led by August Fifteenth argued that its seizure of power was a revolutionary act in the spirit of the Shanghai January Revolution. Furthermore, it argued that bringing in cadres who had made mistakes in its leadership structure was also a revolutionary act, because "Under the leadership of the Party and Chairman Mao and under the historical conditions of proletarian dictatorship, 95 percent of the cadres are revolutionary. Over the past seventeen years, most of the cadres have been on the side of Chairman Mao's revolutionary line. . . . Most of them were not only the executors of the capitalist bourgeois line but also its victims."[42]

The Smashers charged that the power seizure led by the August Fifteenth was not truly revolutionary but rather followed a "rightist opportunist and rightist capitulation line," because the power seizure was conducted mainly by the representatives of the twelve colleges in Chongqing, while major worker organizations were excluded. They further contended that the creation of the provisional leadership structure after the power seizure did not follow the democratic principles of the Paris Commune and that including cadres from the existing regime in the new leadership team only showed that the power seizure was a fake one.

However unremarkable these differences might appear in hindsight, they were viewed as matters of life and death and were debated publicly until verbal debates escalated to physical warfare. Huang Ronghua, a former rebel leader in Chongqing, recalls the intensity of the debates between August Fifteenth and its opponents in her factory and how these debates aimed at swaying listeners into joining their own group:

> In our factory, the various warrior groups still only differed in opinion and had not split. We were still debating and fighting verbal battles under the same roof, trying to persuade those with different views to join our own side. Among students, however, the "conservative" and "smashers" that split from within the citywide August Fifteenth rebels had already formed their own camps. Their main job was to send people to grassroots units to publicize their respective views in order to win over more supporters and expand their ranks. Students from the August Fifteenth of Chongqing University and August Thirty-First of South-West Teachers College set up stages in the Laoguang Square of our factory to hold debates. They attracted tens of thousands of spectators. Some of these went there to show their support; some were there to decide which side to take; and some were there just for the fun of it.[43]

Undoubtedly, local conditions meant that all intrarebel conflicts were not the same. Yet the generality of the phenomenon means that it must be due to some common underlying factor. If we look at the main differences between the moderates and radicals, it is clear that these boiled down to the nature of revolution and revolutionary conflicts. Is it possible that the visible differences between the two factions in fact only masked a deeper but common concern, namely, the concern to carry the revolution forward even if it had to be carried out in violence? Indeed, driving the violent escalation was a conviction that the revolution had to be carried out through violence for it to be worthy of the name of revolution. I will argue that the common factor was the inexorable aspiration to follow and enact the iron law of revolution. This is not to suggest that it had nothing to do with interest, but that the interest was not material but rather political, and interest-based conflicts were wrapped in such a powerful myth of revolutionary struggle that, even for those directly involved, it was not at all easy to separate them, not even almost fifty years later. Li Zimao, a rebel leader at Tsinghua University who was involved in the "hundred days of warfare" at Tsinghua, wrote in his 2014 memoir that the conflicts between the two rebel factions at Tsinghua University were driven by their goal of fighting for university leadership positions; at the same time, he wrote about people's death-defying courage and idealism in an age that worshipped heroes: "Among those of the two factions who stayed to fight, the vast majority had consciously and actively participated in the Cultural Revolution from the very beginning. They had idealistic aspirations, were full of hot-blood passion, and firmly believed in Mao Zedong's judgment that 'the bourgeoisie is within the communist party.' They were determined to 'carry it to the end' and to devote themselves heart and soul to the movement."[44]

THE JANUARY REVOLUTION IN CHONGQING

In Chongqing, the period that split the rebel faction into two opposing factions decisively was the January Revolution in 1967. During this period a majority of rebel organizations led by August Fifteenth of Chongqing University built a coalition, staged power seizures in the city, and established a preparatory revolutionary committee. A minority of organizations led by August Thirty-first of Southwest Teachers College contested the power seizure activities of the August Fifteenth, arguing that the power seizure was "fake" because the new authority structures included party leaders who had been overthrown in the earlier stage. Citing theories of revolution from the international communist movement, they reiterated that an intrafactional split was a necessary step in all revolutionary movements. They argued that the iron law of revolution dictated such a split.

The Shanghai January Revolution had already positioned itself in the pedigree of sacred proletarian revolutions in modern world history. The series of power seizure events that happened in Shanghai in January 1967 was probably first named the January Revolution at a meeting of Shanghai rebel leaders on January 19. The manifesto declaring the triumph of the January Revolution, issued on February 5, 1967, gave the name of Shanghai Commune to the new leadership structure that was created with the revolution. The names *January Revolution* and *Shanghai Commune* thus put the action of Shanghai rebels explicitly in the lineage of the October Revolution in Russia and the Paris Commune of 1871, a tradition of proletarian revolution held sacred in China.

Nationwide, the language of January Revolution was disseminated through the publication of the manifesto proclaiming the victory of the January Revolution in Shanghai's *Liberation Daily* on February 7, 1967, and of a *People's Daily* article on February 5, 1967, titled "Long Live the Spirit of the Great January Revolution." In Chongqing the earliest public mention of the term *January Revolution* I came across was in an article published in the inaugural issue of the rebel newspaper *October 5 Storm* on February 1, 1967. The same issue carries polemics in praise of power seizure, arguing for the inevitability of intrarebel struggles as a reflection of an "objective law" that defies human will.

The launching of *October 5 Storm* coincided with the temporary closure of *August Fifteenth Battle News*. On January 27, 1967, the newspaper stopped publishing because its editors decided that the revolution had triumphed and no more polemics were needed. It resumed publishing on February 17, 1967, however, when August Fifteen felt a renewed need to defend the power seizure in Chongqing and the United Committee. The February 17, 1967, issue published the following short notice explaining why the paper was relaunched:

After *August Fifteenth* stopped publishing, some people used newspapers as a front to distort truth and exaggerate matters and launched attacks against August Fifteenth at Chongqing University and the United Committee. Their activity seriously sabotaged the great alliance and great power seizure of the revolutionary rebels and deflected the general orientation of the struggle. To defend Mao Zedong Thought, to defend the general orientation of the struggle, to advocate for the guidelines and policies of the Party, responding to the strong demands of the great masses of workers and peasants, our newspaper decided to resume publication on a temporary basis beginning with this issue.

In its next issues, the *October 5 Storm* continued its polemics against the "fake" power seizure led by the August Fifteenth. An article in the February 20, 1967, issue argues that internal splits between rebels are an inevitable law of proletarian movements:

> The great polemics also show: The struggles over power seizure and counter power seizure between proletarians and the bourgeoisie inevitably find their way into the rebel factions. Engels said, "Proletarian movements of necessity undergo various stages of development. At each stage, some people will come to a stop." With the development of our movement, opportunism of all colors will inevitably grow out of the rebel ranks. This will inevitably lead opportunists to engage in separatist activities in opposition to Marxism-Leninism. At the same time, it will also inevitably lead Marxists-Leninists to struggle against opportunism and separatism.[45]

In countering the attacks from their opponents, August Fifteenth and United Committee also invoked the tradition of the Russian October Revolution and the Paris Commune. Here is an excerpt from an article that appeared in *August Fifteenth Battle News* on February 25, 1967: "The new things of revolution will inevitably defeat the old things of the counter-revolution. That the new things of revolution will inevitably triumph—this is historical dialecticism. Such was the case with the Paris Commune. So was it with the October Revolution. Such was it with the founding of the People's Republic of China. And such inevitably must be the case with the United Committee!"[46]

These polemics suggest that the rebels deliberately followed theory when they tried to explain the divisions between themselves. They were fitting their practices to the scripts of revolution in the pedigree of Marxist theory of dialectical materialism. In so doing, they enacted what was prescribed only in theory. A cynical reader of the twenty-first century might suspect that all this was a rhetorical smoke screen for hiding self-interest. Yet to those directly involved in those activities, reenacting the script of revolution was a perfectly authentic revolutionary experience. Basking in a sense of triumph, Zhou Ziren, the editor of *August Fifteenth Battle News*, wrote a diary entry on March 6, 1967, that conveyed the joys of revolutionary experience:

> I was late for a mass meeting. When I got there, people had left. This was the first time I entered this auditorium since I came to the city five years ago. When I entered the main lobby of this magnificent palace, my heart was beating like waves in the ocean. I thought of a painting: After their battle attacks on the Win-

ter Palace in the October Revolution, two marines were smoking a cigarette in the quiet lobby. The beautiful palace was full of bullet holes and the floor was a complete mess. Hadn't I just walked into a historical painting? Looking at the scraps of wall posters and slogans from the past few months, I thought: weren't they like the bullet holes left from fierce battles? I felt exhilarated. I ran like wild up the tall stairways. How I felt like singing loudly into the east wind in the city, "We have made sacrifices to a glorious cause, we feel boundless joy and pride."[47]

His memories of the heroic scenes of the Russian Revolution show that people were consciously linking their experiences in the Cultural Revolution to the tradition of proletarian revolutions in world history. The vividness with which he imagined the Russian Revolution suggests that the images of that tradition had been implanted deeply in their minds. On occasions like these, those images became a source of inspiration for their own revolutionary performances. Linked to the pedigree of the October Revolution and the Paris Commune, the January Revolution was apotheosized as a sacred event. As the *People's Daily* article on February 5, 1967, states, the spirit of the January Revolution would live on forever.

The January Revolution provided legitimacy for radicals to challenge what they considered to be the "fake" power seizure in Chongqing. At the same time, August Fifteenth used it to justify its own power seizure as an act of revolution. Thus, the period of power seizure split the rebels from within, not because of a presumed human hunger for power, but because in the sacred chronicles of world proletarian revolutions seizing power was viewed as an essential goal of the revolution and a sign of its triumph. In this sense, the Chongqing rebels' split over power seizure resulted from a shared consciousness of the sacred tradition of revolution. When August Fifteenth and the United Committee, with the support of Chongqing's Fifty-fourth Army, hunted down the Smashers in the period known as the "February suppression of counterrevolutionaries," not only did they fail to quash the Smashers, but, on the contrary, they sealed their split with the Smashers once and for all.[48] For everyone, being labeled a counterrevolutionary was all the more reason to display one's revolutionary credentials. Thus, by mid-May 1967, the stage was set to move from verbal battles to war.

"A PEOPLE'S WAR"

The third period of factional struggle in Chongqing, May 16, 1967, to October 15, 1968, was a "people's war," to use the rebels' own words. This "people's war" included prolonged and deadly battles with heavy casualties. Armed battles occurred in streets, factories, and schools. During this period, both factions were organized like military units, with special units for combat.[49] Each faction came to occupy sections of the city as its base, and opponents were often chased out. At one point, in the tradition of Mao's guerrilla warfare, August Fifteenth even established a base area in the nearby Huayin Mountain.

The following is just a short sample list of the major battles in Chongqing.

- June 5–8, 1967: Armed battles between the Smashers and Spring Thunder (a subsidiary of August Fifteenth) in Southwest Teachers College.
- July 7, 1967: Armed battles between 32111 Combat Team of No. 6 New Middle School and February 7 Combat Team (August Fifteenth) and Light Industry Regiment (Smashers). For the first time, a military weapon (rifle) was used in the armed conflicts in Chongqing.[50]
- July 23, 1967: August Fifteenth attacked August Thirty-First at Southwest Teachers College. As a result, August Fifteenth took control of Chongqing's Beibei District.
- July 25, 1967: Gun fights between the two factions led to ten deaths on the side of the Smashers.[51]
- August 1, 1967: Armed battles in Yangjiaping District between the two factions. Two soldiers of the garrison command and three students from Chongqing University were killed. There were many other casualties.[52]
- August 3, 1967: A transportation ship of the Chongqing Military District was sunk by the Rebel to the End (formerly the Smashers). Three soldiers were killed. Battles broke out at No. 29 Middle School, the Construction Machinery Factory, and in several street sections.
- August 4, 1967: The August Fifteenth Propaganda Team of the Finance and Trade Sector was ambushed by the Rebel to the End. Six middle school students and one college student were killed.[53]
- August 8, 1967: The Rebel to the End faction in control of several machinery factories converted three transportation ships into military battleships. Sailing upstream the Jialing River, they exchanged intense artillery fire with the August Fifteenth faction stationed on the river banks; 24 people were killed, with 129 wounded.[54]

Backed by the Fifty-fourth Army, August Fifteenth emerged as the victor. Many members of Rebel to the End fled Chongqing. Central party leaders in Beijing intervened repeatedly, each time with harsher tones. On July 13,

1967, Xie Fuzhi and Wang Li descended on Chongqing to meet with representatives of both factions. Their attempts at peacemaking were interrupted by a brewing crisis in Wuhan (which subsequently erupted into the July 20 Wuhan Incident). They ended their visit abruptly and flew to Wuhan. Fighting continued between the two factions.

On September 5, the Party Central issued another circular, known as the September 5 Order, forbidding anyone to seize weapons from the military. Fighting stopped temporarily, only to intensify again after March 5, 1968, thanks to a speech made by Zhou Enlai praising the Rebel to the End faction, which was on the losing side of the battle. On June 2, 1968, the Chongqing Municipal Revolutionary Committee was established. Nationwide, the establishment of "revolutionary committees" absorbed members from both factions and marked the rebirth of collapsed power structures and the beginning of the end of the Cultural Revolution. On October 15, 1968, the Chongqing Municipal Revolutionary Committee held a mass meeting to celebrate the victory of the Cultural Revolution. At the meeting, the two opposing factions officially announced the dissolution of all their organizations and headquarters. The "people's war" officially came to its end.

Factional warfare happened across the country, often ending in violence. As in Beijing, the main period of factional warfare in Chongqing happened between two rebel factions, not between conservative and rebel factions as in Guangzhou. In Guangzhou the military supported the conservative faction from the beginning, and, as a result, the main factional warfare was between the conservatives and the rebels throughout. In Chongqing the military supported August Fifteenth, the more moderate among the rebel wing.

Although factional battles were intense and deadly in many places, they were especially so in Chongqing, involving the use of rifles, heavy artillery, and even tanks and military battleships. This was probably due to the peculiar mix of local and national elements in Chongqing. Chongqing was an important base of industry with a concentration of military factories. Local rebels themselves spoke proudly of the "eight big military factories" in Chongqing, almost as if they had something to match the "ten big buildings" in Beijing.[55] Weapons were thus more easily available than in most other cities. Sometimes they were handed out; more often they were stolen or seized by force.

The availability of weaponry alone was a negligible factor in and of itself. People had to have legitimate reasons for taking hold of weapons and using them. How did this happen?

There is no doubt that Mao and his policy of "arming the left" fueled factional violence.[56] Yet, in Chongqing and elsewhere, deadly factional battles had already occurred before "arming the left" became a policy. Local Red Guards and rebels had resorted to fighting before they received clear signals of support from the top. Weapons had already been used. Evidence in Red Guard newspapers from Chongqing indicates that the escalation of factional conflicts from verbal battles to armed violence was a gradual process. To extend the metaphor of performance, it was almost as if armed violence was the logical climax of the revolutionary drama of the Cultural Revolution. How so?

To the Red Guard generation, no revolution would be a true revolution without violence. Violence was an integral part and ultimate manifestation of revolution in the imagination of this generation. The sacred tradition of the Chinese revolution, carefully crafted by the party in the same period in which this generation was coming of age, celebrated martyrdom and revolutionary heroes. It exalted violence as a necessary means of revolution and glorified death for the cause of revolution. In the following section I will discuss two critical events in Chongqing to show how factional battles became imitations and enactment of revolutionary warfare in the past.

TWO FACTIONAL BATTLES

The first battle to be examined here was called the June 5–8 Incident. On those days in 1967, August Fifteenth and the Smashers fought each other at the Southwest Teachers' College. The main faction of August Fifteenth at the Southwest Teachers' College was called Spring Thunder, which had occupied the college's newly built library. Spring Thunder's opponent at the college was August Thirty-First. In the afternoon of June 5, August Thirty-First attacked Spring Thunder and took control of the two lower levels of the library, but could not take over the two upper floors occupied by Spring Thunder. As the battle continued on June 6–7, reinforcements from other August Fifteenth groups in the city arrived, but were initially blocked outside the campus by August Thirty-First. Finally, on the night of June 7, major reinforcements from the August Fifteenth at Chongqing University arrived on the scene. Under attack above from Spring Thunder and below from the reinforcements, August Thirty-First could no longer hold out. Some of its members were captured, while others made their escape by jumping off the building. Although no military weapons were used, the battles from June 5–8 marked the beginning of large-scale factional violence in Chongqing.

The second case was the July 25 incident. On July 25, 1967, members of the August Fifteenth faction, armed with knives, pistols, rifles, machine guns, and submachine guns, attacked four hundred unarmed members of two Smashers groups, Red Crag Regiment and September First Column, at the Industrial School in Chongqing.[57] After half a day's battle, August Fifteenth defeated the Smashers and took control of the Industrial School. August Fifteenth killed ten members of the Smashers and lost two lives on its own side.[58]

In each case, after the battle each side was engaged in publicity, attacking the opponent and commemorating its own dead. Those who died in action were conferred with "martyr" status. The commemoration included both public memorial services and newspaper pages devoted to the incident and the martyrs. The newspaper pages contained narratives about the incident in the form of editorials, reportage, and eyewitness accounts. The narratives published by each side viewed the other side as the enemy, yet except for that they were very similar. They would condemn the cruelty and fierceness of the enemy, extol the bravery and fearlessness of their own fighters, and end with expressions of determination to defend Mao and the cause of the revolution and avenge the martyrs.

The narratives were invariably interspersed with quotations from Mao's verse or prose works, which seemed to have a fitting quote for praising all heroic and revolutionary behavior and condemning every reactionary act. Some examples were "Be resolute, fear no sacrifice, and surmount every difficulty to win victory"[59] and "Wherever there is struggle there is sacrifice, and death is a common occurrence. But we have the interests of the people and the sufferings of the great majority at heart, and when we die for the people it is a worthy death."[60] Mao quotations, which had become a treasured household possession in China since they were first issued in the form of the *Little Red Book* in 1964, were core elements of the sacred tradition of the Chinese revolution. They were memorized by people and in turn had a mesmerizing effect, close to that of Scripture.[61]

The narratives in these two cases usually contain descriptions of battle scenes. These battle scenes bear such close resemblance to those in Chinese war films and fiction of the revolutionary romantic style that one might argue that these factional battles were mimetic. They provide convincing evidence for my argument that Red Guard factional warfare was the enactment of an imagined revolution based on scripts familiar to these youth.

Here is a description of the battle scene at the Southwest Teachers' College on June 6, 1967. It is from a story in the June 16, 1967, issue of *August Fifteenth Battle News,* the leading newspaper of the August Fifteenth faction, to which the Spring Thunder group at the Southwest Teachers' College belonged. The first part of the story describes how ruthlessly Spring Thunder's opponents, August Thirty-first, had attacked Spring Thunder. Now a day's battle had come to an end:

> Night fell on the campus of Southwest Teachers' College. The situation is getting more and more serious. "Looking up, we see the north star, in our heart we think of Mao Zedong . . ." Spring Thunder fighters could all be wiped out. But to die, what is so scary about that! Spring Thunder fighters have all made up their mind. "When called upon to die, then be brave enough to die, including losing your own life. To hell with death! On the battlefield, once fighting starts, old-man me just gets ready to die on the battlefield!"[62]

Besides narratives about battle scenes, Red Guard papers devoted to these incidents contained photos, obituaries, diaries, and occasionally letters of the dead, as well as memorial speeches. These mnemonic genres similarly glorify the dead and exalt heroism and sacrifice for the cause of revolution. The standard scripts used in these remembrances were Mao's remarks about the need to memorialize the dead in the *Little Red Book*. Coming from "Mao the storyteller," in the words of Apter and Saich, these remarks seemed to cast a spell on their readers like incantations inviting them to act.[63] The following passage from "Serve the People," for example, was printed in the middle of the page devoted to the "martyrs" of the July 25 battle in the August 8, 1967, issue of *August Fifteenth Battle News*: "From now on, when anyone in our ranks who has done some useful work dies, be he soldier or cook, we should have a funeral ceremony and a memorial meeting in his honor. This should become the rule. And it should be introduced among the people as well. When someone dies in a village, let a memorial meeting be held. In this way we express our mourning for the dead and unite all the people."

Another quotation from Mao, which appeared at the end of the story reporting the August Fifteenth memorial service for its martyrs, is a famous eulogy of martyrdom: "Thousands upon thousands of martyrs have heroically laid down their lives for the people; let us hold their banner high and march ahead along the path crimson with their blood!" As factional warfare intensified and casualties increased, these Mao quotations became staples in the Red Guard press.

About forty years later, one of the August Fifteenth members who participated in the battle, Zhou Ziren, recalled the battle scene in his memoir. In the evening of June 7, 1967, Zhou was in his student dorm in Chongqing University. Two of his friends came and asked: "Do you dare to go fight the Smashers?" Zhou's answer was terse: "Dare I? Let's go and fight!" In the darkness of the rainy night, they joined truckloads of their comrades-in-arms and drove to the Southwest Teachers College to the rescue of Spring Thunder. Zhou recalled that people on the truck were all soaked in the rain, but no one showed any fear. It was as if they were on the way to a carnival.[64] Once they arrived at the battle scene in Southwest Teachers College, what Zhou saw startled him: "The final attack had just started. The battle trumpet blew out sad but loud sounds. Tall ladders were pulled to the third floor using a long rope. The armed fighters dashed to the building from all sides like a flood and began climbing up the ladder. Most of them were students. They had no equipment of any kind. Bare-headed . . . they dashed forward like flying locusts. . . . I watched from afar and was instantly moved by wild impulses. I could not control myself and dashed forward with stick in hand."[65]

THE REALITY OF THE ROLE

Mao quotations and other imagery of revolution were not mere rhetoric with which Red Guards embellished their narratives. It would be difficult to imagine the violent warfare between opposing factions without this rhetoric. One need not have to argue that Mao quotations *caused* the factional violence to see their essential role, as part of the revolutionary script, in Red Guard factionalism. These young rebels were performing a role in a revolutionary drama, often in imitation of roles in the sacred script of the Chinese revolution. When they were in battle, they often consciously imitated the actions of soldiers in the battle scenes in the many Chinese war films and works of fiction they had grown up with. To argue that they were performing the revolution by no means implies that their action lacked authenticity. For them, performance and reality had become one and the same thing. Their role in the drama of the Cultural Revolution was their reality. We can get a sense of this unity of performance and reality from the story of one person who died several days after the battle on July 25, 1967.

On July 29 Li Shengpin, a member of the August Fifteenth of Chongqing University, was killed in an accident while training high school students to use self-made hand grenades. Li was one of the three people conferred "martyr" status in a decision published in the *August Fifteenth Battle News*. The same issue published excerpts of Li's diaries, as well as a letter to a friend he wrote shortly before his death. Zhou Ziren, the newspaper's editor, revealed in his memoir that the friend was in fact Li's girlfriend. The letter provided a valuable glimpse into the inner world of the factional warriors at that time.

Li Shengpin was fully aware of the dangers. His letter expressed intimations about possible death. He recalled the sufferings of his parents and grandparents in the "old society" and mentioned specifically that his mother had to beg for food in the streets when she was ten years old. After this, Li wrote, "I often thought, if our country doesn't have a future, all talk about personal future is deceitful nonsense. . . . The question now is whether to carry the Cultural Revolution to the end or to let it die prematurely. . . . We must exert ourselves, struggle hard, and not fear death."[66] Li asked his girlfriend not to tell his family if he died. He ended the letter by saying that she should not feel too sad about his death and should look to the future. Li's letter had a calm, intimate, and conversational tone, atypical of the Red Guard writing style at that time. It conveyed a sense of authenticity about the meaning of revolution and sacrifice to the young generation. True, the revolution was performed, yet this letter shows the difficulty and perhaps the meaninglessness of any attempt to separate performance from reality. One might argue that Li Shengpin, in writing the letter, in the use of language in his letter, and eventually in his death, was following a script that he had learned through socialization and education. Yet, if he was acting a role, he had certainly taken that role to heart. His role was his reality.

In the middle of such glorification of heroism and martyrdom, the factional warfare in Chongqing continued. The atmosphere of war in the Red Guard press and in the streets intensified, feeding upon each other. The diaries of Wu Mi, a well-known scholar of comparative literature on the faculty of the Southwest Teachers College who lived on the college's campus at that time, contain his disinterested observations of the campus atmosphere. Below is an entry for July 1967:

July 6 Thursday
At 1 AM at night, I heard the sound of a cannon. I got up and got dressed just in case. Then I heard another cannon, slightly louder. Then August Thirty-first began broadcasting to gather its forces. It sounded like war. I opened a corner of the window and pricked up my ears. I heard it declaring war on its enemy, saying, "If you use guns, we will use guns; if you use cannons, we'll also use cannons," etc. Then I heard the explosion of a third cannon, slightly muffled. Then a fourth cannon, the loudest yet, making my windows and walls shake. At this point, the broadcast beamed out music of marching and war making and the slogan "overcome every difficulty, fear no sacrifice, win victory."[67]

Although factional warfare escalated gradually, its ending happened abruptly. This again attests to the performative character of the Red Guard movement. When the factional warfare ended, twenty-two had been killed in Chongqing University alone. Official records show that from the summer of 1967 to summer 1968 there were thirty-one factional battles. One list alone, compiled by He Shu, contains the names of twelve hundred deaths related to factional fighting.[68]

I have argued in this chapter that rebel violence happened as a result of the conscious enactment of an imagined revolution through the uncertain processes of the Cultural Revolution. But what made the young people rise to the occasion? Why would they embrace opportunities for violence knowing their own lives were in danger? Indeed, why did they actively create opportunities for violence? To answer these questions, it is essential to understand, in the words of Qian Liqun, "the way our generation imagined the world."[69] The next chapter delves into the way the Red Guard generation imagined the world.

2

FLOWERS OF THE NATION

RELEASED IN 1955, *FLOWERS of the Nation* (*zu guo de hua duo*) was one of the first children's films produced after the founding of the PRC. It depicts an image of youthful innocence, beauty, vitality, and idealism that was to become an indelible part of the memories of the Red Guard generation. The most memorable part of the film is perhaps the theme song "Let Us Paddle" (*rang wo men dang qi shuang jiang*), sung by a children's choir while the young characters of the film are rowing a boat on the lake in the famous Beihai Park in the center of Beijing. Many years later, in 2012, a blogger remembered: "This beautiful song drifted over my childhood and teenage years. The picturesque view of the White Pagoda gave me boundless imagination. Whenever I go to a KTV, I cannot help but request this song. When classmates hold gatherings and sing together, we often choose this song. Every time I listen to it or sing it, I am so inspired that tears roll down my face and the scenery in Beihai Park—'the beautiful White Pagoda reflections on the surface of the lake'—will appear in my mind."[1] The title of the film, *Flowers of the Nation*, became the symbol of the young generation, the would-be Red Guard generation. It was the pride of the nation. This sense of pride was built into the identity of the generation. The song has a subtle message about the source of children's happy life:

Having done the day's homework,
We come here to enjoy happiness,
I asked you, my dear playmates,
Who has given us the happiness of life?

To the viewers of the film, the answer to the rhetorical question in the last line was self-evident: it was Mao and the Chinese Communist Party. As the blogger's story shows, this song continues to be a favorite for the Red Guard generation sixty years later. It still moves people to tears.

Besides "flowers of the nation," the young generation was also seen as "revolutionary successors." Increasingly common after the Hungarian Uprising of 1956, narratives about revolutionary successors had built to a crescendo by the eve of the Cultural Revolution. To the image of "flowers," narratives about revolutionary successors added a tone of militancy and the sacredness of a historical mission. Stories of revolutionary violence, class struggle, martyrdom, and heroism saturated the media and everyday life in the years before the Cultural Revolution.

How did these images affect the young people? The previous chapter shows that Red Guards and rebels enacted a revolution in their verbal and physical battles, because the category of revolution had become hallowed in Chinese political culture, a central element in the imaginary of that political generation. This chapter explains how that political culture took on such power. Clearly, it is too simplistic to view it purely as the result of propaganda, because such a theory captures neither the complex context in which such powerful generational imaginary was produced nor the sense of agency that accompanied the socialization process.

Accordingly, I will argue that multiple conditions combined to produce the effects. My point is not that this generational imaginary was the cause of factional violence in the Cultural Revolution. In many ways, elements of this generational imaginary, such as a sense of idealism and a passion to change the world, were shared by youth in other countries in the same period. Rather, I argue that this generational imaginary was a necessary and important ingredient in the making of China's Red Guards and rebels and that this ingredient worked because it was an integral part of a larger set of social and political circumstances.

EMBODIED MEMORIES AS EFFECTS OF POLITICAL CULTURE

Understanding the effects of the political culture of the early PRC on the Red Guard generation presents methodological difficulties. Official media material from the 1950s and 1960s, which is abundant, offers little information about how the political culture was received and experienced by its audiences. Even diaries from that period, which I have consulted as much as possible, have their limits when it comes to understanding people's subjective experiences. As Sang Ye points out in his introductory essay written for an exhibition of Chinese diaries and notebooks, diaries could be sources of great personal danger when they could be seized by party officials and used as evidence against the diarist, as often happened in the Mao era.[2] Under these conditions, writing down private thoughts and feelings in diaries took courage, and more often than not, diaries were written with potential public readers in mind. Still, diaries are priceless for gaining insights into the details of everyday life and for knowing some of the things the diarist did (such as "watched a movie") if not what he or she felt and thought. My analysis therefore makes use of as many diaries as I can find for this period (see "Notes on Data" for details).

My main source of data in this chapter, however, is memory narratives. How people remember that political culture and what elements of it are remembered, I believe, reflects the influences of that culture. The assumption is that political culture works most effectively by coming to be embodied in its targeted audiences, through memories, emotions, and other forms of bodily behavior. This is the classical sociological question of how the social and symbolic worlds enfold themselves onto individuals and their bodies. Arthur Kleinman and Joan Kleinman take this approach in their study of the trauma of the Cultural Revolution. Starting with Paul Connerton's insight that societies remember through the incorporation of social memory into the human body (as well as through inscriptions onto cultural texts, e.g., monuments, and commemorative rituals),[3] they argue that bodily complaints such as dizziness, exhaustion, and pain are expressions of social distress and suffering during the Cultural Revolution:

They are lived memories. They bridge social institutions and the body-self as the transpersonal moral-somatic medium of local worlds. The origins and consequences of these symbolizing sensibilities of lived distress and criticism reveal what those local worlds are about; how they change; and what significance they hold for the study of human conditions. That is to say, bodies transformed by political processes not only *represent* those processes, they *experience* them as the lived memory of transformed worlds. The experience is of memory processes sedimented in gait, posture, movement, and all the other corporal components which together realize cultural code and social dynamics in everyday practices. The memorialized experience merges subjectivity and social world.[4]

In the same way, I argue that for the political culture of the seventeen years prior to the Cultural Revolution to influence Red Guard behavior, it would also have to find its expression in embodied memories. Indeed, these embodied memories may persist to the present day. Thus, for example, to understand the prevalence of "red songs" in the popular culture of public square dancing in China today, it is essential to understand that for many of those retirees enthused about such public dancing, the tones and rhythms of the "red songs" are so much a part of themselves and their embodied memories that they are naturally predisposed to favor "red songs" over other musical genres in their daily dancing exercises. Following this reasoning, I will contend that the embodied memories of today, while inevitably reflecting contemporary conditions and concerns, may be studied as vindications of the powerful influences of lived experiences of the past.[5]

Retrospective accounts of members of the Red Guard generation, when touching upon the seventeen years before the Cultural Revolution or the processes and experiences of the Red Guard movement, are full of memories of the cultural symbols of the past. Particularly common are memories of heroic characters and famous scenes from films and literary works; memories of songs, music, and images; and memories of canonic texts such as *Quotations of Chairman Mao* and the Nine Commentaries.

THE NINE COMMENTARIES

The Nine Commentaries (*jiu ping*) are a series of nine polemical articles that the Chinese Communist Party published in *People's Daily* and *Red Flag* to attack Soviet revisionism between September 1963 and July 1964. Masterminded by Mao himself and drafted by CCP's top theorists, the Nine Commentaries made ideological and media preparations for the launching of the Cultural Revolution. The core issues in these polemics concerned the necessity to fight Soviet-style revisionism and prevent its happening in China,[6] the need to forestall the American strategy of peaceful evolution, and the urgency to cultivate China's younger generation as the successors of China's revolutionary cause.

The Nine Commentaries had profound influences on the Red Guard generation. Its polemical style and powerful rhetorical flourishes would soon become a model for Red Guard polemics. A notebook in the Cultural Revolution diary collection at the University of Melbourne was full of excerpts from the Nine Commentaries. That it was dated September 1968 suggests that, although the Nine Commentaries were published in 1963–64, they continued to be popular quotations and reading materials in 1968.

The Nine Commentaries are also among the most frequently remembered texts among the Red Guard generation. Authors of memoirs are still proud of how they used to be able to recite long, famous passages from the Nine Commentaries. They talk about how they were moved by the righteous indignation of the rhetoric, and the solemn and awe-inspiring voice of the famous broadcasters who read the Nine Commentaries on radio.

Qin Hui (b. 1953) is a well-known liberal intellectual and a professor of history at Tsinghua University. When the Cultural Revolution started, Qin was thirteen years old and had just graduated from elementary school and entered junior high school in his hometown Nanning. From then until he was sent down to a village in 1969, he said that he did not have a single day of real school, but spent all his time "doing revolution." Qin wrote that he entered junior high school in earnest search of revolution. He recalls especially the influence of the Nine Commentaries:

At that time I already had "beliefs." When I was ten years old, the blazing "open debate" against Soviet revisionism attracted me powerfully. To this day I remember the scene of my whole family sitting next to the radio and listening to the Nine Commentaries. Although I only had a vague understanding, the righteous and solemn tone of the broadcaster made me feel the power of "truth." I was captivated. For a long time, I was able to recite fluently the Nine Commentaries and some articles in a volume of debate titled *Proletariat of the World Unite Against Our Common Enemy*. I still remember some passages clearly, such as: "Friends, comrades! If you are men enough, step forward! Let each side in the debate publish all the articles in which it is criticized by the other side. That is what we are doing, and we hope you will follow our example. If you are men enough, you will. But having a guilty conscience and an unjust case, being fierce of visage but faint of heart, outwardly as tough as bulls but inwardly as timid as mice, you will not dare. We are sure you will not dare. Isn't that so? Please answer!"[7] Whenever I think of these lines, a passion to debate people in defense of truth surges up from inside.[8]

Xu Hailiang (b. 1944) is a retired hydraulic engineer and hydraulic historian and the author of a memoir about the Cultural Revolution in Wuhan titled *The Chronicles of East Lake*. He says that for him the Cultural Revolution may have begun in the 1950s. At that time he was attending high school in Chongqing, and high school life was just as tumultuous as for those who went to high school in the early 1960s, because in the 1950s they were already hearing news about de-Stalinization and antiparty cliques in the Soviet Union, raising for them serious questions about the future of international communism. He remembers reading *The Young Mao Zedong* (*Mao Zedong de qing nian shi dai*) written by Li Rui and being inspired by Mao's example of a poor young man trying to change China and the world. When Xu started college in 1963 at the Wuhan College of Hydraulic and Electrical Engineering, the historic debate between the Chinese Communist Party and the Communist Party of the Soviet Union had just begun. He found himself fully devoted to studying the Nine Commentaries and believed that the style of the debate significantly influenced the polemical style of the Red Guard movement.[9]

Jin Shan (b. 1948) is a well-known sports commentator and researcher in the Beijing Academy of Social Sciences. In a blog entry dated February 24, 2012, he wrote about how the voices of famous anchors broadcasting the Nine Commentaries on radio inspired him:

> Beginning on September 6, 1963, the Central Committee of CCP, in the name of the editorial boards of *People's Daily* and the *Red Flag* magazine, published a series of polemics against the open letter of the Soviet Communist Party. These polemics were known as the Nine Commentaries. It seems that as newspaper articles their impact was not so clear. But once they were read by Qi Yue and Xia Qing on the Central People's Radio Station, they stirred up cities and villages all over the nation. Their eloquent and uplifting voices were imitated by many people. . . . Undoubtedly, the broadcasting of the Nine Commentaries at that time has become the collective memory of all Chinese above the age of fifty-five. In those years, in many large and small cities, it was almost as if everyone was reading the Nine Commentaries, everyone was listening to the Nine Commentaries, and everyone was talking about the Nine Commentaries. The broadcasting of the Nine Commentaries on Central People's Radio Station caused huge enthusiasm in its audience. After the Fifth Commentary was broadcast, Zhou Enlai, Deng Xiaoping and Chen Yi went to the Broadcasting Bureau and received all the staff members of the Nine Commentary broadcasting team.[10]

FILMS ABOUT CHILDREN, YOUTH, AND WAR

The effective use of films for propaganda in the Maoist period is well recognized by scholars of Chinese cinema. As Xueping Zhong puts it, "the CCP had from the founding of the PRC looked upon film as an important propaganda (and entertainment) tool. As a result, films were made to be, either implicitly or explicitly, the discursive bearer of the CCP's ideology."[11]

In the 1950s and early 1960s, China produced about two hundred feature films, nearly half of which were war movies.[12] In the same period, thirty-nine children's films were produced, eight of which were war films.[13] War films depict revolutionary heroes and martyrs in the War of Resistance against Japan and in the Civil War with the Guomindang troops. Not all films about children and youth had military themes; many of them were about socialist construction in the new China. Yet both types of films create heroic and idealistic characters for China's younger generation to emulate.

War films were especially popular. They were didactic but entertaining, because the film professionals who made the films had war experiences themselves.[14] Overall, as Ban Wang puts it, "Chinese revolutionary films had a tremendous and indelible emotional impact on audiences."[15] And, although they were ideological, many scenes provided emotional pleasures for viewers, allowing them "to enjoy a sensuous and aesthetic delight not dictated by political doctrines."[16] Table 2.1 shows a list of the films that are often mentioned in the retrospective writings of members of the Cultural Revolution generation.

Zhou Ziren was a student in Chongqing University at the beginning of the Cultural Revolution and became the editor of the main newspaper of the August Fifteenth faction, *August Fifteenth Battle News* (featured in chapter 1). His memoir about his experiences during the period contains many stories and reflections about factional violence in Chongqing. Here is one:

> Today, I still clearly remember an experience in Chongqing. It was at dusk and I forgot why, but I took a truck and went to the May First Vocation School on Shiyou Road. That place had been turned into the battle front of the two factions locked in armed struggle. There, the August Fifteenth had set up its headquarters for armed struggle for the Daping District. The dusky sky looked gloomy. On the small campus, the young boys and girls of the vocation school were preparing for war. They were in the prime of their lives. They should be wearing loose T-shirts or beautiful skirts and sharing their dreams and tender love with each other in the garden pathways at dusk. And yet, at this point, they were carrying stones in their dirty clothes and piling them in front of the building for military defense. Others were smashing the stones into small pieces and then carried them inside the building for use as weapons. Some girls were using their notebook paper to wrap limestone powder, one pack at a time. These were also to be used as weapons. All the windows were smashed and were sheltered only

TABLE 2.1 POPULAR CHINESE FILMS
IN THE 1950S AND EARLY 1960S

CHILDREN'S FILMS	*Letter with Feather* (鸡毛信, 1954) *Flowers of the Nation* (祖国的花朵, 1955) *Red Children* (红孩子, 1958) *Little Heroes* (英雄小八路, 1961) *Little Soldier Zhang Ga* (小兵张嘎, 1963)
FILMS FOR YOUTH	*Song of Youth* (青春之歌, 1958) *Ode to Ouyang Hai* (欧阳海之歌, 1965) *The Young Generation* (年轻的一代, 1965)
FOREIGN FILMS	*Chapaev* (夏伯阳, 1934; Soviet film directed by the Vasilyev brothers) *The Gadfly* (牛虻, 1955; Soviet film introduced to China same year)
WAR FILMS	*Defending Yan'an* (保卫延安, 1954) *Railroad Guerrillas* (铁道游击队, 1954) *Shanggan Ridge* (上甘岭, 1956) *Tracks in the Snowy Forest* (林海雪原, 1957) *Ancient City Under Attack from Wild Fire and Spring Wind* (野火春风斗古城, 1958) *Steel Meets Fire* (烈火金钢, 1958) *Behind Enemy Lines* (敌后武工队, 1958) *Red Crag* (红岩, 1961) *Mine Warfare* (地雷战, 1962) *Heroic Sons and Daughters* (英雄儿女, 1964) *Tunnel Warfare* (地道战, 1965)

SOURCE: AUTHOR'S COMPILATION.

with straw curtains. This scene was every bit the same as that in the revolutionary film *Tunnel Warfare*, where the villagers were busily preparing to fight the invading Japanese troops.[17]

Li Musen, a leader of the August Fifteenth's opposing faction Fight to the End (*fan dao di*), also wrote about factional battles in his memoir. He recalled that on August 13, 1967, his faction decided to attack the Jialing River bridge, which was guarded by its rival faction August Fifteenth. On the night of August 14, he and his comrades-in-arms transported heavy artillery to battle position using six trucks. At this point, he wrote, "I walked over to the Jiangbei District party committee compound to check out the best location for positioning the 12.7mm machine gun. . . . I chose a little hill on the right side. It was next to the auditorium. I set up the tripod next to the auditorium and placed the machine properly. I held the machine with my two hands. At this point, the shining image of the hero Chapaev shooting machine guns in the Soviet movie *Chapaev* appeared in my mind."

My last story in this section is about a Mr. Zhang, who was born in 1958 and is currently employed in the international freight shipping business in his home town in Zhejiang. In his spare time, he blogs about books he has read, films he has seen, and about his childhood memories. I came across his blog accidently and then started communicating with him by e-mail. In one e-mail exchange, he wrote to me, "because of the rigorous and orthodox education I received as a child, there is more or less some kind of 'red syndrome" (*hong se qing jie*) in my bones that will not be brushed away."[18] Both in his e-mails to me and in his blogs, he wrote about the deep influence films had on him. In a blog essay he posted on March 30, 2013, he wrote about his deep memories of the 1965 film *The Young Generation:* "Every generation has its own aspirations. Every generation has its own youth and ideals. If in the lives of many people there is always a book or a film that shapes their life trajectories, then undoubtedly in my own memory, one of the most memorable is the film *The Young Generation.*"

Much studied by literary scholars for its depiction of China's idealistic youth right before the CR started,[19] *The Young Generation* tells the story of Lin Lan and her brother Lin Yusheng. Lin Lan is a young woman in Shanghai who gives up a comfortable life and career opportunities to settle in a poor village in order to dedicate herself to socialist construction. In contrast, her brother Yusheng has worked briefly as a geologist in a remote Qinghai Province and, now back in Shanghai on sick leave, wants to get married and settle down in Shanghai instead of returning to his job in Qinghai. The film ends with Yusheng going back to Qinghai after reading a letter left for him by his biological parents written before they were executed in Guomindang's prison. Mr. Zhang remembers that he was in elementary school when he watched the film, and the scene of Yusheng reading the letter always brought tears to his eyes; even after he grew up, when he watched this scene, he still felt deeply moved. Mr. Zhang wrote:

> I can never forget the ending of the film—Lin Lan's awe-inspiring words of farewell, delivered in [actress] Cao Lei's youthful and sonorous voice. Perhaps for many people who came of age in that period, those words are an unforgettable part of our memory: "Good-bye, papa and mama. Good-bye Grandma Xiao. Good-

bye, teachers and classmates! We're leaving. We are going to assume our respon-sibilities on our jobs, just like seeds being scattered on earth. We will take roots, germinate, blossom, and bear fruits. Good-bye, we are setting off, bearing your hopes and blessings to create a beautiful future. Good-bye!"[20]

MUSIC, SONGS, AND IMAGES

Another source of influence for the Red Guard generation was music, songs, and images from posters and children's picture books (*lian huan hua*). These cultural forms were used extensively by Red Guards in their verbal battles. Red Guard newspapers exploded with militant images and cartoons just as campuses and streets were often full of the blasting of Red Guard broadcast-ing stations. Music and battle songs would be broadcast mingled with verbal attacks and propaganda. The "Fight to the End" faction in Chongqing, for ex-ample, had its broadcast station in the post and telecommunications build-ing in the center of the city near the Liberation Monument until the building was attacked and destroyed by the August Fifteenth on August 13, 1967.[21]

Stories of young Red Guards singing revolutionary songs in the face of danger were common in the Red Guard press and retrospective writings. One example is Zhu Qingfang (1951–1967) who died at age fifteen in a fac-tional battle in Wuhan. She was then a junior high school student in Wu-han's No. 8 Middle School and a supporter of Wuhan's rebel organization Wuhan Workers Rebel Headquarters. On June 24, 1967, the Workers Rebel Headquarters, which was based in the Wuhan Workers Union Building, was attacked by its opponent Million Heroes. Million Heroes soon defeated the Workers Rebel Headquarters, but the Workers Rebels' broadcasting station at the top of the building continued to blast out the rebels' military song. Ac-cording to the recollections of Yingji Changkong, a blogger who wrote about Zhu Qingfang's death in 2006, the Million Heroes stormed into the broad-casting station and dragged a young girl out. The girl was Zhu Qingfang. Yingji Changkong wrote:

With crowds of Million Heroes pointing their lance at her chest, Zhu Qingfang was contemptuous and began to sing with deep emotion the popular revolution-ary song "On Top of the Golden Mountain in Beijing." As someone of the same generation, I can imagine what she was thinking at that moment. She must be thinking: In order to defend Chairman Mao's revolutionary line, I will view death as going home. She must be thinking: I'll be like the little hero Liu Hulan, who died at my own age, and face the enemy's murderous knife calmly. She must be thinking: After she dies, her comrades-in-arms will continue to fight for the revolutionary beliefs she deeply upheld.

Exacerbated by anger at the young girl's performance of fearlessness and contempt, the attackers killed her on the spot.[22]

One of the most thoughtful stories about the power of posters is told by Xiaomei Chen, a professor of Chinese literature at the University of California at Davis who grew up in China during the Cultural Revolution. In an essay published in 1999, Chen wrote:

> I have no doubt that in my unconscious, posters became indelibly inscribed as part of my childhood world of wonders, my wanderings, and the emotions associated with growing pains. My weekend visits to history museums in the early 1960s (before the Cultural Revolution when museums, libraries, and other cultural institutions were closed), included bus trips to the architectural marvels known as the "ten great buildings" (*shi da janzhu*), which were constructed in a very short period of time to celebrate the tenth anniversary of the nation's founding. I do not recall whether special posters were prompted to commemorate endeavors of this sort, but these edifices constituted the setting for many posters; the most frequently used was the Great Hall of the People. Surely there would also have been commemorative stamps (*jinian youpiao*), souvenir badges (*jinian zhang*) and postcards that would have found their way into the treasured space of my messy drawers. In this way painting, poster, artifact, museum, and national identities and narratives all become blurred, coalescing into the most valued memories of my childhood.[23]

BIOGRAPHIES AND LITERARY WORKS

Books had a special appeal to the Red Guard generation (if only because of the lack of them), and many of the personal stories of this generation are about reading experiences. As a sacred text propagated nationwide, the *Quotations of Chairman Mao*, or the *Little Red Book*, was memorized by millions and the ability to quote passages from it in the middle of mass debates in the Cultural Revolution could decide the chances of winning or losing an argument. Many retrospective writings also mention the influences of biographies of Karl Marx, Friedrich Engels, and Mao Zedong, as well as works of literature. Cai Xiang (b. 1953), a literary critic at Shanghai University, recalls:

[In my memory], I saw a thirteen-year old boy walking toward me. . . . As I walked to him slowly, I saw again the spirit of that time, a red age of heart-throbbing thrill. At that time, we were no longer having classes. Teachers were busy studying, making self-criticisms, and exposing one another. We took to the streets and angrily stared at those wearing sunglasses, long hair, sharp-pointed leather shoes, and snow-white shirt collars. We condemned all these people as hooligans. We worshipped Pavel Korchagin [hero in the Russian novel *How the Steel Was Tempered*] and emulated everything about the young Pavel. To train our bravery and will, we lined up to jump off the balcony on the second floor of our building. We had our own organization and published our own newspaper. . . . All our sense of crisis was brought out by that age. We congratulated ourselves for finally encountering a revolution.[24]

Mr. Huang Zhenhai, a painter, was born in 1950 and was a junior high school student in Chengdu in 1966. In an interview published in a 2012 issue of the online Chinese journal *Yesterday*, he explained why people got involved in factional fighting: "The cause of factional warfare could be traced to the war education before the Cultural Revolution. When we were kids, we dreamed of fighting wars, because wars produced the heroes we worshipped. The favorite films of young boys were all war films."[25] In addition to war films, Huang mentioned the popular books they read, such as *Red Crag* and *Red Sun*: "These books were all about the war years. . . . Growing up in this kind of atmosphere, many of us hated the fact that we were born too late. Otherwise, we could have joined the war against Chiang Kai-shek or against the Japanese. Who knows, we could have been a Little Soldier Zhang Ga or a Li Xiangyang."[26]

Xie Quan was a high school student in Chengdu at the beginning of the Cultural Revolution. He recalled that he devoted himself seriously to the Cultural Revolution and from the autumn of 1967 to spring of 1968 was engaged in "deep and fearless explorations in search of truth." He remembered, however, that he was in a spiritual crisis on the eve of the Cultural Revolution: "Before the Cultural Revolution began, I was in high school. I was in a state of spiritual crisis. I didn't know clearly why I was studying and did not have a clear idea of the meaning of life."[27]

He recalled that reading the biographies of Marx, Engels, and Mao Zedong gave him a sense of direction. He wrote,

I really like this passage written by the young Engels: "My heart was often fermenting and boiling. My not-always cool brain was burning endlessly. I strove for great thoughts which would cleanse the dross of my heart and turn energy into fiery flames." I wrote these words in my own notebook and felt that they subtly captured my own state of mind. At that time, I worshipped Marx and Engels for their spirit to pursue truth and devote themselves to truth, their great learning, and their noble aspirations. . . . At that time, I also read Li Rui's book *Mao Zedong and the Revolutionary Activities of His Youth*. I very much enjoyed some of the passages in the book. As a young man, Mao Zedong once wrote in his notebook: "As an individual, I'm small; as part of the cosmos, I'm grand. As an individual, I'm but a physical being; as part of the cosmos, I'm a spiritual being." These words left a deep impression on me. I especially liked an axiom which the young Mao Zedong praised highly: "Civilize one's spirit, bestialize one's body." I asked a classmate who wrote good calligraphy to copy these two phrases for me. When he was writing, I asked him to reverse the order of the two phrases, because I thought what was especially innovative about this saying was the use of the word "bestialize," which forms an interesting contrast with "civilize."[28]

CRAFTING A REVOLUTIONARY TRADITION

In his reflections on the Chinese student movement in 1989, the literary critic turned political dissident and Nobel Peace laureate Liu Xiaobo remarks that "in Communist China, there is no word more sacred or richer in righteous indignation and moral force than 'revolution.'" He continues,

> Although ten years of reform have attenuated the sacred quality of "revolution" and weakened the political culture built upon class struggle, we still worship "revolution" in our bones. We are still the "revolutionary successors." As soon as we meet with a large-scale political movement, our enthusiasm for "revolution" swells; as soon as the kindling of revolution is lit, it burns—the fire rapidly becoming flames that reach to heaven, consuming everything. It does not matter whether the movement is of the extreme Right or the extreme Left, autocratic or democratic, progressive or regressive; "revolution" supersedes all. From within any tendency, it is possible to excite our frenzied worship of "revolution."[29]

Liu then goes on to argue that the 1989 protest movement, in its sublime struggles for democracy, was also a revolution born out of the worship of "revolution." Where did this worship of revolution come from?

Although efforts to craft a revolutionary tradition had been an integral part of the process of the Chinese revolution, the most systematic efforts started in the Yan'an period.[30] After the founding of the People's Republic in 1949, such efforts took on a new urgency. A new revolutionary regime must not only rebuild economy and society but must also establish and maintain its political legitimacy through culture work such as the building of traditions. Constructing a revolutionary tradition became an essential part of this effort. By the eve of the Cultural Revolution, as Perry puts it, "China had embarked on a sacred revolutionary crusade to save the nation and the world from the perils of Soviet 'revisionism.'"[31]

This tradition celebrated martyrdom and revolutionary heroes, exalted class struggle and violence as a necessary means of revolution, and glorified death for the cause of revolution. The entire education of the Red Guard generation in the seventeen years prior to the Cultural Revolution, whether it was formal school education or informal education through films, arts, and children's picture books, was suffused with these messages of heroic martyrdom.[32]

Chang-tai Hung's study of political culture in the early PRC may be read as a work on the building of revolutionary traditions. The five parts of the book cover 1. the utilization of space such as the building of the ten monumental buildings in Beijing; 2. celebrations such as parades and revolutionary dances; 3. the treatment of history in museums and paintings; 4. the use of visual images in depicting war, resistance, heroes, and enemies; and 5. the building of memorials in celebration of heroes. Hung shows how Chinese leaders in the early years of the PRC mobilized both traditional and new cultural forms to construct a tradition of revolutionary heroism and glory and affirm the legitimacy of the new regime. The chapter on the "cult of the red martyr," for example, shows that part of the new political culture was about the creation of a national institution in celebration of heroes who died in China's revolutionary struggles. Called the "red martyrs," this institution took on the quality of a political "cult," calling on citizens to worship and emulate the red martyrs. Hung shows that the building of this "cult" was a top-down political project of the CCP created through a whole set of practices consisting of the establishment of a Martyrs Memorial Day, the building of war memorials, the publication of martyrs' biographies, and even public trials of "counterrevolutionaries" charged with murdering communist martyrs.[33] By the eve of the Cultural Revolution, an edifice of "revolutionary tradition" had been erected.

The institutions and practices of the "cult of the red martyr," built in the 1950s, did not just remain in place during the Cultural Revolution. The Cultural Revolution was in fact the ultimate manifestation and proof of the profound effects of the revolutionary tradition. Of all aspects of the Cultural

Revolution, the factional battles were the manifestations in their most con-crete form. They reenacted familiar scenes in the representations of war and revolution that had become an integral part of the social and mental land-scape of the Cultural Revolution generation prior to the Cultural Revolution.

TRADITION BUILDING AS PERSON MAKING

Hobsbawm identifies three overlapping types of invented traditions: "a) those establishing or symbolizing social cohesion or the membership of groups, real or artificial communities, b) those establishing or legitimizing institutions, status or relations of authority, and c) those whose main pur-pose was socialization, the inculcation of beliefs, value systems and conven-tions of behaviour."[34] He finds that type a) was prevalent, while types b) and c) were implicit or derivative from type a).

Types b) and c) were evidently more important in China in the years be-fore the Cultural Revolution. The building of the Chinese revolutionary tra-dition, such as the remaking and sacralization of the political space of the Tiananmen Square,[35] had everything to do with legitimizing the new revolu-tionary regime and its political and moral authority. It also aimed explicitly at the remaking of citizenry, or rather the making of a new citizenry.[36] The prime target of this political project was the Red Guard generation, the first cohort "born under the red flag."

The Chinese Communist Revolution had started as a youth movement, and the Communist Party had always relied on youth as revolutionary van-guards. In the decade after the communist victory, the question of cultivat-ing revolutionary successors took on unprecedented urgency.[37] The socialist state devoted great attention to the making of the new socialist person.[38] Thus, from early on, efforts to craft a revolutionary tradition in the period before the Cultural Revolution went hand in hand with political designs to cultivate revolutionary successors.

In the 1950s, shortly after the founding of the PRC, the "First National Conference of Cadres Involved in Adolescents' and Children's Work" formu-lated the educational objectives of the new nation: "Our educational aim is to nurture the new generation in correct ideological consciousness and revolutionary qualities, to give them basic cultural and scientific knowl-edge and healthy bodies, in short (to bring up) virtuous and wise future masters of a new society, outstanding sons and daughters of new China."[39] Throughout the period, but especially after 1956, an intense social and po-litical atmosphere was created for the cultivation of the young generation as revolutionary successors. An editorial (June 1) in a 1959 issue of *People's Daily* claimed that children were "the army for building communism in the future." Another called for "stories about the revolutionary struggle and heroic and exemplary exploits in actual life" (June 1, 1960).[40] In his analysis of the "revolutionization" campaign in the early 1960s, Townsend writes,

> In short, Chinese youth were given a clear message to revolutionize themselves through study, struggle, and self-cultivation. They received, too, a list of the virtues they were to develop and the evils they were to oppose. But the revolutionary struggles in which they were to steel themselves were non-existent, and the evils were pervasive phenomena scattered throughout society without connection to specific classes or social strata. During the Great Leap, revolutionary spirit could be cultivated and used in a struggle against nature and all manifestations of conservative thought. By 1962, however, nature had proved unconquerable and some of the "conservative" notions of 1959 had acquired official sanction. The problem that lay beneath the propaganda appeals of 1962 was how youth were to revolutionize themselves in a non-revolutionary situation.[41]

The Red Guard cohort was cultivated as revolutionary romantics. According to a study of elementary school readers in use between 1957 and 1964, the political and behavioral values being taught included 1. devotion to the new society, 2. benevolence of the new society, 3. glorification of Mao Zedong, 4. the evils of Guomindang China, 5. social and personal responsibility, 6. achievement and altruistic behavior.[42] The ideal socialist person would have an unquestioning belief in the Communist leaders and the socialist state and be ready to make self-sacrifices for their sake.[43]

A careful study of the emulation of heroes published in early 1968 shows that Chinese political culture prior to the Cultural Revolution had built an image of revolutionary heroism that directly fed and fired Red Guard factional struggles. Analyzing the diaries of officially promoted heroes, Mary Sheridan wrote that "a hero openly courts death, and when it comes it elevates him to a higher plane. There is a thrill of achievement which overrides the sense of loss . . . for a revolutionary hero, death holds neither pain, nor fear, nor disfigurement. Transfixed by inner visions, the hero watches himself pass into immortality. He dies in spiritual certainty."[44] This revolutionary romanticism had always been in the Maoist vision of revolution. Sheridan further wrote, "but in the Red Guard period this proclivity for the images and symbols of romanticism was carried to new extremes: (1) youth as the ideal condition of life; (2) the Faustian struggle to break through the physical constraints of tradition and old age by returning to or emulating the condition of youth; (3) destruction and renewal through perpetual rebellion of younger generations against older; (4) the glorification of death and sacrifice; (5) freedom conceived as service to an immortal ideal."[45]

This extraordinary identification with the socialist state was characteristic of Chinese youth before the Red Guard movement. Patriotism had been a dominant force in the making of twentieth-century Chinese history. It was a major inspiration for Chinese youth dedicated to national liberation and modernization. The socialist state successfully inducted this historical energy into new circumstances and transformed it into a passion for the socialist state and its charismatic leaders.

Parallel to this passion was a utopian vision of the future. Gloating over their recent revolutionary victory, Chinese communist leaders imagined the imminent realization of Marx's vision of a communist society. National projects of industrialization were launched to accelerate this process.[46] With an historical identity of revolutionary vanguards, Chinese youth were the "moral elect" to whom the call of utopianism appealed directly. As Mi Hedu puts it,

> The political education that was poured into us in the 17 years before the Cultural Revolution played an important role in forming our world views. In short, it was a Marxist idealism and a sense of social responsibility and mission centered upon the theory of class struggle. . . . The excessive political education cultivated a grandiose political zeal in our generation, which, compared with other social groups, was much more radical and had a much stronger sense of political participation and sense of intervention in social life.[47]

How did top-down approaches to the building of a revolutionary tradition and the molding of revolutionary successors appeal to their targeted audience? Two factors were indispensable to the success of these policies. One was the multiple, all-encompassing cultural forms that were mobilized for the molding of the youth just discussed. The other was the social world of the youth, which gave a sense of reality to the narratives of revolution by creating a sense of enchantment and danger.

A SOCIAL WORLD OF ENCHANTMENT AND DANGER

The idyllic and romantic atmosphere of the film *Flowers of the Nation* shows that the youth of the Red Guard generation lived in a fairy-tale world in the

1950s and early 1960s. This was a world of enchantment, mesmerization, and danger, one that combined a sense of infinite possibilities and hopes with a sense of danger and threat. It was this world that gave reality, urgency, and potency to the political culture of that historical era. These two worlds were juxtaposed in the mass media campaigns, policies, and the entire cultural atmosphere of that time. The result was a peculiar way of imagining the world and imaging the purpose of life. The liberal intellectual Qian Liqun conveys the sense of danger in his essay "The Way Our Generation Imagined the World": "In the 1950s and 1960s, Mainland China underwent two external embargoes—the blockade by the Western societies led by the United States in the 1950s, and the blockade by the international communist movement led by the Soviet Union. This had a profound impact on the thoughts, characters, culture, and psychological structures of the intellectuals who grew up during these twenty years. Even to this day the impact has not yet been adequately appreciated."[48]

Qian's essay also captures that sense of enchantment in his generation: "In our minds, the world consisted of 'oppressors and the oppressed,' the former being our enemies and the latter our brothers, sisters, and friends. Our ideal and our historical mission was to eliminate all of that, both in China and abroad: all the phenomena of oppression, exploitation, and slavery. Perhaps it was a Utopian ideal and pursuit, but we were utterly sincere. We tended to view international issues as extensions of the national issues, and this way of thinking is a particular trademark of our generation."[49]

The construction of this social world was influenced by Mao's theory of permanent revolution and Mao's perception of domestic trouble and international threat in a cold war context.[50] Propagated in 1958, Mao's theory of permanent revolution reflected his deep anxieties over and contradictory assessments of the conditions of Chinese socialism. The completion of the first Five-Year Plan in 1956 was hailed as a milestone, marking the young nation's successful transition into the stage of socialism in the Marxist vision of human progress. Mao was apparently euphoric about China's economic achievements. On his Moscow visit in November 1957 to attend the Conference of World Communist and Workers' Parties, Mao heard Nikita Khrushchev's speech commemorating the fortieth anniversary of the October Revolution, when Khrushchev pledged that the Soviet Union would overtake the United States in major industrial indicators in fifteen years. In his own speech Mao surprised his fellow communists from around the world by boasting that China would surpass the United Kingdom in fifteen years.[51] He returned from his Moscow visit to prepare and launch the "Great Leap

Forward" so as to leapfrog China from socialism into what utopian Marxism viewed as the final destiny of humankind—communism.

While preparing to launch China into a communist society, Mao was burdened with worries about both domestic challenges and international threats. This led to a series of polices and campaigns aimed at forestalling Soviet-type revisionism and American imperialism. First was the perceived danger of Soviet revisionism to the international communist movement. De-Stalinization by Khrushchev led Mao to fear a future de-Maoization in China. Such concerns were exacerbated by the large-scale popular demonstrations in Poland and Hungary at the end of 1956. Reflecting on these events, Mao was quoted as saying: "It is destined that our socialist revolution and reconstruction will not be smooth sailing. We should be prepared to deal with many serious threats facing us both internationally and domestically. As far as the international and domestic situations are concerned, although it is certain both are good in a general sense, it is also certain that many serious challenges are waiting for us. We must be prepared to deal with them."[52]

To forestall similar happenings in China, Mao decided to reform the party. A rectification campaign was launched in May 1957, calling for a "hundred flowers" to bloom. In a short period of five weeks, intellectuals and students poured out so many pent-up grievances against the party that the party hurriedly gathered itself together to fight back. As a result, about four hundred thousand rightists—persons who had spoken against the party—were seized and subjected to punishments, including imprisonment.[53] From the unexpected and unprecedented outspokenness of the intellectuals, Mao and other Chinese party leaders derived the message that "it would be extremely hazardous to base the country's economic future on their skills."[54] Mao's hope rested on the young generation.

On his same visit to Moscow in November 1957, at a meeting with Chinese students studying in the Soviet Union, Mao expressed his faith in China's young generation in the following terms: "The world is yours as well as ours, but in the last analysis, it is yours. You young people, full of vigor and vitality, are in the bloom of life, like the sun at eight or nine in the morning. Our hopes are placed in you."[55] These remarks were to inspire millions in the following years to live up to Mao's high expectations. That Mao made these remarks in the context of the imminent Sino-Soviet split and Mao's prediction of a third world war added a somber premonition to what may now sound like simple words of encouragement to young people.[56] As Perry notes in her study of the construction of the Anyuan revolutionary tradition, paranoid as those warnings about "hidden counterrevolutionaries" and "secret agents" may seem today, "events on the ground at the time did lend some credence to these dire admonitions. In the early years of the PRC, the Communist Party's hold on power appeared more tenuous than is sometimes remembered."[57]

The international environment became more treacherous in the years after the 1957 Moscow conference. In May 1957 the Nationalists in Taiwan reached an agreement with the United States that permitted the emplacement on Taiwan of U.S. matador surface-to-surface missiles, capable of delivering a nuclear warhead into the Chinese mainland. The most serious event was the Taiwan Strait Crisis in 1958, which, according to recent studies, almost pushed the world to the verge of a nuclear war. Although Jian Chen argues that China's abrupt bombing of the Jinmen Island, an outpost of the Guomindang regime in Taiwan, was Mao's strategy of using anti-imperialism to mobilize domestic fervor for the Great Leap Forward, Nancy Tucker shows that American policy makers seriously considered the possibility of launching nuclear warheads at targets in mainland China.[58]

Although the military crisis ended soon when China abruptly stopped shelling Jinmen Island, Mao came to be preoccupied with the threat of "peaceful evolution." According to the memoirs of Bo Yibo,[59] who was the PRC's first minister of finance and then a vice premier from 1957 to 1966, although Mao paid attention to the U.S. secretary of state John Dulles's strategy of "fading" Chinese communism through "peaceful evolution" as early as in 1953, it was not until 1958 and 1959 that Mao brought up the issue of preventing "peaceful evolution." By then the mass protests in Poland and Hungary and the de-Stalinization in the Soviet Union had convinced Mao that the American strategy of peaceful evolution was already taking effect.

Other developments further enhanced the Chinese regime's perception of threat. In September 1959, the Soviet leader Khrushchev met with President Dwight Eisenhower on a visit to the United States. He then briefed Chinese leaders that Eisenhower wanted peaceful coexistence. The Chinese leaders did not share Khrushchev's view. Chinese analysis of the situation pointed to the "irreconcilable hostility of the imperialists to the socialist camp."[60] Eisenhower's strongly worded State of the Union address in 1960 served to confirm Chinese fears. Then on July 16, 1960, the Soviet Union notified the Chinese Foreign Ministry of its decision to withdraw Soviet advisers from China, marking the final rupture between China and the Soviet Union. From 1961 to 1963, while President Kennedy was in office, American commitment to South Vietnam increased. After Lyndon Johnson assumed office, the American commitment escalated. Johnson and his advisers "came to see the struggle in Vietnam as one which the West had to win."[61] Subsequently, Chinese aid to North Vietnam increased.

By 1964 the Chinese foreign minister was assuring foreign experts that "the Chinese were prepared for attack by the United States from the south, the Russians from the north, and the Japanese from the east."[62] On April 12, 1965, the Central Committee of the Chinese Communist Party issued a directive on preparing for war.

It was in this tense international context that China waged its sustained polemics against Soviet revisionism, flooding the nation with warnings of imminent danger. And it was this social world that made texts such as the Nine Commentaries and films like *Tunnel Warfare* so meaningful and relevant to the youth of the time.

3
THEORY AND DISSENT

THE FACTIONAL WARFARE IN Chongqing was so complicated that one chapter can hardly do justice to it. Besides the violence, for example, Chongqing was home to one of the "big five" articles of dissent that appeared in the Red Guard movement. In the language of the Cultural Revolution, they were called counterrevolutionary "poisonous weeds" (*du cao*). One of the editorials published in *August Fifteenth Battle News* caused Mao's personal displeasure and was declared heresy. Nationwide, there were other such Red Guard writings that were denounced as "poisonous weeds." These writings expressed heterodox thoughts, or ideas of dissent, and are the subject of this chapter.

While factional warfare was prevalent across the nation, voices expressing dissent were more limited in scale or influence. This chapter therefore moves out of Chongqing to survey the broad landscape of Red Guard dissent. If a case study of factional warfare in Chongqing reveals much about the logic of revolutionary performance in the Red Guard movement, it takes a broader survey to bring to light the less visible currents of dissent.

Theoretically, my argument is consistent with the thesis about factional violence in Chongqing developed in chapter 1. I argued there that the escalation to factional violence was the result of Red Guards and rebels consciously enacting a hallowed revolutionary culture in response to political circumstances that called for such enactment. This chapter will show that, besides a commitment to revolutionary practice, Red Guards and rebels were also actively performing revolutionary theorizing. Just as factional violence was the result of practical revolutionary action, so dissent was, ironically, the outcome of theoretical revolutionary action. I will show that the same myth of revolution that fired Red Guard passions for revolutionary practice and led to violence also fed their passion for revolutionary theory. And it was in the pursuit of revolutionary theory and in attempting to apply theory to the analysis of Chinese reality that a small minority of youth began to formulate and express ideas of dissent.

The major texts of dissent in the Cultural Revolution are collected in a volume edited by Song and Sun.[1] These are arranged under nine groups of essays. Eight of these groups of essays appeared during the Red Guard movement, whereas the last one, a wall poster by Li Yizhe, appeared in 1974. The nine groups of essays are as follows:

1. Bloodline theory
2. Theories of family origin
3. "Doubt everything"
4. The April Third new trends of thought
5. The May Sixteenth trends of thought
6. Shengwulian in Hunan
7. Bei-jue-yang in Wuhan
8. New trends of thought in Shanghai
9. Li Yizhe's wall poster

This chapter does not intend to offer a comprehensive analysis of all expressions of political dissent in the Red Guard movement. My analysis will focus on four clusters of heterodox essays: 1. theories of family origin, 2. "Doubt everything" or the "December black winds," 3. the April Third faction and new trends of thought, and 4. Shengwulian in Hunan. These four groups of heterodox writings contain both the key ideas of dissent expressed in the Red Guard movement and well represent the conditions and dynamics under which dissent was expressed. An analysis of these samples will be sufficient to demonstrate that dissent, like violence, was the result of factional competition to perform the revolution.

THE MEANING OF RED GUARD DISSENT

An important feature of the Red Guard movement was the mutual attacks between opposing factions conducted through wall posters and factional newspapers, leaflets, handbills, and other such publications. In these publications, rival factions would accuse each other of spreading counterrevolutionary ideas, "poisonous weeds," "counterrevolutionary black winds," or "ultraleftist thoughts." Some of these fall under what I refer to as dissent, but most do not. While rival factions challenged each other, they both subscribed to the same regimes of truth as represented by Mao and the official theories of the Cultural Revolution. I will consider as dissent only those ideas that either challenged Mao and the rationale of the Cultural Revolution or were denounced as such by Mao and his lieutenants.

Dissent is a form of heterodoxy, and heterodoxy is what it is through its relationship to orthodoxy.[2] The orthodoxy about which dissenting ideas were expressed in the Red Guard movement had many components. Foremost among them were Marxism and Maoism. The core idea taken from Marxism was class struggle. Mao's main contribution was the idea of *ceaseless* class struggle even *after* a proletarian revolution. Enunciated as the theory of "continuous revolution under the conditions of proletarian dictatorship," it provided the theoretical basis for launching the Cultural Revolution. For the practice of the Cultural Revolution, these abstract ideas were translated into concrete political terms in the official party document "Decision Concerning the Great Proletarian Cultural Revolution," known as the "Sixteen Points."[3]

The "Sixteen Points" set out two basic rules of the game for the Cultural Revolution. One is that individual party leaders may be attacked, but not the party itself, not the socialist system, not Mao Zedong or his ideas.[4] Further, the raison d'être of the Cultural Revolution was beyond doubt because it was launched by Mao Zedong as a new stage of the Chinese socialist revolution.[5] Dissent, then, refers to ideas that violated these terms of the Cultural Revolution, or, as Xu Youyu puts it, "all attitudes, ideas, theories that disagreed with officially promulgated doctrines."[6]

To the extent that ideas of dissent were not isolated slogans but formed "*trends* of thought" (*yi duan si chao*), they had a systemic nature, aiming at more or less systemic critiques of the political system and the official establishment. If individual party leaders were denounced, it was mainly in order to attack the system and orthodoxy that the individuals represented. It is in this sense that Andrew Walder considers these subversive ideas as dissident radicalism and their authors as dissident radicals: "Dissident radicals were descended from heterodox radical groups that came to dissent from the officially defined orientation of the Cultural Revolution. . . . These radicals developed a *systemic* critique that did not place blame on degenerate individuals within the Party. . . . Rather, there was something about the Party system that encouraged this degeneration, and so the system of power and privilege must be restructured in order to prevent similar degeneration in the future."[7]

Ideologically oppressive atmospheres anywhere have chilling effects on voices of dissent. How was dissent possible in a movement whose zealous participants pledged themselves to be the loyal red guards of "red power" and fervently performed their loyalty even if it they had to resort to violence?

It is worth emphasizing that almost all the heterodox writings appeared in small waves of a sequence of essays. Such was the case of the "December black winds," Yu Luoke's "On Family Origins" series, the Bei-jue-yang manifestos and investigation reports, and Yang Xiguang's series of essays discussed below. It seems that these young authors could not, or would not want to, stop writing. They seemed to be driven by an imperative to theorize.

I propose that these ideas of dissent did not originally appear as dissent, but rather as the efforts of sincere believers to theorize the Cultural Revolution. They were the product of the conscious imitation and enactment of what their authors imagined orthodox Marxists would do in these contexts. In their imagination, these young authors were playing the role of revolutionary theoreticians personified by Marx, Engels, Lenin, and Mao. They were performing the revolution theoretically, just as their comrades were doing the same practically. And they were doing so consciously and passionately in order to provide guidance to practical revolutionary action. It was the same kind of emulation and enactment that characterized Red Guards' performance of revolutionary violence discussed in chapter 1.

This interpretation would put our understanding of Red Guard dissent in a new light. Some scholars view these critical voices as prophetic thinkers who were ahead of their times. Thus in his study of the "new trends of thought" in the Cultural Revolution, Shaoguang Wang considers the theorists of new thought to be "clairvoyants who were trying not only to reshuffle the bureaucracy but also to create a new society, a society modeled after the Paris Commune of 1871."[8] They "sought to make fundamental changes in the existing social and political order."[9]

The desire to create a new society modeled after the Paris Commune could be as genuine as the dissatisfaction with the existing social and political order. But it was also true that the Paris Commune was the only imaginable model for these young people and that was the model that had been planted in their minds in the years prior to the Cultural Revolution. Zheng Qian, a historian of the Chinese Communist Party, argues that there was such an obsession with the Paris Commune among both party leaders and the grassroots during the Chinese Cultural Revolution that there existed at that time a "Paris Commune" complex. The reason for the existence of this Paris Commune complex was that the Chinese Communist Party, before the Cultural Revolution, had conducted national campaigns to study the Marxist classic *The Civil War in France*, where the ideals of the Paris Commune were most powerfully stated and were made popular to Chinese youth through the promotion of the Marxist classic.[10]

Another important reason for the appearance of dissent was that it had an organizational context. Dissent had more of a collective than individual character. It was likely to be formulated in the context of a Red Guard organization, often as an attempt to thwart opposing factions ideologically and theoretically. For this reason, the appearance of dissent was related to another distinct feature of the Red Guard movement—the booming of a Red Guard press. Almost all the "new trends of thought" were publicized in Red Guard newspapers, handbills, or big-character posters, big-character posters so named because the posters were typically written in extra large calligraphy with traditional Chinese writing brushes.

The officially endorsed practices of voluntarily forming "mass organizations" and using "mass publications" to carry out the Cultural Revolution inadvertently provided the conditions for expressing dissent. These conditions allowed a small minority of individuals with intellectual aspirations to take what they imagined to be the historically unprecedented revolutionary movement to a new theoretical level by emulating Marx, Mao, and other revolutionary theorists. They enthusiastically imagined themselves to be revolutionary theoreticians, and it was in this process that they formulated and published ideas of dissent. It is essential, therefore, to examine how the Red Guard press was conducive to dissent.

THE RED GUARD PRESS

The voicing of dissent in the Red Guard movement was inseparable from the Red Guard press. Most Red Guard organizations or coalitions had their own newspapers or "little papers" (*xiao bao*). Red Guard newspapers were published and distributed without any official registration, although some were designated as "internal publications" not for public circulation. They were, by and large, distributed locally, but the most influential ones were distributed nationally through post offices.

The Red Guard press encompassed a wide variety of forms, including wall posters, leaflets, handbills, magazines, newsletters, pictorials, and newspapers. The contents of Red Guard newspapers resembled those of an official newspaper. Typically, they carried editorials, reprints of articles from *People's Daily* or other national newspapers, news items, leaders' speeches, essays, poems, cartoons, songs, letters to the editor, and so forth. Red Guard publications also carried much that would normally not appear in official newspapers, including grapevine stories about party leaders at the top and regional politics, which added popularity to the Red Guard press. Even in the middle of the Red Guard movement, there were underground black markets for trading Red Guard publications.

Red Guard publications exploded with information related to factional conflicts. Many papers carried detailed accounts of incidents of conflict in order to challenge and discredit opponents and justify one's own action. Photographs of those wounded or killed in factional battles were published along with stories hailing them as heroes or martyrs. Polemics against rival factions were a staple feature.

The Shanghai-based historian Jin Dalu differentiates among four types of "mass newspapers and journals" (*qun zhong bao kan*) in Shanghai.[11] The first type was the official newspapers, such as *Liberation Daily* and *Wenhui Daily*. In most cases these official newspapers were taken over by rebel groups after the 1967 January Revolution. In some cities the official newspapers were simply suspended, which affected the local print runs of national newspapers. This caused concern at the top and a central policy document was issued on January 3, 1967, to warn that even if it was OK to suspend the operations of local government newspapers, the local printing of major national newspapers such as *People's Daily*, *PLA Daily*, and *Guangming Daily* should continue.[12]

The second type was newspapers run by "mass organizations" at the municipal level or in major universities, while the third type included newspapers run by district-level or department-level and other grassroots organizations. Jin calls the fourth type "underground" newspapers (*di xia bao kan*) because they were run by miscellaneous social groups who did not belong to any legitimate "mass organizations." Of these four types, the second and third were the largest in number and influence. Generally speaking, this Shanghai-based typology applies to the Red Guard press nationally.

Nationally, the Red Guard press produced enormous numbers of newspapers, tabloids, and journals. According to one source,[13] the Chinese National Library has 2,611 different titles of Red Guard tabloids in its collection. From 1975 to 2005, the Center for Chinese Research Materials (CCRM) in the United States published 148 volumes of reprints of *Red Guard Publications* with a total of 3,155 titles.[14] In the city of Chongqing alone, over 1,639 Red Guard papers were in circulation.[15] In Chengdu there were about 200 different Red Guard papers.[16] In Shanghai, according to a survey conducted in July 1967 by the city's political propaganda department, there were 256 mass newspapers at that time. Of these, about 50 were newspapers and 65 were magazines or journals (kan wu). Twenty-five of the newspapers and 36 of the journals were printed by the municipal printing press.[17]

REASONS FOR THE EXPLOSION OF RED GUARD PUBLICATIONS

The crucial condition responsible for the blossoming of the Red Guard press was Mao's support and the institutionalization of mass debate and wall posters in Chinese politics. During the Cultural Revolution, people were officially encouraged "to air their opinions in a big way, to contend in a big way, to debate in a big way, and write big-character posters." The "Sixteen Points" states: "Make the fullest use of big-character posters and great debates to argue matters out, so that the masses can clarify the correct views, criticize the wrong views, and expose all the ghosts and monsters. In this way the masses will be able to raise their political consciousness in the course of the struggle, enhance their abilities and talents, distinguish right from wrong and draw a clear line between the enemy and ourselves."[18] After Red Guards newspapers began to appear, Mao took a special interest in them and reportedly read Red Guard papers every day. Wang Li, for example, told the personnel of Beijing Daily that "Chairman Mao pays special attention to the newspapers of rebel factions. You must run your newspaper well."[19] Such messages were undoubtedly an important legitimating factor for Red Guards.

Besides upholding the principle of using posters and mass publications for the Cultural Revolution, there were specific policies from time to time about "mass publications" that showed clear official support of Red Guard publications. For example, the "Recommendations About Improving Propaganda through Newspapers and Magazines Run by Revolutionary Mass Organizations" ("关于改进革命群众组织的报刊宣传的意见") issued by CCP on May 14, 1967 has the following points:[20]

1. The publications of mass organizations must follow the instructions of Chairman Mao, Vice Chairman Lin Biao, the CCP, and the Military Committee of the CCP. They should conduct their work with reference to the editorials of People's Daily, Red Flag, and PLA Daily.

2. These publications must not publish the private writings and speeches by Chairman Mao and Vice Chairman Lin Biao. They must not publish the internal documents and minutes of meetings of the CCP or the speeches of leaders of the CCP.
3. They must not publicly attack the People's Liberation Army in the newspapers.
4. They must not publish information that discloses state secrets.
5. The papers should focus on serious political issues and not publish trivialities, rumors, and "yellow news."

This policy is revealing in that it attests to the messiness of the Red Guard newspapers, suggesting that in addition to the ongoing political debates, a great deal was published to appeal to readers' curiosity about grapevine news and news of human interest.

Another reason for the explosion of Red Guard publications was official financial support, at least for those that were edited and published by major Red Guard and rebel organizations. Again, Jin's study of the Red Guard press in Shanghai sheds light on this issue. He finds that by April and May 1967, there were so many Red Guard publications in Shanghai that they began to become a serious financial burden. A policy recommendation issued by the Politics and Propaganda Department of the Shanghai Revolutionary Committee (市革委会政宣组) recommended that it continue to financially support the publication of seven major papers. As for others, if they insisted on continuing publication, "we will not be responsible for providing the paper or the printing costs."[21] This shows that at least before publication costs and paper shortage became a serious issue, major Red Guard newspapers were financially supported with government budget.

There was a limit to how much financial support was available. As the Shanghai case indicates, Red Guard publications put such burdens on the city's finances that eventually efforts were made to reduce their numbers after mid-1967.

Not all Red Guard newspapers were financed with government budgets, however; some papers had to raise their own funds and resources. In some cases, printing equipment and paper sheets used for printing were appropriated or forcefully seized from printing factories. And while in the earlier period most Red Guard publications were distributed for free, after mid-1967 more and more of them charged a subscription or retail fee. One newspaper in the city of Yangzhou ran an advertisement as follows: "This paper now wishes to expand its subscribers. All work units and revolutionary masses are welcome to take subscriptions at the local post office. We publish six times a month. The subscription fee is 12 cents for every month."[22] In addition to political and financial support from the top leaders, the most important reason for the proliferation of Red Guard publications was that they were crucial weapons in factional conflicts and their editors and authors threw themselves into the editing, production, and distribution of their papers with great passion and dedication.

WEAPONS OF FACTIONAL WARFARE

Red Guard publications served many functions. A few classmates could proclaim the founding of an organization by putting up a poster or by launching a "small paper," much as an organization today might declare its existence by setting up a website. More established Red Guard organizations had editorial offices with a staff, much as regular newspapers did, and their newspapers would serve as hubs of information and organization, publicizing organizational activities or announcements for a rally or demonstration.

The most important function of Red Guard publications, however, was as a weapon of factional warfare. Up until the Red Guard movement, posters had been used mainly for two purposes—they were a means of state propaganda and mobilizing public support for official policies. The major official wall poster campaign before the Cultural Revolution happened during the Great Leap Forward. As Chinese communication scholar Xu Jing details, the poster campaign in 1958 was an official effort to mobilize public support for the Great Leap Forward. In many places, individuals and work units alike competed to see who put out the most posters.[23]

Posters had also been used for political debate and political dissent in earlier times. The earliest cases are traced to the Yan'an period in 1942, when Wang Shiwei wrote a poster challenging party leaders for suppressing dissent.[24] The most important case before the Cultural Revolution was the "Hundred Flowers campaign" in 1956–1957. Its background was similar to the Cultural Revolution in one crucial aspect: Both started with Mao's support. And Mao himself lauded the wall poster as a "great development in our democratic tradition."[25] A precedent was thus set for using posters as an institutional means of social and political criticism. Red Guards followed this tradition. Many posters were declarations of support for official policies, while others staked out positions in public debates. It was in the midst of these verbal battles that ideas of dissent found their channels of expression.

Red Guards used their publications as tools of propaganda in their factional struggle. They promoted their own political views and positions and
attacked their opponents. For this reason, Red Guard newspapers often became the targets of attack. Opposing factions sometimes sabotaged each
other's publishing facilities and distribution centers. The May 22, 1967, issue
of Xin Nankai, the paper of a rebel organization in Tianjin's Nankai University, published a blank front page with only a notice and a slogan that reads:
"Long, Long, Long Live Our Great Teacher, Great Leader, Great Commander-
in-Chief, Great Helmsman Chairman Mao!" The notice says that their newspaper printing facilities had been destroyed by a rival faction, that they
printed the current issue only with the assistance of another unit, and that
the first page of the current issue had been seized by their opponent and
therefore could not be printed.[26] A July 1967 issue of Lu Xun Battle News (Lu
Xun zhan bao) announced to its subscribers and readers that its distribution
center had been attacked and the paper's mailing list had been seized by
"rioters," which prevented the staff from promptly putting the papers in the
mail for its subscribers.[27]

Besides sabotage, Red Guards engaged in endless debates and polemics.
It was in the middle of these polemics that the most radical heterodox ideas
of dissent were published and disseminated. In the following section I will
discuss some of the most influential cases of dissent in roughly chronologi-
cal order.

"AN OPEN LETTER TO COMRADE
LIN BIAO," NOVEMBER 1966

This open letter first appeared as a poster in Qinghua University on November 15, 1966. It was signed by Yilin-Dixi, a pseudonym for two students from
the middle school attached to Beijing Agricultural University. The letter
attacked a speech by Lin Biao that exalted Mao's genius and placed Mao's
thought over any other Marxist thinker in history. It advocated a historical
approach to understanding Mao Zedong's thought, implying that it was not
the absolute truth Lin Biao claimed it to be. This letter thus challenged two
"sacred" symbols of orthodoxy—both Mao and Lin. Although mass criticism
was an integral part of the Cultural Revolution, and Red Guards everywhere
wielded the Marxist banner of "Doubt Everything!", it was an unacknowl-
edged rule that, besides Mao, his comrade-in-arms Lin Biao was also beyond

doubt. Tao Zhu, the No. 4 person in the Chinese communist hierarchy, explicitly made remarks to that effect in an interview with Red Guards.[28]

Yet the letter was more than an attack on Lin Biao. It questioned the legitimacy of the Chinese political system since 1949:

> You stressed the correct side of the dictatorship of the proletariat—that which needs no improvement. But you did not acutely perceive the problems that have become so prominent since the launching of the Great Cultural Revolution, e.g., the need to ameliorate the dictatorship of the proletariat and to improve the socialist system. It is necessary to change the organizational form of our Party and government in a major way. The People's Republic of China with its people's democratic dictatorship set up seventeen years ago is already obsolete.[29]

This open letter was an important sample of the first wave of political dissent that directly challenged the orthodoxy of the Cultural Revolution. The context was as important as the content of the letter. This wave of dissent started among "old Red Guards" (*lao bing*) who had initially dominated the Red Guard movement but whose fortunes began to suffer with the campaign to "criticize the bourgeois reactionary line," officially launched with the publication of an editorial in the thirteenth issue of *Red Flag* in October 1966. With Mao's sponsorship, this campaign dealt a fatal blow to conservative Red Guard organizations and catapulted rebels groups into prominence and power.

These "old Red Guards," as they were known then, were mostly children of high-ranking cadres and military officers. With a strong sense of their elite status, they supported the so-called bloodline theory, according to which they were the natural heirs of the revolution, whereas children from nonelite families were excluded. When the political winds turned against them in early October 1966, they launched daring attacks against all the key supporters of the Cultural Revolution by putting up anonymous posters.

This wave of dissent was quickly denounced as the "November black winds" or "December black winds."[30] The "black winds" consisted of 1. slogans supporting Liu Shaoqi, who had already been publicly denounced as a capitalist roader; 2. a series of posters by conservative Red Guards attacking the Cultural Revolution Small Group; and 3. even an open letter to Mao himself questioning the "criticism of bourgeois reactionary line" campaign.

The December black winds was thus a counterattack launched by the "old guards" against the rising rebels. As such, it was part and parcel of factional conflicts. The goal was to challenge and undermine their factional rivals, and political dissent appeared in the form of challenges against opposing factions. Thus factional struggles provided the organizational spaces for dissent.

Although the countermaneuvers of the "old Red Guards" against the Cultural Revolution Small Group may have been motivated more by a desire to undermine the radical Red Guard organizations than to challenge the Cultural Revolution orthodoxy, their opponents, not surprisingly, framed their ideas as premeditated attacks against the revolutionary orthodoxy. A whirlwind of counteroffensives from the rebels quickly overwhelmed the "black winds" stirred up by the "old guards," denouncing their ideas as "poisonous weeds" and "reactionary," "opportunist" and "bourgeois" trends of thoughts.[31]

Again attesting to the complex circumstances of dissent, public denunciations of these "reactionary thoughts" inadvertently helped to spread them to a wider audience. At Beijing University a liaison station was formed to criticize To the Tiger Mountain (*hu shan xing*), one of the many old guard organizations associated with the December black winds. In a lengthy editorial the liaison station named the five members of Tiger Mountain and enumerated their "reactionary crimes." Their first "crime" was that they "malignantly attacked Chairman Mao and Comrade Lin Biao." As evidence of their "crimes," one of the five members was accused of saying, "I'm currently at a stage of doubt about Mao Zedong Thought." Another allegedly said, "I am afraid what's happening now is a replay of the late Stalin." Members of Tiger Mountain were also charged with the crime of viciously attacking the Cultural Revolution and the Central Cultural Revolution Small Group. Thus a third member had reportedly written the following in a letter: "I think [the Cultural Revolution] has a pretty dark side. The first two months were devoted to mobilizing the masses, the next four months to letting the masses fight among themselves. . . . I would say that in a sense the Cultural Revolution is a failure."[32] These were the unpublished "heterodox thoughts" among some of the "old guards," yet, in exposing their "reactionary crimes," the rebels gave publicity to these ideas.

"ON FAMILY ORIGIN," JANUARY 1967

Another powerful expression of dissent was a series of essays that systematically critiqued what was then referred to as the "bloodline theory" (*xue tong lun*). All these essays were authored by one person, Yu Luoke, who was a twenty-four-year-old worker in 1966. The most important of these essays was titled "On Family Origin" (*chu shen lun*).

The systematic use of social and political labels by the Chinese socialist state was a major cause of symbolic immobility.[33] Among these labels was a category based on class origin. Three broad types of class origin, good, middle, and bad, respectively dubbed "red," "gray" and "black," were distinguished on the basis of the head of household's economic and political status in the years before the Communist Party took power.[34] Different class origins bestowed different political and social statuses on their incumbents. Thus the good ones ranked highest socially, the bad ones were condemned and stigmatized, and the middling ones occupied a limbo space between the red and the black. Like a caste system, class labels both divided the society and put its members under strict control. Class labels, once assigned, went into everyone's dossiers and would permanently affect almost all aspects of one's life, from educational opportunities to careers. Labels like these created and perpetuated ascribed statuses or social stigmas.

Before the Cultural Revolution, this "class line" controlled the nerves of Chinese society, giving those from red categories a sense of superiority and treating those from nonred categories as second-class citizens, if not criminals. This class line cast its dark shadows over the education system. The first contingent of Red Guard organizations in Beijing consisted of students from "red-category" families. Their core members were the children of high-level party, government, or military leaders. To show and sustain the sense of superiority of these elite students, these early Red Guard organizations recruited members on the basis of the bloodline theory. On this theory, only students from families of "red categories" were eligible to join Red Guard organizations. Those from "black categories" were not only excluded, but in many cases became the targets of attack. Whereas before the Cultural Revolution such a theory was in de facto effect but not publicized as a party doctrine, the Red Guards lost no time in pronouncing it publicly, and they did so in the most blatant manner. The whole theory was condensed into the following notorious couplet, which spread nationally in June 1966:

> If the father's a hero, the son's a great fellow;
> If the father's a reactionary, the son's a rotten egg.

This was merely a cruder version of the theory that implicitly guided the official practice of dividing Chinese society into various class categories.

Just as the class categories had been a political yardstick used by the party-state in evaluating individuals, so the ideas expressed in the couplet became widely adopted by some Red Guards as the basis for excluding certain groups of students from Red Guard organizations, making them vulnerable to political persecution.

Yu Luoke wrote the long essay "On Family Origin" in July 1966 to refute the bloodline theory. The essay was first publicized and distributed in a leaflet by his brother Yu Luowen, a student in Beijing's No. 65 Middle School. Initially only several hundred copies of the leaflet were printed and distributed. It was not until it was published in the *Middle School Cultural Revolution News* (*zhong xue wen ge bao*) that it gained wide influence. This "little newspaper" was launched on January 18, 1967, through the joint efforts of Yu Luowen, Yu Luoke, and Mu Zhijing, a student in Beijing's No. 4 Middle School.[35] The paper ran six issues before it was forced to shut down in April 1967. The sixth and last issue was published on April 1, 1967. Each of the six issues carried a major article by Yu Luoke, all attacking the "bloodline theory," but authorship was attributed to a "Beijing Family Background Study Group," and Yu Luoke was never named.

"On Family Origin" argued that a new hereditary caste system (*zhong xing zhi du*) had formed in China that resembled the feudal caste system. In this system, Yu Luoke argued, social groups that belonged to the so-called seven black categories of family origins became the oppressed class, while those in the red categories were the ruling class. Yu further argued that the criteria for making this distinction was entirely arbitrary and based on ascribed and not achieved status. He contended that the reason for the appearance of the new caste system in China was political. It was for the more effective ruling of the people, as he wrote in another article, "On the Life and Death of Zheng Zhaonan the Martyr." On the basis of these analyses, Yu Luoke called on all oppressed youth to rise up in struggles against the injustices of politically imposed social inequality.

These essays struck a chord among many. In a 1996 interview, Mu Zhijing, the original editor of the newspaper that carried Yu Luoke's essay "On Family Origin," described the popularity of his little paper:

> Thirty thousand copies of the first issue of the paper were printed. Later, sixty thousand more were printed. Altogether, 110,000 copies of "On Family Origin" were printed. The newspaper became very influential. We received large numbers of letters from readers. . . . Because too many letters were sent to us, the post office refused to deliver them. Everyday, we had to go to the post office to bring

back two big bags of letters. The price of our paper was set at two *fen* [equivalent to pennies], but it could be sold as high as five *yuan* in the street.[36]

The diffusion of Yu Luoke's "On Family Origin" owed much to the chaotic political conditions of the Cultural Revolution, which provided relative freedom for people to form organizations and publish their views in small papers. It was a typical case of a small group of people voicing dissent through a small paper. At a time when thousands of such small papers were mushrooming, dissenting voices such as those carried in the *Middle School Cultural Revolution News* found their outlets.

Yet the movement-countermovement dynamics were also essential. As a refutation of the "bloodline theory" of the "old Red Guards," Yu Luoke's "On Family Origin" provided theoretical support to the insurgent zaofanpai, many of whom had suffered persecution in the hands of the "old guards." Not surprisingly, although his essay was written in July 1966, its widespread circulation through the publication of *Middle School Cultural Revolution News* happened only in January 1967, after the old guards had lost their domination of the Red Guard movement. In this sense, the voicing of dissent became possible because the insurgent rebel ranks needed these voices to challenge their rivals.

As soon as the voices of dissent had spread, however, their power became a threat not only to the "old Red Guards" but also to the political establishment. Yu Luoke's challenge against the bloodline theory could be easily interpreted as a challenge to China's political system. Thus, before long, in April 1967, Yu's "On Family Origin" was denounced by top leaders as "counterrevolutionary" and the *Middle School Cultural Revolution News* was shut down. Yu Luoke was arrested on January 5, 1968, and ruthlessly executed on March 5, 1970.

Such was the irony of radical mass action during the Cultural Revolution. Sponsored by the very center of political power in China, mass action inadvertently provided the conditions for political dissent that challenged the same power that had sponsored the mass action.

"ON NEW TRENDS OF THOUGHT—A MANIFESTO OF THE APRIL THIRD FACTION," JUNE 1967

The notion of the existence of a specially privileged class was the theme of the manifesto of the "April Third" faction among Beijing's middle school students. After party authorities issued orders in March 1967 for schools to resume class and sent military teams from the Beijing Garrison to provide military training to middle school students, rebel Red Guards in Beijing's middle schools split into two factions. The April Third faction came to be known as such after Zhou Enlai, Kang Sheng, Jiang Qing, Xie Fuzhi, and other central party leaders met with Beijing's college and middle school students on April 3, 1967.[37] At that meeting, Jiang Qing, Kang Sheng, and Xie Fuzhi took the Beijing Garrison to task for suppressing rebel organizations in Beijing's middle schools and supporting the conservative United Action (*liandong*). Encouraged by these speeches, the rebel students who had been the target of suppression by the military immediately launched a counteroffensive by putting up posters around the city the next day. These rebels came to be known as the April Third faction.

Perhaps to prevent the rebels from going too far in their counterattacks, but certainly reflecting the whimsies of the dynamics of the Cultural Revolution, several other members of the Cultural Revolution Small Group, including Wang Li, Guan Feng and Qi Benyu, met with rebel students in Beijing's middle schools on April 4 and told them that although the military teams from Beijing Garrison might have committed mistakes in conducting military training, overall they had done a good job and should not be publicly attacked. These speeches were taken as words of support by April Third's opponents, who became known as the April Fourth faction. After the conservatives or royalists were crushed at the end of 1966, the Red Guard movement in Beijing's middle schools was carried on mainly between these two rival rebel factions.

Although April Third and April Fourth were both rebel organizations, as opposed to conservatives, there were several important differences between the two. First, there was a clearer class line dividing the two than that dividing rebel factions in colleges and universities. The more extreme and radical April Third faction gathered children from "ordinary families" (平民子弟), whereas the April Fourth faction was dominated by children of elite cadres or military families. Second, this difference partly explained their different attitudes toward students of Liandong, who were uniformly from elite families and had vehemently promoted the idea of born-reds in August and September of 1966. The April Third faction argued that members of Liandong were all counterrevolutionaries to be vanquished, whereas the more sympathetic April Fourth faction maintained that not all Liandong members were bad and at least some of them were redeemable and should be won over. The third difference was their attitude toward the army, the PLA. Because the April Third faction accused the PLA of suppressing rebel organizations, they were charged of being anti-PLA, whereas April Fourth had the support of the PLA.

The rivalry between the April Third and April Fourth factions was carried out both verbally through wall posters and little papers and through physical violence.[38] "On New Trends of Thought—a Manifesto of the April Third Faction" was born in the middle of these conflicts. It was published in the first issue of *April Third Battle News* (*si san zhan bao*) on June 11, 1967.

Theorizing the revolution was just as important as conducting the revolution in the street. Much of the political dissent in the Red Guard movement was born as a result of such theorizing. The theorizing itself was deliberate, indeed often done in imitation of the great "revolutionary teachers" such as Marx, Lenin, and Mao Zedong, but the dissent was often accidental and expressed as the applications of Marxist theory to the analysis of Chinese realities.

Relatively little is known about the background of the writing of the April Third manifesto. According to Bei Dao's recollections,[39] the author was Zhang Xianglong, whose elder brother Zhang Xiangping was a writer for a rebel group known as the "Commune of New No. 4 Middle School." No. 4 Middle School was an important hub of rebel radicalism for Beijing's middle school students. It was Mu Zhijing, a student there, who had started the *Middle School Cultural Revolution News*, which published Yu Luoke's articles attacking the bloodline theory. Besides *Middle School Cultural Revolution News*, rebel students there published several other small papers. It was not surprising that the publication of the April Third manifesto was connected to rebel activities in No. 4 Middle School.

The manifesto tried to provide theoretical justification for the practical actions of the April Third faction. Its claim to a "new trend of thought" derives from its argument that the Cultural Revolution was a revolution to promote the redistribution of property and power, encourage revolutionary changes in the society, and break up the privileged class. At the beginning of the CR, the Sixteen Points had defined the main target of the CR as "those within the Party who are in authority and are taking the capitalist road."[40] The question about redistribution of power and property was never mentioned. Yet the April Third manifesto argues that a privileged class had formed in the socialist period and that the Cultural Revolution should aim to achieve the redistribution of property and power. In this respect, the class theory in this document was consistent with Yu Luoke's theory of family origin. Both provided theoretical support for students from marginalized social groups to challenge the "old Red Guards."

The impact of the April Third Manifesto may be seen from the counterattacks it incurred. It was soon labeled and denounced as reactionary heresy. On September 19, 1967, a Red Guard newspaper in Huhhot of Inner Mongolia published an essay titled "Also on New Trends of Thought" (*ye lun xin si chao*), which was a denunciation of the spreading of similar ideas in Huhhot.[41] Another kind of impact was that the manifesto inspired Yang Xiguang to produce his famous essay "Whither China," which I will discuss.

"WHITHER CHINA?" OCTOBER 1967–JANUARY 1968

Both Yu Luoke's essays and the manifesto of the April Third faction influenced Yang Xiguang's thinking. Yang was an eighteen-year-old high school student in Changsha No. 1 Middle School and a member of *Shengwulian*, shorthand for Hunan Provincial Proletarian Revolutionary Alliance Committee. *Shengwulian* was an umbrella name for many rebel organizations consisting primarily of individuals from disadvantaged social groups. The social background of members of Shengwulian clarified to Yang Xiguang the class nature of the political struggles. Yang saw it as a struggle of the oppressed social groups against a ruling bureaucratic class, which he called "red capitalist class." According to Yang's own account, the idea of the existence of a "red capitalist class" first occurred to him when he was exposed to the ideas of the April Third faction on a linkup trip to Beijing in 1967.[42] Back in Changsha, Yang traveled to the rural areas to study local social conditions. It was at this time that he began writing "Whither China?"

In this essay Yang Xiguang argued that in the seventeen years of communist rule after 1949, a "red capitalist class" consisting of over 90 percent of the high-ranking officials had formed in China. The relationship of this class with the people was that of rulers and ruled, oppressors and oppressed. Because of the existence of this antagonistic relationship, the author further argued, the struggles of the Cultural Revolution were between the oppressed class and the oppressors:

> Facts as revealed by the masses, and the indignation they brought forth, first told the people that these "Red" capitalists had entirely become a decaying class that hindered the progress of history. The relations between them and the people in

general had changed from relations between leaders and followers to those between rulers and the ruled and between exploiters and the exploited. From the relations between revolutionaries of equal standing, it had become a relationship between oppressors and the oppressed. The special privileges and high salaries of the class of "Red" capitalists were built upon the foundation of oppression and exploitation of the broad masses of the people. In order to realize the "People's Commune of China," it was necessary to overthrow this class.[43]

In targeting a "red capitalist class," Yang argued that the Cultural Revolution was not an internal party struggle for purging a few power holders. Rather, it was the struggle of an oppressed class against the oppressors, who were none other than the communist party leadership. The essay proposed to establish a new political party "that will lead the people to overthrow today's class enemy–the new Red bourgeoisie."[44] In a separate essay, Yang suggested that this new party could take the incipient form of "Maoist groups." The mandate of these groups was to unite all those who were "willing to learn and bold enough to think, and think independently," so that they could openly and critically analyze the conditions in China and reach their own conclusions instead of accepting wholesale the theories promulgated in official newspapers ("Suggestions About Establishing Maoist Groups"). Yang suggested that Shengwulian could be viewed as the prototype of such a party. As Jonathan Unger puts it,

> Shengwulian . . . was a congeries of groups that held one element in common: they all had been persecuted and shortchanged by the state and Party apparatus before and during the Cultural Revolution. . . . To be sure, elsewhere in China, too, there were obvious distinctions in the overall social composition of the Rebels as against the Conservative faction. But, by 1967, these differences had become partially obfuscated by the twists and turns of the Cultural Revolution, as the alignments of various subgroups and organizations shifted and split and recoalesced in accordance with the vagaries of local repressions, desperate efforts to secure vengeance and to end up on the winning side, and subsequent alliances of convenience.[45]

Yang Xiguang's articles drew immediate condemnation from the authorities. Yang himself was charged by party authorities as a "counterrevolutionary," arrested in February 1968, and imprisoned for ten years.

Scholars generally agree about the radical nature and significance of Yang's ideas as expressed in "Whither China?" In particular, Yiching Wu's book analyzes the tortuous trajectories of Shengwulian and the radicalism of "Whither China."[46] Still, an important question remains: Why the imperative to theorize the revolution?

The stylistic features of Yang Xiguang's radical essays suggest that he was consciously imitating the style of Mao the revolutionary theorist. He borrowed Mao's words both in the title of his essay "Whither China?" and in its opening sentences. Yang's use of Mao's classic texts was an act of emulation and reenactment of an ideal, namely, Mao and his revolutionary practices, and it was by means of such emulation that the young radicals wished to become the revolutionaries of their own times. Yang Xiguang's borrowing of Mao's words was not limited to "Whither China?" Another important essay he wrote, titled "Report on an Investigation of the Youth Movement in Changsha," was modeled on Mao's famous "Report on an Investigation of the Peasant Movement in Hunan." Here is a famous passage from Mao's 1927 essay:

> "IT'S TERRIBLE!" OR "IT'S FINE!" The peasants' revolt disturbed the gentry's sweet dreams. When the news from the countryside reached the cities, it caused immediate uproar among the gentry. Soon after my arrival in Changsha, I met all sorts of people and picked up a good deal of gossip. From the middle social strata upward to the Guomindang right-wingers, there was not a single person who did not sum up the whole business in the phrase, "It's terrible!"[47]

Below is a striklingly similar passage from Yang's 1967 essay:

> "IT'S TERRIBLE!" OR "IT'S FINE!" Educated youth who returned to the city to make rebellions disturbed the sweet dreams of the bourgeois masters, mistresses, young masters, and young misses. From the middle social strata upward to the rebels' right-wingers, there was not a single person who did not sum up the whole business in the phrase "It's terrible!"

The emulation of the young Mao was not just a matter of prose style, though the significance of style must not be underestimated. The young radicals of the Cultural Revolution emulated Mao's whole way of being a revolutionary, his method of social investigation, his boldness and ambition, and his theoretical vision. In the steps of the young Mao, reading Marxist and Maoist theories and applying them to Chinese realities became a way of clarifying the goals and methods of the Cultural Revolution when many young people began to entertain doubts and ambivalences about the gaps between the Cultural Revolution and Chinese realities. Hence the rise of what Yang Xiguang calls "theoretical movements" in the second half of 1967. Yang saw such a "theoretical movement" happening when he was studying the educated youth and preparing his report on the educated youth movement:

> Financially, educated youth had the most difficulties, yet they ran the largest number of newspapers. Whenever a new view appears which offers an explanation of the conditions of educated youth, in less than a day's time it can spread to every educated youth. Therefore, when you visit the educated youth, you will find a special characteristic, that is, that their views about the educated movement was almost entirely the same. Among educated youth, theory has become a flourishing movement.[48]

Unger's detailed study of Yang Xiguang's intellectual trajectory explains this well:

> On the one hand, Yang Xiguang was seeking out such complaints at the bottom of society, while on the other he was searching feverishly for explanations and, idealistically, for alternate ways of organizing society that would avoid inequalities and repressive hierarchy. In particular, he and two other students of like mind ruminated over Lenin's "State and Revolution," and discussed the 1966 Cultural Revolution articles commemorating the 95th anniversary of the Paris Commune.[49]

There was, in Yang Xiguang and other self-designated young theoretians of the time, a confidence and audacity that was both the result of the idealistic education the Red Guard generation received and a mark of the times. Even in their most dangerous and difficult moments, these young people carried with them a strong sense of optimism and idealism. Thus Unger writes of how Yang Xiguang faced his arrest: "The turmoil of the Cultural Revolution thus far had provided him with an adventure in self-education, and he looked forward to more of the same. It was a reaction akin to that of other interviewees—Rebel Red Guards similarly crushed in 1968. Yang Xiguang recalls: On the way to prison, I felt excited, not scared. I felt I had been living in upper-class society. I felt I'd now have a chance to experience a fuller variety of society—what the bottom felt like. It was idealistic."[50]

Lu Li'an of Wuhan, another important author of essays of dissent, who was also imprisoned for ten years like Yang Xiguang, writes about a similar kind of optimism and sense of mission in his 2005 memoir. He said that he and his friends often proudly imagined themselves as belonging to the "young Mao Zedong group": "At that time we were thinking: If the cannons of the October Revolution and the outbreak of the May Fourth Movement had led Mao onto a career of rebelling against the old society, then the Proletarian Cultural Revolution that he personally launched and led must lead us onto to the revolutionary road to accomplish the historical mission of 'permanent revolution under the conditions of proletarian dictatorship.'"[51] Lu wrote about how he and his friends gathered at the East Lake in Wuhan to discourse on the nation: "It was October on the East Lake. The autumn sky was high and the air was clear. It was refreshing and pleasant. The warm sunshine was as gentle as silk. We gathered on the lakeside, talking, laughing, and feeling so happy that we did not want to leave. We felt we were the pride of the nation, the brave swimmers in the tidal waves of the times. We sang [Mao's poem] Pointing to our mountains and rivers, / Setting people afire with our words, / We counted the mighty no more than muck."[52]

THE HISTORICAL SIGNIFICANCE OF RED GUARD DISSENT

The Red Guard movement was a period of intensive protest and counter-protest. Because of incessant conflicts and factional struggles, ideologically driven polemics were prevalent. Most of these polemics fell squarely within the party orthodoxy. In the vortex of political rhetoric, voices dissenting from the party orthodoxy formed only a minor current. They were eventually suppressed without exception.

Dissent was not a cause of the Red Guard movement, but its unintended outcome. As the movement progressed and conflicts escalated, dissent became more widespread and more radical. This progression indicates that the Red Guard movement itself was not about the voicing of dissent, but it unwittingly furnished the conditions for its expression. This attests to a paradox of the Cultural Revolution—the making of the revolution contained its own seeds of destruction. So far as the Red Guard generation is concerned, the paradox is that at the very moment when it imagined itself to be making a revolution it was undoing its own revolutionary convictions. The rise of dissent in the course of making a revolution shows that the transformation of the Red Guard generation was coeval with the revolutionary process.

What is the significance of Red Guard dissent? First were the new revelations and analyses of social conflicts in Chinese society. While the official decisions on the launching of the Cultural Revolution designated "bourgeoisie" as the revolutionary target, the authors of dissent redefined the "bourgeoisie" as the "red capitalist class," a new class formation consisting of the majority of the leaders within the Chinese communist party itself. At the same time, the experiences of factionalism exposed and deepened the cleaveages between the chidren of the "red" elites and those from "black" or "gray" family backgrounds. Once formulated by Yu Luoke into a theory of social inequality and oppression, these class differences, which had already been in existence, became unusually threatening to the regime. At least theoretically, therefore, there was a perceptual shift of the locus of social conflict from between the people and the bourgeoisie to between the people and the privileged class within the party.

This new understanding of social conflicts and social relationships implied, however vaguely and incoherently, a new understanding of the self. In Yu Luoke's writings this notion of the self was implicit in his theoretical defense of human equality and choice. He wrote, for example, that "human beings are capable of choosing their own directions for progress" and that "we reject any right that cannot be achieved through individual efforts." In Yang Xiguang's essays, this notion of the self was adumbrated in his championing of original and critical thinking. In a political context where the goals of national development were set by the party, Yang and his associates in Shengwulian called on all social groups to search for alternative routes based on independent analyses of China's actual social conditions. The popularity of the essays of Yu Luoke and Yang Xiguang suggested that this notion of the self was not limited to a few individuals or small groups.

The subversive elements in the political agendas that contained this notion of the self were so obvious to the party authorities that politically divided factions within the party lost no time in joining forces to crush the proponents of these ideas. The harsh punishments dealt to Yu Luoke, Yang Xiguang, Lu Li'an, and others prevented them from developing their ideas further and for a short period of time even curtailed the spreading of their ideas. But, as we will see in later chapters, the seeds of dissent that were sown in the Red Guard movement would grow in new soil.

Despite the radical nature of political dissent, the heterodox "theoreticians" of the Cultural Revolution shared a fundamental commonality with the practitioners of the revolution who were engaged in violent battles like those in Chongqing, and that is that they had a strong sense of idealism and passion about revolution and radical social change. Their faith in the leadership of the Cultural Revolution may have been shaken, but revolution remained a sacred category in the heterodox thoughts in 1967 and

1968. It continued to be the linchpin of the meaning of a "good life." It was only when the drama of the revolution came to an end that alternative visions of a good life began to emerge. Yet it is crucial to see the persistence of revolutionary idealism even in the middle of radical revolutionary theorizing, because it helps to understand a distinct trait in the formation of the Red Guard generation, that is, that whatever they became later in their lives, once upon a time they were true believers, and that experience of true belief decisively shaped their personal identities and experiences. Xu Xiao captures this trait quite well in her characterization of Mu Zhijing, who helped to disseminate Yu Luoke's theory of family origin in 1967. In her memoir *Half of My Life* published in 2005, Xu Xiao writes:

> Mu Zhijing is still a spiritual wanderer to the present day. To a great extent, his mental journey is a proof of the spiritual journey of our generation. Our spirit of doubt grew out of experiences of belief. Even if we rejected something, we must have first accepted it. This is our difference from the skeptics in the younger generation. They doubt and reject something for the sake of doubting and rejecting it. They do not care whether it is a kind of nihilism. Or maybe nihilism is precisely what they are after.[53]

4
ORDINARY LIFE

THE RED GUARD MOVEMENT came to a dramatic end on July 28, 1968. In the early hours of that day, Mao called an urgent meeting with the five major Red Guard leaders in Beijing in the Great Hall of the People. Four of the five arrived at the meeting promptly, but Kuai Dafu of Tsinghua University was nowhere to be found; he was trapped in the middle of violent factional battles on campus. When he was finally located and brought to the meeting room, Kuai burst into tears upon seeing Mao. Mao stood up to shake hands with Kuai, who then reported to Mao that Tsinghua University was in grave danger and the students there were being attacked by workers under the control of a black hand behind the scene. Mao's response was firm and stern: "If you want to catch the "black hand," the "black hand" is me. What can you do to me?"[1]

Kuai's rise to power and stardom had depended on Mao's personal support. He had been tutored and cultivated as a storm trooper of the Red Guard movement in Beijing and then nationally. He had always thought Mao would stand behind him. The moment that Mao told him, with the other student leaders and all the top party leaders listening, that Mao himself had sent a worker militia to suppress the Red Guard movement, was highly symbolic. The same young "storm troopers" who had enjoyed the national limelight for two years were now cast out of favor. The curtain fell inexorably on the Red Guard movement.

The story of Red Guard generation, however, did not end there. Back in October 1967, small groups of middle school students had already started going to the countryside in what would soon become a new national campaign known as "Up to the Mountains, Down to the Villages." From then to the end of 1969, in over a period of two years, about 4.6 million middle school students were sent from their urban residences to settle in China's vast rural areas.[2]

In the previous chapters I have argued that the escalation of Red Guard factionalism was inseparable from the competition between rival factions to enact a great world-historical revolution. The Red Guard movement was a drama of revolution. The question now is this: What happened to the "characters" of the drama once the curtain fell?

In a way, what happened in this case was not so different from what happens to actors performing a drama in a theater. Like dramatic characters, students returned to their routine lives. Yet this was no ordinary return, but one that was full of new drama. For one thing, the young people did not return to their pre–Cultural Revolution school life, but instead left school for entirely unexpected and new destinations and occupations: that of being farmers in agricultural rural areas. There were of course other trajectories. Small numbers of lucky ones, more likely than not from cadre or military families, joined the army, the dream occupation of the youth of that generation. Others became factory workers, probably the next best job, second only to joining the army. Still others suffered persecution of one form or another in the campaign to "cleanse class ranks" that followed the Red Guard movement. Some, such as the dissenting authors Yang Xiguang and Lu Li'an, were sentenced to long years in prison. But the vast majority were sent away from home to rural areas, some at the young age of fifteen or sixteen. And for the vast majority, the end of the Red Guard movement and what came afterward was an experience of falling from grace. Coming in the wake of the Red Guard movement, the sent-down campaign added a painful sense of betrayal to disillusionment. There was a feeling of loss. In a 1968 English newspaper report, a former Cantonese Red Guard was quoted as saying, "We were already refuse when we went to the countryside."[3] Yet, as the authors of the same report wrote, the banishment of the Red Guards to the villages gave them time "to think and brood."[4]

In this chapter and in chapter 5 I trace how youth of the Red Guard generation made sense of their new life experiences and how their new experiences affected their sense of personal identity and their understanding of politics and society. Historical circumstances, partly of their own making and partly beyond their control, decisively taught them that their role as characters in the grand historical drama of an imagined revolution had come to an end. With the end of that drama, the script that had guided their thinking and action had lost much of its magic. Thrust into new circumstances, they would have to learn new scripts of life—indeed, new outlooks, new values, and new moral frameworks. The new scripts they gradually learned contradicted and further eroded the scripts that had guided them in the Red Guard movement. Thus, by the end of the sent-down movement and the Cultural Revolution, they had experienced a deep personal transformation and attained new understandings of self and society. These new understandings, I will argue, provided the social foundation for China's great reversal from the ideology of class struggle to the ideology of economic development at the beginning of the reform era, as well as for new forms of political activism that would have reverberations all the way until the student protests in 1989.

This chapter first reviews the history of the sent-down campaign and discusses its connections with the Red Guard movement. Then I will turn to aspects of their experiences that shaped, or rather reshaped, their moral frameworks. Unlike earlier chapters that have either a regional focus (Chongqing) or a thematic focus (dissent), this chapter is not confined to a region or a narrow theme, but rather surveys the experiences of the Red Guard generation in broad terms. My evidence is drawn from personal documents such as diaries, letters, songs, and literary works produced in the middle of the Cultural Revolution as well as retrospective writings and interviews. The nature of my evidence puts some limits on the generalizability of the findings. I do not pretend that the conclusions I draw apply to the entire Red Guard generation. They represent, rather, the views and experiences of the more articulate members of the generation, those who have contributed to the vast library of works about this generation through their own writings. Yet the vast size of the treasure trove of works produced by this generation attests to some degree of commonality in the experiences.

Given the extraordinary character of the about-face from the Red Guard movement to the sent-down campaign, it is necessary to introduce a few new concepts for framing the analysis in these two chapters.

THE VALUES OF ORDINARY LIFE

"Ordinary life" refers to the productive and reproductive activities of individual persons, in contrast to the Aristotelian "good life" deemed morally superior to mere "life." Daily labor and family life are among the concerns of an "ordinary life." The affirmation of ordinary life is thus the affirmation of the values of everyday existence. Max Weber speaks of the affirmation of "worldly life," which developed as an unintended consequence of a religious movement and its associated doctrines.[5] For Charles Taylor, ordinary life refers to "those aspects of human life concerned with production and reproduction, that is, labour, the making of the things needed for life, and our life as sexual beings, including marriage and the family."[6] Taylor argues that the rise of the values of these aspects of human life was a modern phenomenon in Western culture. Earlier Western views of human life were dominated by Aristotle's distinction between "life and the good life." For Aristotle, life was mere existence and hence played only an infrastructural role in relation to the good life. In a good life, as Taylor puts it, "men deliberate about moral excellence, they contemplate the order of things; of supreme importance for politics, they deliberate together about the common good, and decide how to shape and apply the laws."[7] The citizen ethic contained in this view of the good life endorsed an ethical hierarchy. It exalted the lives of contemplation and participation and degraded the lives of the common householder. It was analogous to the aristocratic ethic of honor, in which the life of the warrior or ruler was deemed superior to the life of the ordinary people.

The affirmation of the values of ordinary life thus upset the ethical hierarchies endorsed by the ethic of the "good life." In Taylor's words, this change "displaces the locus of the good life from some special range of higher activities and places it within 'life' itself. The full human life is now defined in terms of labour and production, on one hand, and marriage and family life, on the other."[8] As I will show later in this chapter, it is the growth of similar values among sent-down youth that justifies characterizing this twentieth-century Chinese phenomenon as the affirmation of ordinary life. To understand its historical significance, it is useful to put this trend in longer historical perspective. The next section provides such a historical perspective by discussing the neo-Confucian notion of the moral self.

THE NEO-CONFUCIAN NOTION OF THE MORAL SELF

There is a rich literature on Confucian morality and self-cultivation,[9] as well as historical studies of key Confucian figures in modern and early modern China.[10] However, Thomas Metzger's work provides the most relevant background for my argument, because he not only shows clearly the key characteristics of the neo-Confucian notion of the moral self but also demonstrates its continuity with notions of the self still influential in the Maoist era. The historical significance of the affirmation of the values of ordinary life among sent-down youth cannot be fully appreciated without an understanding of the enduring influence of the neo-Confucian notion of the moral self.

Metzger's analysis is based on an explication of the works of the modern-day neo-Confucian scholar Tang Junyi (1909–1978). Tang's works were chosen as his focus, not because they were the most popular or the most philosophically rigorous, but because they provide "a richly detailed and comprehensive interpretation of the neo-Confucian position within an analytical framework easily accessible to those accustomed to modern days of thought."[11]

According to Metzger, Tang's vision of the neo-Confucian notion of the self "can be summed up as the participation of the self in a noumenal flow of empathy. Instead of a Humean self cut off from the cosmos except for a flow of fragmentary sense impressions, T'ang describes a self that shares feelings of empathy with the cosmos's immanently ordered processes of transformation" (33). The mutual empathy between self and heaven not only means that the self is a conscious self, but also that it is aware that this feeling of empathy is "given" by the objective noumenal world and that the self is engaged in constant interchanges of empathy with the cosmic force. Such interchanges have a context of inexhaustibility and are inherently subsumable under universal and transcendent categories. It is this relationship between the self and the cosmos—an ethos of interdependence—that gives the Confucian notion of the self a "pathos of immensity" and "a kind of Panglossian optimism" (36). Metzger further explains,

> For Confucians, man in his ordinary condition has available to him a power which the Judeo-Christian tradition reserves for god. Because man draws on sources of moral power "given" to him by "heaven," man is not god. But man is godlike because he is the sole existing vehicle of that moral assertion needed to put the world right. Other aspects of human experience ... also contribute to the godlike quality of Confucian self-assertion: a feeling of oneness with "heaven," involving a pathos of immensity; the direct experience of a noumenal, Panglossian world free of grounds for angst and teleologically unproblematic; an intellectual ability to know this world, both as fact and as value, with complete objectivity; and the ability, based on utilizing man's unique moral energy with complete intellectual objectivity, to achieve a society free of the distortions of self-interest.
> (38–39)

THE NEO-CONFUCIAN PREDICAMENT
AND THE MAOIST SYNTHESIS

The notion of a godlike autonomous self is also the source of the neo-Confucian predicament. The belief in the presence of the divine in the self cannot preclude the anxiety that the divine force of the cosmos has an eternal tendency toward elusiveness, because the divine "was almost imperceptible in its subtlety" and typically "in the process of being 'lost'" (198). What was important was the belief in the existence of a transformative power within the cosmos and in the activation of this power by human efforts.

According to Metzger, this belief was the foundation of a wide-spread optimism among twentieth-century Chinese. The optimism arose and kept growing because now it seemed that "the material as well as the political and ideological means were at hand" of building a society according with the neo-Confucian morality of interdependence (214). It is at this point that Metzger turns to show the links between neo-Confucianism and Maoism.

One of Metzger's central arguments is that Confucian values, instead of quickly fading away in China's modernization project, have actually persisted as "the inertia of the past." These indigenous values, moreover, account for China's success after 1949, as economic and technological conditions had accounted for China's failures in the early period of modernization (197). How had Confucianism meshed with Maoism to sustain its vitality?

Metzger notes that many Chinese intellectuals in the twentieth century struggled in vain to explain how a focus on the external instrumentalities of life could be a way of realizing one's "inner" moral nature within the context of an "interdependent" society and cosmos or how a transformative outer cosmos could be linked to the inner self. The problem was solved by Mao: "Part of the importance of Maoism lies in the fact that it offered an answer to this problem, using dialectical cosmological laws to show how selfless participation in mass movements constituted the very essence of the personal quest for truth and morality. In Mao's thought, the *kung-fu* (efficacious moral efforts) of the individual were once more organically connected to the processes of transformation" (230–31).

For my purpose, what is important is not the degree of successful connection between the self and the cosmos in Mao's thought, but the persistence of the kind of Panglossian optimism and "pathos of immensity" in the neo-Confucian notion of the moral self in twentieth-century China. Earlier in the century, one of the great modern Confucians, Kang Youwei, pronounced: "The purpose of my creation was to save the masses of living things, even if instead of residing in heaven, I would go to purgatory to save them; if instead of going to the Pure Land, I had to come to this unclean world to save them; and if instead of being an emperor or a king, I became a common scholar in order to save them. . . . Thus every day the salvation of society was uppermost in my thoughts and every moment the salvation of society was my aim in life, and for this aim I would sacrifice myself."[12]

In 1966 members of the first Red Guard organization pledged: "We are the guards of red power. The Party Central and Chairman Mao are our mountain of support. Liberation of all mankind is our righteous responsibility. Mao Zedong Thought is the highest guiding principle for all our actions. We pledge: to protect the Party Central and our great leader Chairman Mao, we are determined to shed our last drop of blood!"[13]

Despite differences in content and context, these pronouncements both effused over a sense of divine power of the kind typical of the neo-Confucian notion of the self. They both exhibited an aspiration to purportedly higher orders of life and an implicit rejection of the values of ordinary life. The Red Guard pledge was characteristic of the identity of the Red Guard generation at the beginning of the Red Guard movement. It was only in the course of the movement and then in the rustication period that this self-understanding began to change. The affirmation of the values of ordinary life in the rustication period constituted a crucial aspect of this change.

RUSTICATION BEFORE THE CULTURAL REVOLUTION

The policy of sending urban youth to settle in rural areas had existed for over a decade before the Red Guard movement. That early practice aimed to accelerate agricultural development and resolve problems of urban unemployment and the shortage of educational opportunities for youth.[14] A national agricultural development program issued in January 1956 first proposed plans for reclaiming wasteland, increasing the area of arable land and developing state-run farms. According to this program, the labor force for this development plan would be drawn from the unemployed urban population, including elementary school students who could not go on to middle schools or middle school students who could not enter college. On April 8, 1957, People's Daily editorialized about "Questions Concerning the Participation in Agricultural Production of Elementary and Middle School Students." For the first time, it clarified the policy for elementary and middle school students who could not go on to a higher grade to migrate to the countryside and take part in agricultural labor.[15] In 1957, over ten thousand urban students were sent to settle in the countryside.[16] From 1958 to 1959, about fifteen thousand more were sent down.[17] Beginning in 1962, the government consolidated its campaign by setting up a special commission under the State Council to take charge of this issue. From then until 1966, 1.29 million urban youth settled in the countryside or on state farms.[18] The Red Guard movement inadvertently put a stop to this rustication policy because, during the movement, many of these youth went back to the cities and established their own Red Guard organizations, demanding to return to work in the cities.

CONTINUITIES AND DISCONTINUITIES

The sent-down campaign was launched again in the middle of the Red Guard movement and did not come to an official end till about 1980. In this period, 17 million students were sent to the countryside.[19] Of these, 4.6 million belonged to the generation that experienced the Red Guard movement. This 4.6-million cohort left for the countryside over a two-year period, from the latter half of 1967 to the spring of 1969. Chinese historians have divided this two-year history of rustication into three stages.[20] The first stage started in October 1967 and lasted till the spring of 1968. The symbolic beginning of the first stage took place on October 9, 1967, when ten students in Beijing made a pledge on Tiananmen Square and then set off to Inner Mongolia as "educated youth" amidst great media fanfare. Overall, departures at this stage were voluntary. Many enthusiastically embraced rustication as an opportunity to carry the Red Guard movement to the countryside. Some resorted to extreme actions to show their will to go to the countryside. One woman I interviewed told me she cut her own finger and wrote a letter in blood to show her determination. Table 4.1 shows the number of forerunners of rustication, the time they started rustication, and their destinations.

The second stage lasted from the summer of 1968 to December 21, 1968. During this period, local authorities mobilized students vigorously to leave for the countryside and the program turned into a political campaign. The third stage covered the period from December 22, 1968, to the spring of 1969. This stage opened with the publication of a speech by Mao on December 22, 1968, calling on Chinese youth to embrace the campaign and receive reeducation among the peasants. The slogan, "Up to the Mountains, Down to the Villages, to receive reeducation among the poor, lower, and middle peasants" splattered the front pages of local and national newspapers. From then until

TABLE 4.1 FORERUNNERS OF RUSTICATION, 1967-1968

NUMBER OF INDIVIDUALS	STARTING TIME	DESTINATIONS
Ten students from Beijing: Qu Zhe, Guo Zhaoying, Wang Ziping, Wang Jingzhi, Ning Hua, Jin Kun, Zheng Xiaodong, Hu Zhijian, Gao Feng, Ju Songdong	October 9, 1967	Inner Mongolia
Twelve hundred middle school students from Beijing, including He Fangfang	November 11, 1967	Inner Mongolia and Beidahuang
Fifty-five middle school students (thirty-one males and twenty-four females altogether) from Beijing, including Li Zhenjiang	February 8, 1968	Yunnan
Cai Lijian, Beijing	March 1968	Shanxi
Fifty-two students from eleven schools in Shanghai	August 1968	Jinggangshan in Jiangxi Province
One thousand students from the Middle School Attached to Nanjing University and No. 9 Middle School in Beijing	October 21, 1968	Inner Mongolia
Thirty students and one teacher from Tianjin	December 1968	Shanxi

SOURCES: COMPILED BY AUTHOR.

the spring of 1969, the vast majority of middle school students of the classes of 1967, 1968, and 1969 were dispatched to the countryside through cajoling or coercion, later coming to be known as the *laosanjie*, the old three classes.

There were important continuities between the Red Guard movement and the first stage of the sent-down campaign. Both involved students who were in middle school from 1966 to 1968. This biographical continuity meant that a degree of continuity would retain in the activities of those involved. For example, many Red Guards thought of rustication as a new stage of the Red Guard movement or a new revolutionary alternative.

Red Guards came to embrace rustication as a revolutionary alternative through a learning process. This process involved two crucial lessons. The first lesson came from the disillusionment with the Red Guard movement. On the one hand, there was dissatisfaction with the decline of the movement after military training teams took over control of the middle schools in Beijing after March 1967. On the other hand, there was dissatisfaction with the factional struggles that had been raging among middle school and college Red Guards. One former Red Guard in Beijing recalls, "In April 1967, Red Guards broke up. At this time, I began to feel that factional fights really were quite meaningless. . . . Therefore, I approved of taking a road of integrating with workers and peasants."[21] Another one said,

> By the end of 1966 and early 1967, many Red Guards became confused about how to carry on the movement. Some became tired of the previous stage of the movement. Therefore, in some schools, people started to debate about the situation. We studied the works of Chairman Mao in search of theories. At this time, some people raised the question of integrating with workers and peasants. They believed that student movements would come to nothing if they did not integrate with workers and peasants. The Red Guard Movement must take this necessary step.[22]

The second lesson came from Red Guards' experience in the Great Linkup (*da chuan lian*) period of the Red Guard movement. One unintended consequence of the Great Linkup was that it broadened the horizons of the participants. They visited new places and saw new people. The destitute living conditions they saw in rural China began to change their understanding of Chinese society. Small groups even began to think about how to further study China's rural conditions and help transform them. Under these circumstances, some Red Guards conducted "social investigations" on their linkup trips as a means of improving their understanding of China's social problems.[23]

In addition to "social investigations," some Red Guards on linkup trips stayed in the villages they passed through to live and work with the peasants. The best-known example is that of Cai Lijian, a female student in the Changxindian Railway Middle School in 1966. In December 1966, together with three other Red Guard friends, Cai went on a "long march" to Yan'an by foot. On their way, they entered a small village called Dujiashan. There were only five families in the village, with a total of sixteen family members. Of these, only four could be counted as labor force, and the youngest of the four was over forty years old. Life was difficult in the village. After a one-day stopover, the Red Guards continued on their way to Yan'an. Several days later, however, Cai parted company with her friends and walked alone back to the village they had just visited. Soon, school resumed and she was called back to Beijing. Cai deposited all her luggage in a peasant's home and returned to school. Upon seeing the widespread factional struggles in Beijing, Cai put up a poster and expressed her yearning to go and live in the village of Dujiashan in search of a new revolutionary path. She eventually returned to the village in March 1968 and was joined by four classmates two months later.[24] Many other Red Guards chose to go to the countryside because of their exposure to rural conditions during the Great Linkup. It is in this sense that, as one Chinese scholar argues, the sent-down movement may be viewed as a continuation of the Red Guard movement.[25]

There were fundamental differences, of course. The social context had changed. The Red Guard movement was mostly an urban phenomenon, whereas the sent-down movement had a rural setting. The Red Guard movement involved rebellion and protest, whereas the sent-down movement was about rural labor. The goals of the Red Guard movement were amorphous and varied with factional alignments in different regions. Nationally, the abstract goal of the Red Guard movement was about defending the party from the dangers of revisionism and about "rebellion" against authorities and "capitalist roaders." The official goal of the sent-down movement was the reeducation of students by peasants. In Mao's own words, "It is very necessary for sent-down youths to go to the countryside and receive reeducation by the poor and lower-middle peasants."[26] Behind the ideological smoke screen of the term, Thomas Bernstein's analysis shows that the purpose of reeducation was to resocialize the elitist attitudes of urban youth so that they would become qualified "revolutionary successors," a concern of Chinese leaders since the mid-1950s.[27] In addition, as Bernstein argues, the sent-down movement had two other unstated goals: to remove fractious Red Guards from the cities to restore order and stability and to tackle the worsening problem of urban unemployment. More recent studies confirm Bernstein's conclusions, although Michel Bonnin argues that the sent-down movement was more about the political transformation of the young generation's consciousness than about solving the problem of urban unemployment.[28]

MAKING A LIVING IN VILLAGES

The continuities and discontinuities between the Red Guard and the sent-down movements complicated the process of reaggregation such that it became a new beginning in the life journey of the Red Guard generation. It was new because members of the generation faced profoundly new problems in the rustication period. These were the problems of subsistence and meaning.

The destinations of rustication were mainly of two kinds, villages and the so-called production and construction corps (*sheng chan jian she bing tuan*). The corps were state farms with a paramilitary organization. Because construction corps were state enterprises, the sent-down youth there earned salaries in addition to a variable amount of housing and medical care. Materially, they were better off than youth sent to villages. In the words of one interviewee, "youth in construction corps did not experience hunger, while those sent to villages did."[29]

Students sent to the villages were provided for only in the first year. Afterward, they had to make their own living. This was no easy job, even for the villagers. Urban youth faced additional difficulties because they had to learn from scratch. For them, farm labor was hard and the pay was often excessively low. In many villages a full day's labor could only earn a few cents. As a result, after several years in the countryside, many urban youth could still not support themselves and had to depend on their parents for some financial assistance. According to a government document issued in July 1973, of the total number of 4.2 million youth remaining in the villages or corps in 1973, only 1.43 million or 34 percent could earn their own food, clothing, and some pocket money to spend; 35 percent could earn their food, but needed family assistance for clothing and other daily necessities; and 31 percent could not even earn their own food.[30] Apart from the difficulties of earning a meal, housing was another serious problem. The same document shows that in 1973, 64 percent of the 4.2 million youth, or 2.68 million, had been provided with housing, but the other 1.52 million lived either with local peasants or in temporary housing facilities.[31] Rural life was an utterly unexpected challenge for the sent-down youth.

The hardships were recorded in diaries. According to an entry dated April 18, 1969 written by a young man sent to Yan'an, Shaanxi: "We are extremely short of grain. Every day, we had to eat a lot of wild herbs and husks as substitute food. We mix dandelion, hare's lettuce, buckwheat, and things of this kind into our food. Life is very hard."[32] Another entry dated June 3, 1969, written by a sent-down youth in Yanggao, Shanxi has the following:

Why are we sent to the countryside as peasants, but are not provided with living expenses? Does the government have financial difficulties? Why is there no explanation then? . . . This makes me very doubtful. If this problem is not solved within half a year, I will go to the commune to borrow money. I cannot depend on my parents for my whole life. I'm dissatisfied, because the value of work is low here, there are no subsidies, and there is no way I can support myself. Even if this is a thought reform, basic living should be guaranteed. It is correct to work by living a hard life, and I will never work for my personal interests, property, or family in my life. However, I want to live an economically independent life, to be able to make a living for myself. . . . Let me plan how to spend the 5 yuan that I borrowed: a little over two yuan for a lampshade, sesame oil, vegetables, salt, soy sauce, newspapers, and stamps; about 53 cents as pocket money; and then there is a little over 1.7 yuan left. Unbelievable! More than two yuan for half a month. I would need at least more than 5 yuan a month.[33]

As this diary entry indicates, faced with the hardships of material existence, sent-down youth were compelled to ponder many things—the adequacy of government policies regarding rustication, the contradictions between ideology and material existence, the importance of living an economically independent life, of being able to make a living by oneself, and so forth. The bare necessities of life and the difficulties of making a living raised fundamental questions about the meaning of life, and, as one interviewee puts it, "it was the experiences of hunger, the most brutal aspect of human existence, that forced sent-down youth to return to humanity."[34]

THE MEANING OF LIFE

Questions about the meaning of life centered on two contradictions experienced by the sent-down youth. One was between the political rhetoric of socialist revolution and the realities in rural China. An awareness of this contradiction had already appeared in the middle of the Red Guard movement. It became acute in the rustication period, when this awareness sprang directly from the personal experience of daily life. In a diary entry dated April 10, 1969, one individual wrote about peasant life in the following terms: "At lunch time, I saw Gou Wa standing at a distance from us and kept smacking on his tobacco pipe alone. I asked Suo Di, who told me that Gou Wa had no lunch. . . . He could only afford to have two meals of thin porridge each day. . . . After hearing these things, I became very upset for a long time. What I saw today was different from what I learned about socialism in the past."[35]

Related to this contradiction between the rhetoric of socialist revolution and the actual social conditions was the contradiction between altruism and self interest. As mentioned earlier in this book, one of the dominant values inculcated in the Red Guard generation was altruistic dedication to the revolutionary cause and the relinquishment of personal interest. However, for sent-down youth who had to make their own living, to talk about altruism or relinquishment of personal interest was a self-contradiction. Thus a young woman asked herself in her diary, "People say that no one should care about pay and rewards in labor and work. But if I don't care, what do I have to eat? I can't survive by feeding on air only."[36]

These contradictions brought into relief many concrete questions about life and existence. If the socialist revolution had not even solved the basic problem of subsistence, what did it mean to talk about carrying on the revolution? Where was the purpose of life to be located? Was it to earn a living? But how to earn a living under extremely harsh conditions? How did the peasants manage it? Was it wrong to pursue personal interest, abandon the rural life, and scurry back to the city? How to deal with the conflicts between personal and collective interests? These questions appeared frequently in the diaries and letters written by sent-down youth, indicating the depth of their inner tensions. This sense of inner crisis, coupled with the new social conditions, turned the sent-down experiences into a process of reorienting the self or, rather, finding a new self.

PERSONAL INTEREST

A former sent-down youth in Beijing told me about her understanding of rustication in our private correspondence on March 30, 2000. She wrote in a rather impassioned style that it was a step "from heaven to earth, from fantasy to reality, from speculation to confrontation, from self-being to self-consciousness. Knowing the peasants, knowing the countryside, knowing China, knowing the world—in this process, I knew my self. In a worn-out cotton-padded coat, with a belt made of straw, I bid farewell forever to the 'delicate girl' (*jiao xiao jie*) that I had been. From then on, I began to learn 'life as a struggle.'"[37]

What she said here was a down-to-earth nosedive that she went through in the rustication period. By "life as a struggle," she literally meant struggling to live, yet it was not to live a life of revolutionary glory, but just an ordinary life of labor.

This down-to-earth attitude entailed not only a metaphoric "fall from heaven" but also an understanding of the practical necessities and values of everyday existence. At the same time, the ideals of the "good life" as Mao's loyal "Red Guards" and revolutionary storm troopers faded. At the heart of this new outlook was the growing valuation of personal interest. It is not that this generation had been unconcerned with personal interest. Until then, however, to be publicly concerned with personal interest had been viewed as morally wrong and politically unacceptable. Within the moral frameworks into which the generation had been socialized, the pursuit of self-interest for the sake of personal fulfillment had been thoroughly condemned. The core values had always been collective goals and revolutionary causes. Slogans such as "Down with the self!" once filled the pages of Red Guard newspapers, when being "selfish" (zi si) was denounced as criminal.[38]

Sent-down youth learned to value personal interest in their struggles for daily existence. In diaries and letters as well as in recent recollections, I came across many accounts of young people's initial responses to what they saw as the pursuit of self-interest among peasants when they first settled down in the villages. These responses had an element of "cultural shock" similar to what travelers to strange lands may experience. Recalling his experience, a former sent-down youth wrote that the day after he and a few others settled in their designated village, the village party committee convened a welcome meeting. The party secretary opened the meeting by saying, "From now on, you will be the educated new peasants in this village. You should remember: farming is for yourself." As this individual recalled, this statement came as a total shock for a generation that had been accustomed to being told to "study for the sake of revolution."[39]

> From the first day of our rustication life, the contrast between school life and rural life was brought into relief. The fervor "for the revolution" was instantly transformed by the necessity of taking care of oneself. Each of us had a small room, a stove, an iron rake, a sickle, a pair of shoulder poles. We labored and lived; we looked after ourselves; we produced all that we needed ourselves. . . . Here all glamorous slogans and empty words paled into insignificance. The work points that we earned to support ourselves, peasants' trust, young people's friendship—all this had to be earned through one's own labor and production.[40]

In a letter to his family, a young man wrote in meticulous detail about his income:

> Several days ago, we were paid our wages in order for us to celebrate the Dragon Boat Festival. One work-point was worth 10 cents. I earned 5 yuan and 70 cents. . . . The one who earned the most got 9 yuan and 40 cents. Zhao Wenzhong earned

9 yuan and 30 cents. Among females, the one who earned the least got 2 yuan and 90 cents. Among males, the one who earned the least got a little over 4 yuan . . . My analysis of this situation is consistent with the conclusion I reached earlier: when your work-points are low, your income will suffer. Compared with the one who has so far got the most work-points, I'm lagging behind by about 30 work-points. If by the end of the year one work-point is calculated to be worth 80 cents, then it means I earn at least 20 yuan less than the top-earning one in the first five months of this year.[41]

Not only did sent-down youth come to relinquish their contempt for personal interest, but they began to actively pursue it. As Xu Huiying recalled, "In our confusion and pain, we eventually embarked on the road in search of our own personal interest. Many sent-down youth who had initially wanted to dedicate themselves to the rural revolution later left the countryside and went back to the cities, joined the army, entered the factory, or went to college."[42]

In the active pursuits of personal interest, sent-down youth began to plan their lives and design their future according to the new values of ordinary life they had learned. One person recalls the significance of this change in the following words:

After they lost confidence in achieving the social goals they had cherished, many people began to take notice of the existence of "I." They began to cultivate their personal world. They studied scientific and cultural knowledge and plunged themselves into the ocean of books. They designed their futures, drew up three- or five-year plans to achieve their personal goals. They tried to earn more work-points and more money. They strategically looked around them for better positions. For a period of time, they conspicuously parted company with the values they had adopted since childhood: the unconditional melting of the self in society and the collectivity. They had isolated the "I" from society and from the authoritarian will. They had a new understanding of the meaning of personal existence.[43]

Diaries and letters provide detailed evidence of the young people's life-planning efforts. They worked out budgets in order to make both ends meet, made daily schedules to plan their time, and designed short-term and long-term goals. They were tortured by internal tensions caused by the conflict between personal goals and collective values and experienced confusions and frustrations when they found their personal goals unattainable. In a letter to a friend, one sent-down youth gave his view about the relationship between economy and politics, emphasized the importance of economic development, and expressed his worries about the future. He wrote, "Recently we are very hard at work—eight hours a day and only two Sundays off in a month. We get our meals and clothes for free and in addition earn 7 yuan a month. What is the future? No idea. If we follow the principle of "distribution according to work" (and what is distribution according to work anyway?), as some people think we should, then the tens of thousands of us will have to feed on northeast wind, with nothing to eat, because we are in deficit each year."[44]

Also in a letter to a friend, one sent-down youth explained his understanding of future plans, emphasizing immediate goals over grandiose projects such as the attainment of the Marxist vision of a communist society: "As far as future plans are concerned, I understand them as the goals within a particular period of time, the immediate purposes of life. Of course, this does not mean we have any doubt about the future prospect of communism. It's just that we have more immediate goals."[45] Another advised his friend to be realistic: "It's been five years since 1968. We are no longer small kids. In another five years, that is, in 1978, what changes will have happened to you and me? This is difficult to say, but I think at present we should be realistic. We should read some books to enrich ourselves."[46]

The biggest concern among sent-down youth was whether to permanently stay in the countryside and labor as a farmer or to find a way to move back to the cities. For many, this question was a source of great inner anxiety. To reject the idea of "taking roots" in the countryside went against the official rhetoric and propaganda. For those who had initially expressed their determination to carry on the Red Guard movement by integrating with peasants, it was a self-renunciation. Thus there were many discussions and personal reflections about the meaning of rustication. These discussions often led to the conclusion that rustication was not an irreversible necessity in China's modernization project, an argument that helped justify, morally and politically, efforts to rechart one's future career by leaving the villages. One diary entry has the following words: "Things always change. They do not stay the same. . . . China's countryside will change, will be mechanized, use fertilizers, develop industry, commerce and entertainment, eliminate the differences between factory workers and rural peasants, between cities and villages. . . . That means it doesn't make sense to be a peasant for life."[47]

In a letter written to a friend, a young man recounted how he explained his views about rustication to two government cadres:

> I told them that most sent-down youths were not prepared to remain in the countryside for life and that there were historical, class, and social factors involved. . . . This problem cannot be solved in a short period of period, because it is determined by the material conditions of the society. . . . I think that in the long run, industrialization is the main direction. This is a general law in political economy. Industrialization develops at a geometric speed . . . while agricultural development is a mathematical development. . . . With industrialization . . . the industrial population will increase, and the agricultural population will decrease. Does anyone doubt this?[48]

By this point, it is clear that the affirmation of personal interest eventually led to the complete rejection of the official policy of sending young people to do farm labor in rural areas.

THE RHETORIC OF CLASS STRUGGLE

The experience of rural life gave sent-down youth a new understanding of ordinary people. First, they began to see the emptiness of the rhetoric of class struggle that they had learned at school and practiced in the Red Guard movement. Second, they developed a personal understanding of the daily worries and concerns of the rural people. The result was a new kind of identification with the ordinary people.

Before the Red Guard movement, the moral frameworks into which members of the would-be Red Guard generation were socialized and within which they defined themselves and their social relations hinged on three axes—party, state, and socialism. The building of a new socialist society in a process of class struggle provided the ultimate value orientation.[49] In the party ideology, devotion to the party and its leaders was promulgated as a necessary part of the central value orientation. Aggression against the "class enemy" was affirmed in the new political culture of the early decades of communist China.[50]

The Red Guard movement turned the classification of the class enemy into a field of political struggle. At stake, for example, were issues such as who had the right to rebel against whom. Both the subjects and the targets underwent change in the course of the movement. One unintended consequence was the blurring of the political discourse about who counted as the real "class enemy." It began to dawn upon some Red Guards that the class enemy was not an objective existence, but a political label that could be applied to very different social groups.

For many, however, the notion of class struggle still commanded great influence. There was still a strong belief in it and a revolutionary fervor to expose class enemies. As they migrated to the countryside, Red Guards carried the belief and enthusiasm with them. As one individual recalled, "When I first settled in a village in Shanxi, I was still full of revolutionary fervor. Keeping in mind the teaching 'Class struggle will be effective as long as you pay attention to it,' I pondered how to wage a class struggle against the landlords or expose a handful of hidden class enemies." What he found was utterly contrary to his expectations, because, he continued, "Yet our village was so poor it didn't even have a landlord. There were only a few middle peasants. . . . Soon I found that the peasants in the village had no interest at all in class struggle. On the contrary, they repeatedly dampened our enthusiasm for class struggle."[51]

One respondent I interviewed expressed the same idea through a personal story of the first night she spent in the village. She said to me,

> As students, we had always considered landlords as class enemies—they were parasites and oppressors. They were dangerous. When we went to the village, we five girls lived next to a former landlord's cave-house. The first night we were there, we were scared to death. We stacked stools, basins, brooms, and all sorts of stuff behind our door. In the night, we heard noise pushing at our door and seemed to see a dark shadow. The next day, we accused the landlord neighbor of attempting to take advantage of us. But the villagers did not believe us—they seemed to stand on the side of the landlord! They said that was not possible. Still, we made the landlord stand in front of Mao's picture to make a confession. Later we knew it must have been the landlord's black pig that had snouted at our door.[52]

The villagers' indifference to the rhetoric of class struggle was a source of initial confusion for sent-down youth, but the sense of confusion did not last long. An intimate knowledge of the daily struggles of the ordinary people would soon drive home a simple but decisive point: that all individuals who labor to earn their living deserve respect and those who suffer the misfortunes of life do not do so through their own fault.

WHO ARE THE PEOPLE?

Class struggle had another dimension—it was about the people as well as the class enemy. In the Cultural Revolution, the rhetoric of class struggle was dominated by a venomous atmosphere to expose the class enemy. In the crusade of class struggle, "people" was invoked as an abstract category endowed with moral persuasion and political power. Those who were disowned as members of the "people" could be classified as class enemies and persecuted. The party and the government spoke and acted as the sole representatives of the people.[53] This produced a natural logic of identity: to be identified with the party and the government was nothing but an identification with the people. This was a central element of the identity of the Red Guard generation up until the Red Guard movement. It was this identity that began to undergo change from then onward.

A new understanding of the people developed in the rustication period. It was a notion of the people as ordinary individuals with personal likes and dislikes, thoughts and feelings. They live a hard life, are hardworking, may be selfish or generous or both. In short, they are ordinary individuals.

The life documents, interviews, and retrospective accounts collected for this study provide abundant evidence of this notion of the people. In an interview, a sent-down youth who stayed for three years in a village in Shanxi Province explained to me how they changed their attitude toward beggars:

> In Beijing we were brought up to think that beggars were social outcasts, that they were lazy and undeserving of help. In Beijing, when we saw a beggar we would hurry away, as if staying away from a disease. In the village where we were sent, most of the villagers had been poor migrants from further north—they had begged their way to the village and then settled down there. Therefore, the villagers had a very sympathetic attitude toward beggars. No matter how poor they were, they would never let a beggar go away empty-handed. When we first went there, we used to drive away the people who came to beg. We had a dog that was especially wary of beggars. Later, the villagers talked to us about the way we treated beggars and we began to change our ways.[54]

A young man who was sent down for four years in a village in Liaoning Province wrote about the good-natured humor of the local peasants. The author was a good storyteller. Quite by accident, he told a story to several village women and soon became popular for his storytelling skills. Thus, during work breaks in the farm field, peasants would ask him to entertain them with stories. Once, he was telling them the story about the monkey king from the well-known novel *Journey to the West*. When it was about time to resume work, they found Uncle Gao, their team leader, had fallen asleep. They decided not to wake him up in order for the young man to continue the story. So they made a shade to block the sunshine from Uncle Gao's face, and the storytelling continued for two more hours. When the sun was about to set, Uncle Gao woke up, and said, "It's late. Let's get back to work!" In the evening, back in the village, the storyteller asked Uncle Gao, "Why did you sleep so fast?" Uncle Gao smiled and replied, "You think I was dozing off? I heard everything you said!" The fact was that Uncle had pretended to sleep because he also liked the story.

Another sent-down youth described his surprising discovery of peasants' openness toward sex, as well as their selfishness. As students in Beijing, they had been brought up in an urban culture that repressed sexuality. Talk about sex had been considered shameful and immoral. Among villagers, however, he found that sex was a perpetually fascinating topic. Villagers even had a popular saying, "The sun will not set in the west, if there is no talk about the vagina." He also found that villagers were not so selfless as they had thought they were. He discovered that when peasants' private interests were in conflict with collective interests, almost no one would sacrifice personal interests for the sake of the collectivity. Eventually, the image of the perfect socialist peasant evaporated from his mind. At the same time, as the young man puts it,

> the hollow and abstract idea [of the peasant] also evaporated. At this point, I discovered the agreeable and respectable character of the peasants. . . . I discovered that only after you had really immersed yourself among the "ignorant and backward" peasants and only when you had developed similar feelings with them could you really understand the term "people." They never hid their likes or dislikes, just as they were undisguised in their ideas about sex. They were very frank. They were not fond of empty talk. They believed that "one practical action is better than a dozen programs." They were down to earth to the extreme. They might be cunningly selfish, yet at the bottom of their hearts, they were gentle and kind.[55]

The new understanding of the people that developed among sent-down youth has had far-reaching consequences for both the Red Guard generation and Chinese society. As a result of such an understanding, the Red Guard generation began to identify itself emotionally with the people, an identity that would continue to influence their moral outlooks and political action for decades to come. Appropriately, a poem was posted during the Democracy Wall movement, at the end of the Cultural Revolution, that expressed this understanding of the people:

Perhaps some day,
When we begin to talk about the people,
It will no longer be hollow and abstract.
At that time,
Each and every painful moan,
Will gather its force like drops of water gathering into the sea.
And high waves will rise that are powerful enough to topple the mountains
    and overturn the seas.
Every piece of vague thought,
Will condense into nuclearlike power,
And release energy powerful enough to destroy everything.
At that time, the people
Will no longer be an alibi for the bureaucrats to issue orders.[56]

CONSEQUENCES OF THE AFFIRMATION
OF THE VALUES OF ORDINARY LIFE

The affirmation of the values of ordinary life among the Red Guard generation provided the necessary sociocultural foundation for the implementation of the state's economic policies in the reform era. This is a simple and yet important argument. It is simple because the link seems to be too obvious to be ignored; it is important because, surprisingly, it *has* been ignored. Even sociologists concerned with explaining the socioeconomic changes in the post-Mao era have focused mostly on the consequences of state policies. Little attention has been given to the social basis of these policies.

Retracing the steps from the mid-1980s to the late 1970s, when the reform "officially" took off, it is easy to say that the changes in this period resulted from state policies.[57] This state-centered perspective on social change, however, gives short shrift to the grassroots impetus for change. Other scholars have looked beyond the party-state for sources of change. Works with a focus on the rural origins of reform have produced what may be termed a "rural initiative perspective."[58] A useful counterpoise to state-centered approaches, it nevertheless leaves open the question of whether or not there was a parallel urban initiative. With a partial focus on the role of local governments in China's economic transition, the chapters in *Zouping in Transition: The Process of Reform in Rural North China* edited by Andrew Walder give an affirmative answer to this question. A similar answer emerges from a study by White, who shows that local interests supported by local networks pushed and pulled state decision makers toward change.[59] To these works, my analysis of the affirmation of the values of ordinary life adds a bottom-up perspective that highlights the changes in the attitudes, values, and daily concerns of the Red Guard generation.

I argue that the formulation of the reform policies in the early post-Mao period was in part a response to the grassroots demands for socioeconomic change. Their implementation, furthermore, was not as difficult as it might have been, given the dramatic nature of the policy reversal, because members of the Red Guard generation had already been predisposed, through their experiences of rural life, to support economic development in order to attain a better material life.

Two historical developments associated with the Red Guard generation contributed to major policy changes in the early years of the reform era. One was the growing demand among sent-down youth to return to the city and the eventual return of the majority of them. The other was the unemployment problem in China's urban centers in the late seventies and early eighties.

Beginning from the early 1970s, sent-down youth began to drift back to the cities through various channels. But the policy of rustication remained in place, and many people had to resort to illegitimate means to achieve their goals of returning. After Mao died and Hua Guofeng assumed office as the party leader, Hua reaffirmed the rustication policy in his report to the Eleventh Plenum of the Chinese Communist Party in August 1977.[60] A national conference was convened in Beijing from December 12, 1977, to January 13, 1978, to discuss the rustication policy. At this conference the rustication policy was upheld by Hua's new leadership. Although the resumption of college admissions in 1977 absorbed about 350,000 sent-down youth in 1977 and 1978,[61] there were still 8.6 million of them in the villages or on collective farms in 1978. Some began to publicly protest against the rustication policy and demand urban jobs. The first of these collective protest activities took place in April 1978 in Fushun City, Liaoning Province.[62] Large-scale demonstrations took place in the second half of 1978 in other cities in Liaoning Province, with national reverberations. At a Politburo meeting on October 18, 1978, the concern was expressed by top party leaders that "if all the 8 million people start to make trouble, who could deal with it?"[63] Soon after this, at the end of October, sent-down youth in Yunnan Province began to petition government leaders to allow them to return to their home cities. About forty thousand signatures were collected from a total of eighty thousand sent-down youth in Yunnan Province.[64] A strike was announced and won when the party secretary of Yunnan Province finally accepted sent-down youth's demand to return home (I will discuss this case in greater detail in chapter 6).[65]

The return of sent-down youth from Yunnan marked the beginning of a national wave. Youth in other parts of the country soon followed suit. Altogether over 4 million of the total number of 8.6 sent-down youth returned to the cities in 1979 alone. Their return exacerbated unemployment in the cities. Urban unemployment was a serious problem in the late seventies and early eighties. Tom Gold identifies four social groups that constituted the population "waiting for employment" in the decade from 1978 to 1987.[66] One of these four groups were youth who had returned to the cities. Exactly how many were "waiting for employment" is unknown. According to one source, from 1979 to 1982, Shanghai provided jobs for 1.54 million unemployed. Fifty-eight percent of these, or 886,000, constituted youth who had returned from the countryside.[67] Of course, the unemployed population included other social and age groups, but sent-down youth posed the most serious challenge. By 1979 the typical age of the Red Guard generation had reached thirty. Many of them were unmarried. Without jobs, they had to be supported by their parents. They had grievances and, as the process of their return to the city indicated, they could use the tactics of protest they had learned as Red Guards to champion their cause.

Under these circumstances, semiprivate or private business practices began to be endorsed by the state as legitimate economic practices in a socialist economy.[68] Such practices had existed before the Cultural Revolution. They came under attack during it, most vehemently by Red Guards themselves in the early days of the Red Guard movement. Thereafter they mostly disappeared, but began to reemerge in the 1970s, first in the countryside and then in urban areas. In the early days of economic reform, state actors had ambivalent attitudes toward private business,[69] because official recognition of such practices would have far-reaching implications for interpreting the nature of Chinese socialism. The acute problems of unemployment, however, raised serious doubts about the efficacy of China's existing economic structure. The analysis of these problems led to the conclusion that other forms of economic activities, market oriented rather than centrally controlled, must be encouraged to deal with these problems.

How many sent-down youth were engaged in semiprivate or private businesses after they returned to the cities? Some estimates may be made on the basis of data on the channels of returning to the cities. There were four main channels for leaving the countryside. One was to be recruited as a worker by an urban factory. The second was to be admitted into a college or university. The third was to join the army. The fourth was to return to the cities under the excuse of an illness (called *bing tui*) or extreme family difficulties (*kun tui*). People in the first three categories did not have to worry about jobs, but those in the fourth group returned to the cities without job assignments. They had to consider how to support themselves. Of the four categories, those who returned as factory recruits numbered the most, roughly 1.3 million in 1978 and 2.2 million in 1979. The number of those who returned to the cities under the excuses of illnesses or family difficulties ranked second, about 800,000 in 1978 and 1.3 million in 1979.[70] This means that about one-third of all youth who returned to the cities had no official job assignments. In addition to these, many youth had simply sneaked back to the cities without official authorization. They too had to worry about earning a living, because they had no chance of finding a job without legal urban residence status. Many had to do odd jobs of all kinds to make a living.[71] Others engaged in small-scale individual business practices, such as repairing radios or bicycles on the streets. These practices belonged to what Solinger called activities in the "petty private sector,"[72] the embryonic forms of a privatization that was to occur in large scale as China's economic reform forged ahead.

It remains to consider the attitudes of sent-down youth toward such business practices. I have argued so far that 1. the valuation of personal interest was an underlying factor behind sent-down youth's return to the cities; 2. their return to the cities exacerbated the existing unemployment problems in the urban centers; 3. they engaged in semiprivate and private business practices that had been viewed as illegitimate; 4. this situation pushed state actors to recognize their legitimacy; and 5. such practices were the embryonic forms of privatization in the process of economic reform. A counterargument may be raised that members of the Red Guard generation had been *forced* to undertake private business activities after they returned to the cities, because for many of them, that seemed to be the only option for making a living. This may well be true, but it does not refute the hypothesis that the rustication experience significantly contributed to a more positive attitude toward such politically ambivalent undertakings. As noted previously, in the early days of the reform era the political discourse about privatization was ambivalent. There was hostility toward privatization because of its potential ideological challenge to the socialist economic system then in place.[73] To engage in such practices, therefore, demanded a self-understanding of the legitimacy of what one was doing, to say the least. For the Red Guard generation, such self-understanding had by then become available. What they had learned in the countryside they could not put to better use after they returned to the cities: that ordinary life embodied the meaning of existence and that social respect is due to all who earn a living through their own labor. It is in this sense that, as one of my interviewees put it, "Without the rustication experience, these people would never doff their stinking airs and go into petty business."[74] In other words, by the time they returned to the cities from the countryside, members of the Red Guard generation had rejected their earlier attitude toward what they considered bourgeois practices.

5

UNDERGROUND CULTURE

IN THE NEW CULTURE movement in early twentieth-century China, key intellectual figures such as Lu Xun, Chen Duxiu, and Hu Shi rejected traditional Confucian culture and argued that rejuvenation of the modern Chinese nation must be based on the construction of a new culture. This new culture would promote a new philosophy of life with strong beliefs in individualism, freedom, science, technology, and democracy. This New Culture movement remains one of the most significant defining moments of modern Chinese history.[1]

Many other cultural movements have since appeared, none as influential as the New Culture movement. It thus came as a surprise when I learned in conversations with a former Red Guard and sent-down youth that during their years of rustication, she and her friends were involved in what they called a second New Culture movement.[2] In my research I had often read about the sort of underground cultural activities among sent-down youth, but had not associated these activities with another new culture movement, particularly one that claimed to be the successor of *the* New Culture movement. But the analogy made sense to me. Despite the differences in the quality and quantity of the output of the two new culture movements, they share one key similarity, namely, the theme of a growing new consciousness. This new consciousness is an important component in the mental journey of the Red Guard generation. This chapter traces the development of this new consciousness through a study of this "second new culture movement."

AN UNDERGROUND CULTURAL MOVEMENT

Unlike the first New Culture movement, this second one had a surreptitious character. It consisted of an amalgam of semiopen, underground, or sur-reptitious cultural activities and it was primarily a phenomenon involving the Red Guard generation.[3] On the production side, there was the writing of letters, diaries, poems, songs, political essays, short stories, and novels. The output of letters and diaries was presumably large, because diary writing and letter writing were prevalent.[4] Letters were not only written for private communication but also for sharing ideas. Some letters went into under-ground circulation because they contained serious discussions about social and political issues.[5] The output of poetry was similarly large. Exchanging a self-composed poem (in classical or modern free verse) was common among sent-down youth. Many such poems were a way of expressing personal con-nection and friendship. However, fine poetry did emerge, as evidenced by the volumes of "misty poetry" (*meng long shi*) later published in the post-Mao era.[6] The most influential poets and artists who began to publish after the Cultural Revolution were already honing their skills in the early 1970s.[7] There were fewer stories, songs, and political essays, though they were equally widely circulated. Dozens of "sent-down youth songs" (*zhiqing ge qu*), for instance, were in underground circulation, the best-known of which was "A song of sent-down youth from Nanjing."[8]

The reception-side story was even more fascinating, because it was more multifaceted and involved many more people. It was about the reading, copying, and circulation of forbidden books and unpublished manuscripts, about singing, storytelling, and listening to foreign radio stations. The most popular hand-copied manuscripts were unpublished works, which Perry Link refers to as hand-copied entertainment fiction.[9] Link classifies them into six story types, namely, detective stories, antispy stories, modern his-torical romance, modern knight errant stories, triangular love stories, and pornographic stories. They are estimated at over a hundred in number, but only fewer than half are extant today. Their authorship is usually unknown, though some of them were likely to be written by Red Guards or sent-down youth.[10]

Unpublished manuscripts were only a small part of the reading materials. The majority were published works. Because of the scarcity of books, people would read anything they could lay their hands on. Works of Mao, Marx, En-gels, Lenin, and Stalin were legitimate readings and available in book stores. Other books they read were published before the Cultural Revolution but were then banned. These included masterpieces of Chinese and Western literature, modernist Western literature, works about Soviet revisionism, and the international communist movement. Some of these were internal publications.[11]

To help cadres understand the Chinese Communist Party's critique of Soviet revisionism and the alleged decadence of Western modernist thought, the propaganda department of the CCP inaugurated a publishing project in 1962. Works of Western modernist literature and Soviet revisionism were selected, translated, and published as internal materials for criticism. Their readership was limited to high-ranking party cadres. By 1965, over one thousand titles had been published, but many titles had a print run of only about nine hundred.[12] Literary titles were published with a uniform yellow cover, and nonfiction works were published with a gray cover. In the wake of the Red Guard movement, these yellow-cover (huang pi shu) and gray-cover books (hui pi shu) became popular readings among young people. The following is a list of sample titles with the date of the publication of the Chinese edition in brackets.

The Stranger by Albert Camus (December 1961)

Waiting for Godot by Samuel Beckett (July 1965)

On the Road by Jack Kerouac (September 1963)

Look Back in Anger by John Osborne (July 1965)

The Catcher in the Rye by J. D. Salinger (December 1962)

Nausea by Jean-Paul Sartre (April 1965)

One Day in the Life of Ivan Denisovich and The Gulag Archipelago by Aleksandr
    Solzhenitsyn (February 1963)

Men, Years, Life by Ilya Ehrenburg (3 vols., 1962–1964)

The Thaw by Ilya Ehrenburg (1963)

Khrushchevism by Theja Gunawardhana (November 1963)

The Revolution Betrayed by Leon Trotsky (December 1963)

The New Class: An Analysis of the Communist System by Milovan Đilas
    (February 1963)

The forbidden books circulated among young people thus included political dissent, critique of socialism, and the international communist movement, as well as works of world literature. Circulating and reading these titles entailed varying degrees of personal risks, from public humiliation to imprisonment. Some authors were subject to political persecution. Ren Yi was arrested on February 19, 1970, and sentenced to ten years in prison under the charge that he had written a "counterrevolutionary" song.[13] Zhang Yang, the author of the novel *The Second Handshake*, also suffered from persecution. For these reasons I consider such cultural activities to be manifestations of an amorphous underground cultural movement.

TRANSGRESSION, SELF-CULTIVATION, AND DESACRALIZATION

Several scholars have studied the underground cultural movement in the Cultural Revolution. Yang Jian's history of underground literature is among the earliest and most systematic treatment of the literary products of the period.[14] Yin Hongbiao's book provides a comprehensive history of what he calls "trends of thought" among youth, from the Red Guard movement through the April Fifth movement.[15] However, these two important works focus on the contents of the cultural products created by the "elites" of this generation. My interest differs in two ways. First, I explore the meaning of cultural activities for the Red Guard generation in the decade after the Red Guard movement. Here my focus is less on the contents of culture and more on culture as a social activity. I argue that from this perspective the meaning of the underground cultural movement was in transgression and self-cultivation. Second, I examine the relationship of this underground culture to the "high" political culture of the Red Guard period. I argue that the underground culture desacralized the revolutionary culture of the earlier period and produced a new sense of self and society.

A distinct feature of the underground cultural movement was not organized activism, but transgressive communication. Copying, borrowing, and returning a book; writing, reading, singing, storytelling—these were all acts of communication, discursive or nondiscursive. In form or content they deviated from the social norms and political ideology of the time and thus had a transgressive character. They were transgressive not in the sense of the reversal of the high and the low or of the dominant and the subordinate, as argued in the works of Mikhail Bakhtin, Peter Stallybrass, and others.[16] Nor was it exactly the same as the notion of the weapons of the weak in James Scott's work.[17] Transgressive communication refers to communicative acts that occur on the margins of power. These acts may or may not be intended as deliberate transgressions upon power. Often they are not intended as such. Transgressive practices may have subversive effects, but usually slowly and accumulatively. They may or may not express dissension, though they often deviate from the orthodox and the mainstream. Their transgressive character is less about engagement or confrontations with power and more about disengagement and distancing from power. There is a hidden pleasure and thrill to transgressive practices. In this sense, transgressive practices were the extraordinary in the ordinary routines of daily labor. As I will show, part of the attraction of underground culture for youth in the Cultural Revolution derived from the pleasures and risks of transgression.

Cultural practices, transgressive or not, were technologies of the self and self-cultivation. Writing diaries, reading books, singing songs may be about self-improvement, self-planning, and self-entertainment. After universities and colleges were reopened in 1972 to admit students from among workers, peasants, and soldiers, sent-down youth began to entertain hopes of going on to college, and many of them spent their leisure time studying math, English, philosophy, literature, and other subjects. Despite all the fierce attacks on culture in the Red Guard movement, culture retained its attraction and prestige among the youth. In fact, the revolution against culture had in all likelihood intensified rather than weakened the appeal of culture, and the underground cultural movement was merely a sign of the resurgence of culture's undying status and appeal in Chinese society.

Yet the "new" culture that appeared and circulated among sent-down youth was radically different from the revolutionary culture that led to the violent performances of Red Guard factionalism. Hence its unofficial and underground character; yet its widespread circulation underground ultimately eroded the sacred aura of revolutionary culture. New understandings of self and society emerged through this process.

In the rest of this chapter, I will analyze the many ways of producing, accessing, and consuming underground culture among sent-down youth. The chapter ends with an analysis of the contents of the cultural products and the new ideas they expressed.

LETTER WRITING

The production and reception of culture among sent-down youth can be distinguished only loosely. In many cases, the cultural activities combined production and consumption. Writing a letter to a friend was an act of production, but the letter writer expected a reply and was thus also a would-be reader. The act of note-taking, a common practice among youth at that time, was an act of reading as well as producing something new. The product could be a collection of quotations and sayings, like the commonplace books popular in early modern Europe, which could then be shared with friends.

Letters were a dear part in the lives of sent-down youth. A letter dated April 18, 1971, has these lines: "In the boring and monotonous days of rural life, it is always a delight to get a letter from a friend."[18] A former sent-down youth writes that in the villages "letter-writing became an important matter in our lives. When we were lonely, hopeless, sad, and homesick, we relied on letters for mutual care, mutual comfort, and mutual encouragement."[19] The poet Shu Ting recalls that "writing and reading letters was an important part of the lives of educated youth and my greatest joy."[20]

Letters were written to families, lovers, friends, and classmates. They linked up those scattered in isolated rural areas into friendship circles. A collection of 124 letters written between 1966 and 1977 shows that the letters were sent to or from almost all the provinces in mainland China, weaving together a web of connections from places such as Shaanxi, Inner Mongolia, Yunnan, Sichuan to Heilongjiang, Beijing, and Shanghai.[21]

Letter writing was not only a means of keeping in touch with the outside world but also of sharing ideas. Some letters may run as long as ten or more pages in which their authors would engage in serious debates about practical and political issues. For example, among the most famous letters were two exchanged between Huang Yiding and Liu Ning in 1975. Huang and Liu had been classmates. They had both left Beijing for Heilongjiang as sent-down youth in 1969. In 1975 Huang moved back to Beijing. In a letter to Liu, Huang advised Liu also to return to Beijing. He wrote: "My life at home was OK. Every day, I read, go out in the street, do grocery shopping, clean the house, do the laundry. I've changed. I've changed from a farmer to a loafer, from a Marxist to a bourgeois liberal. I have no clear goal now. I want to stay away from politics and study technology. However, I know Beijing is a big world. My greatest wish is to study all the 'secrets' of this world, to understand its general conditions and the various types of human beings in this society."[22] In his reply Liu chided his friend for having abandoned the revolutionary ideals and dreams they used to share. He criticized his down-to-earth practicality and bourgeois liberalism. And he expressed his own wish to continue to pursue his revolutionary ideals as an educated youth. This debate reflected the dilemmas of many young people at the time. Several months later, the two letters were published in Beijing Daily. The newspaper editors, however, used Huang's letter as a negative example and added comments in praise of Liu's attitude toward rustication.

Only rarely did a letter get published in a newspaper, however, and if it did, it would be surely because it served official political purposes. Letters by sent-down youth were normally written to share private feelings, thoughts, and the details of everyday life. I examined 162 letters published in three collections.[23] Of these, 98 were written to friends or classmates, 47 to family members, and 17 were love letters. The expressions of personal feelings and thoughts were a remarkable feature of these letters. Generally, letters to family members—parents and siblings—included more details about daily life and activities, whereas letters between friends and classmates featured more discussions of personal thoughts and feelings. Here is an excerpt from a letter addressed by a daughter to her parents, dated September 1, 1968: "I bought 1.5 *jin* of honey. It is delicious. I plan to have one *jin* of honey each month. It cost one yuan a *jin*. There is no fish here, probably because the Russians are making trouble. There are no eggs to eat either."[24]

An excerpt of a letter from a son to his mother and brothers, dated July 4, 1969: "We start working in the field at 8 in the morning and stop at 12:30. Then we work from 2 PM to 6 PM. There is a short break in the middle of the day. In fact, we now start working after 9 in the morning, and do not start working in the afternoon until after 3. . . . We have three meals a day. There is not quite enough to eat. The toughest part is that we are going without vegetables. It has been like this since the 28th day of last month."[25]

Finally, here is an excerpt of a letter addressed to a friend, dated March 15, 1969:

You raised many questions in your letter. This means you are concerned with these questions and you want to find answers to them. That is very good. Only those who are good for nothing are not concerned about these issues. However, some of the questions you raised should not have been raised. I am being frank because I know you will listen to me. For example, questions concerning the future and methods of the Chinese revolution and the directions and methods of agricultural reform. Also, the question about what the main problems of the Chinese revolution are. In my view, these questions have been resolved. There is no need for further discussion. . . . In my view, discussions are necessary, but they should be more about practical issues. Then we can go deeper from there step by step.[26]

This letter is a fascinating sample of the mental world of the sent-down generation in a moment of transition. Its addressee had apparently posed "big questions" such as the future of the Chinese revolution, a habit among youth in the Red Guard period. Yet the letter writer did not think they should ponder such "big questions" any more, but rather be concerned "more about practical issues."

ACCESS TO BOOKS

Forbidden books were hard to come by. The main channels of book distribution in the Cultural Revolution were state-owned bookstores, uniformly called the New China Bookstore (xin hua shu dian). The number of New China Bookstore branches grew slowly up to the eve of the Cultural Revolution, from 3,584 in 1957, to 3,791 in 1963, and 4,076 in May 1966.[27] After the CR started, some bookstores were closed, and many stores locked away most of their books. The Central Branch of the New China Bookstore was shut down in 1969 (to be reopened in March 1973), and all its cadres sent to cadre schools or villages.[28] Nationwide, 576 million copies of books were sealed off in bookstores. Bookstores in Beijing alone locked away 8 million copies of 6,870 titles.[29] In Shanghai the biggest bookstore on Nanjing Donglu had 1,792 titles in social science in early 1966. After the CR started, only 200 titles were for sale.[30]

Books available in bookstores mainly consisted of the selected works of Mao Zedong, Marx, Engels, Lenin, and Stalin, political pamphlets of newspaper editorials and articles published for all kinds of political campaigns, technical and agricultural manuals, and children's picture books, mostly about the eight model Peking operas. Table 5.1 shows the types and numbers of books published in China from 1966 to 1970.

Mao's works flooded the nation. A village in Anhui had 20 households and 97 people, but these 20 households had 21 sets of Mao's Selected Works, 100 copies of Mao Quotations, and 1,003 Mao portraits.[31] When Nixon visited China in 1972, Zhou Enlai wanted to present him with a set of the complete works of Lu Xun. Yet the set that was published in the late 1950s had been banned and was considered inappropriate as a gift. Zhou ended up giving Nixon a set from the Lu Xun Museum that was published in 1938.[32]

The Cultural Revolution thus changed the supply-demand conditions of the book market. Books with strong ideological contents, as shown in table 5.1, flooded the market. Works of foreign and classical Chinese literature were scarce, because most of them were banned. And many libraries

TABLE 5.1 TYPES OF BOOKS PUBLISHED IN CHINA, 1966–1970

TITLE	QUANTITIES
Selected Works of Mao Zedong (in Mandarin, 5 minority, and 36 foreign languages)	4.2 billion copies
Works of Marx, Engels, Lenin, and Stalin	8.9 million copies
Elementary and middle school textbooks	248 titles, 1.7 billion copies
Political pamphlets	584 titles, 2.6 billion copies
Arts and literature	137 titles, 422 million copies
Culture and education	5 titles, 6.7 million copies
Science and technology	1,739 titles, 243 million copies
Readers for children and youth	287 titles, 165 million copies

SOURCE: COMPILED FROM *DANG DAI ZHONGGUO DE CHU BAN SHI YE*, 1:76–78.

were closed. It was under these conditions that youth resorted to transgressive acts to obtain books to read. Two main forms were stealing and borrowing.[33]

STEALING BOOKS

One way of obtaining books among the young people was stealing. A favorite place to steal books from was libraries, many of which were closed down, but there were other unexpected locations as well. According to one memoir,[34] three friends in Shaanxi once saw a carriage of books being taken to paper mills for pulping. They wanted to buy a few, but the driver turned them away. They followed the carriage to the paper mill and went back at night to steal the books. In another case, two sent-down youth on a state farm learned that there were some books locked away at the headquarters of their regiment. They traveled many miles there and stole several bags.[35]

Stealing books had its risks. People might steal a few at a time or at most a few bags. In one case in the early 1970s, four young men systematically stole over three thousand volumes of foreign literature, books for internal circulation (*nei bu fa xing*), and works of theory and philosophy. When they were arrested, the charge against them was not theft, but involvement in a nationwide counterrevolutionary clique of reading groups. They were imprisoned for four years.[36]

In another case, a young student out to steal books from his school library almost lost his life: "The books that were not destroyed in our school were kept in a room on the fourth floor. Everyone knew that since most books had been burned, the remainder wouldn't last either. Some students who loved books were unwilling to give up. They wanted to steal the books. Risking his life, one student . . . climbed out of the window of another room on the fourth floor, and stepping on the thin edge of the wall, inched toward the room where the books were kept. He fell from the fourth floor . . . but luckily didn't die."[37]

Eager readers sometimes got unexpected help from librarians. Once, during his vacation, a young man visited his sister back in the city, who introduced him to a librarian who gave him the key to a sealed library. Thus he spent his vacation reading in the library. There were a few favorite books that he really wanted to take away with him, but he decided not to steal them because it would be a betrayal of his sister's friend's trust. On the day when he was leaving town, the librarian came to see him off and offered him a copy of classical Chinese poetry, one of his favorites from the collection. Seeing him hesitate, she said, "Just take it. Many books were burned anyway. It is better to take it away than have it burned."[38]

This example shows a social dimension of book stealing that was common in these transgressive practices. The act of transgression was made possible by trust between friends and acquaintances. We will see this pattern repeated again and again in other transgressive acts.

BORROWING BOOKS

Another common way of obtaining books was borrowing from friends and acquaintances. Book-borrowing had a culture of its own. People were willing to make great efforts to borrow books. The following account by a young man sent to a village offers an example: "To borrow books, I had to cover long distances, from the near to the far. I would start with the near, walking for three or five kilometers, and borrow [from people] in the few nearby villages. . . . Then I reached out to the commune . . . walking for twenty or thirty kilometers. After that, with horizontal ties increasing among educated youth, I would borrow books from youth in other communes. In that case I had to walk very *long distances.*"[39]

Borrowers were usually bound by honor to return books promptly. Because books often passed through many hands, however, they did get lost often, but this did not mean it would cause friendship to break up. "I never heard of people breaking up with their friends because of not returning borrowed books," one person recalled, "Those who wanted to monopolize their own books would probably be viewed as sinful."[40]

In explaining why he decided not to return a favorite book to a friend, this person conveys vividly the passion for books that was common among these youth:

Many popular books passed through my hand at that time, including those yellow-cover and gray-cover books that were hard to come by. I never thought of keeping one for myself. I kept my innocence until I came across the Soviet writer [Konstantin Georgiyevich] Paustovsky. The first time I read the selected works of Paustovsky, I did it in a hurry as I was being rushed. I didn't know why I was touched so strongly [by his works]. . . . The deep and melancholy beauty that was unique to Russian culture flowed through my heart slowly. I felt as if my soul was melted and purified by it. For days after I returned the book, I experienced the pain of lost love. I asked all around to find the whereabouts of that book, but never heard of it again. One day about a year later, I accidentally saw the book in a pile of books at a friend's home. . . . Grabbing it, I said to my friend casually, "Let me take a look at this book." My friend took a glance and replied just as casually, "Sure." . . . From the moment when I got hold of the book again, I decided not to give it up anymore. . . . After a long time, the owner of the book casually asked me about the book. I replied just as casually that I had loaned it to somebody and didn't know where it was. . . . I did loan it to my friends many times . . . but each time I repeatedly warned them to return it in time, and they had kept their promise. Another year passed. Then one day . . . the book's owner came to visit me. I had already considered that book as my own . . . and did not think of hiding it away from the visitor. As we were chatting, my friend saw the book and ask casually: "Is that mine?" I was completely taken off guard and realized my carelessness with frustration and embarrassment. It could not be helped. I put on an air of casual indifference and said, "It was just returned to me. Take it back." That moment, I felt like a knife had been struck into my heart.[41]

Among such passionate book lovers, it is not surprising that books became an important medium of social exchange. On the one hand, sharing forbidden books became a means of social bonding. It relied on trust and it strengthened friendship, as we see from the foregoing story. Forbidden books gathered friends around them, which at least partly explained the rise of underground salons in cities and study groups in villages.[42] On the other hand, however, ownership of and knowledge about forbidden books became status symbols in underground cultural circles. Those with access to forbidden books gained an advantage over those without. They were more likely to learn new ideas. The first and most important group of poets to emerge out of the CR began to publish poetry with a strong Western modernist flavor after the Cultural Revolution because they were mostly from elite families in Beijing with access to internal publications.[43] Thus they had access to and read works like *Catcher in the Rye*, *On the Road*, and *The Stranger* in the early 1970s, while experimenting with new poetic techniques. In the same period, there was an underground group in Yunnan Province whose members were also writing poems. Yet their works lacked the modernist flavor because they had no access to masterpieces of Western modernism.

READING

Reading practices varied with location and context. Compared with urban life, overshadowed by a social control system built on neighborhood committees and work units, life in the villages was relatively free of outside interference. In some regions, peasants were not at all interested in Cultural Revolution politics or class struggle.[44] The relative freedom of rural life gave sent-down youth the space and time to pursue their own interests, such as reading forbidden books:

> "Reading forbidden books on a snowy night behind closed doors"—that was one of the ultimate pleasures of life for the ancients. For us educated youth, such pleasure was easy to come by. In the years of the Cultural Revolution, most books were banned. Fortunately, Northern Shaanxi was a place "far from where the emperor lived," and nobody interfered with what books you read. We could openly read Fan Wenlan's *An Abridged History of China*, Anna Louis Strong's *The Stalin Era*, Liu Qing's *A Pioneer Story*, Gunawardhana's *Khrushchevism*, and whatever other books we could find. We didn't have to worry about being criticized or having the books confiscated. Thus, although material life was extremely hard, our spiritual life turned out to be richer than in Beijing.[45]

Life on state farms known as "production and construction corps" was more regimented. With a paramilitary organization, and functioning like "work units," these state farms had much tighter control over the lives of youth. They also developed systems of organized cultural activities (such as singing contests) to provide organized entertainment as a safety valve to channel unregulated energies and sentiments. As a result, the pursuit of independent intellectual activities was more difficult. Yet resistance is a creative art; it produces its own artists under different circumstances. Some young people made use of the free time after a day's farmwork to read or write. Others read or wrote after their dorm mates went to bed. Their writings may not express direct political dissent, but may frame discontent and grievances in ironic or ambiguous terms. Thus poems and stories still circulated in intimate circles on state farms. Some of these activities were not without high costs. On a state farm in Yunnan Province, a young man accidentally overturned an oil lamp while reading a forbidden book at night. The lamp caused a big fire and killed ten people.[46]

NOTE-TAKING

Note-taking and reading groups were especially important aspects of the reading experience. People had a limited amount of time to read a borrowed book, because others might be lining up for it. They would give a quick read and then go over it to find things to copy into their notebooks.

Notebooks were a common gift item for many ordinary occasions during the Cultural Revolution, just as music CDs and books are common gift items today. They were common gifts for friends, classmates, and even lovers. If it was a gift to a friend, then words of friendship would be written on the cover page. These could be a quote from Mao, a favorite aphorism, or a self-composed poem.

Notebooks were used to take notes and write diaries. They contained collections of aphorisms, poems, songs, and book excerpts. Mainly for personal use, they were also shared among friends. Lin Mang, a member of the Baiyangdian Lakes poetry circle, recalls: "We all had a pile of notebooks for copying poems. I had about four or five of them. In them there were works by educated youth or works copied from books. Duo Duo had a notebook, which was passed around quite widely. Song Haiquan had a notebook, and he kept saying that I borrowed it and never returned it. I did borrow it from him, but I thought I returned it. Perhaps he loaned it to someone else again!"[47]

Writing about the circulation of forbidden books, Lin continues: "These books were circulated rapidly. Usually you had one or two days to finish it. Some people took notes. Others copied entire books. When he had time, Jiang

He also copied several books. These books were a great boost to the poetry-writing circles at Baiyangdian. They changed people's way of thinking."[48]

There were extreme cases of note-taking as well. On one of his overseas trips, the novelist Han Shaogong met a former sent-down youth who seemed to have become a note-taking machine. Han wrote, "Probably because he copied too many books when he was a sent-down youth, even today [late 1990s] whenever he got hold of a pen, he wanted to write something. He said that when he was a sent-down youth in Jiangxi Province, he used up close to one hundred notebooks just taking notes from books."[49]

These activities of copying and note-taking were primitive forms of media. One had to use one's hands and feet as means of communication. In these activities we see a form of writing that is truly about self-making. If one has to walk many miles to borrow a book, the meaning of the book clearly goes beyond its contents.

SINGING, STORYTELLING, AND RADIO LISTENING

Group activities were not limited to reading. People sang forbidden songs, listened to foreign and "hostile" radio programs, and told stories in group settings. The following story is about listening to foreign radio programs in Yunnan Province:

> In the 1970s we listened to foreign radio stations, called enemy radios at that time. I don't know how common it was among sent-down youth nationwide, but it was very common in Yunnan. Yunnan had a special geography. The radio programs of the Central People's Radio were hardly audible. Newspapers reached the mountain regions many days late. . . . So we listened to enemy radio programs, not just for political news but mainly for entertainment. I remember there was a Taiwanese radio drama series on an Australian radio station called "Small Town Story." Because short-wave radio signals drifted around, we would line up several radio sets together . . . so that there was always one radio with clear signals. In their straw huts, young men and women huddled around and cried and cried over the stories.[50]

Songs were carriers of relationships. Dozens of "songs of sent-down youth" were in circulation. Although banned, these songs spread far and wide. Like folklore, they seemed to have caught on a life of their own once they were born. Ren Yi, the author of the popular "A Song of Sent-down Youth," wrote the song in May 1969 after spending a night singing melancholy songs with his fellow sent-down youth friends. The village where he was sent down had a large farmers' market. On market days, sent-down youth from neighboring villages would gather in his village. They were among the first to learn to sing and spread the song. After summer harvest, Ren Yi spent two months at home in Nanjing. On the ship back to the village, he was surprised to hear several young women singing the song. Pretending not to know the song, he asked them what they were singing. "Are you a *zhiqing*?," one of the women asked. Upon hearing a "yes" for an answer, the woman laughed, "Then how can you not know the "Song of Sent-down Youth?"[51]

A woman who was sent to Beidahuang (Great Northern Wilderness), in Heilongjiang Province, recalls her singing experience: "In the barren wilderness, we loved Russian literary songs. They sang of humanity, love, nature, and more important, the fate of the exiles. . . . A helpless old horse, the driver of a horse-carriage at the edge of death on the vast grassland, the banished who persevered for the sake of their beliefs . . . these were the images that filled our hearts and our days and years."[52]

Mr. Wang recalls that on one of his home visits to Beijing, he read several hand-copied entertainment stories. Back in Beidahuang, where he had been sent down on a state farm, he told these stories to his friends. The winter nights in Beidahuang were long and drab and there was little to do after dark. Thus storytelling became an entertainment, and he soon acquired something of a reputation for his tall tales. Here is how he describes the storytelling atmosphere:

> Seeing how sad and distressed my friends always were, I really wanted to cheer them up and give them some fun. . . . I would sit in the middle of the room, ask someone to turn off the light and light a candle to create some atmosphere. At this point, the entire room would be so quiet that you could hear a needle drop on the floor. Everyone would open their eyes wide, hold their breath, and wait for me to start. I was not in a hurry. I would have a sip of tea, slowly take a cigarette, put it under my nose to smell it, lick it from one end to the other, and casually light it. I would spin out a mouthful of smoke ever so lightly and sweetly. By now, I would have cultivated my mood well and I was ready to start. Once I started, I would talk away for two hours on end. No one would feel tired.[53]

Because of the covert nature of such storytelling, it could be regarded as a form of ironic and ambiguous cultural dissent. Once discovered, it could bring trouble. The aforementioned individual was chastised for telling ghost stories and disrupting production and subject to the punishment of supervised labor for a period.[54]

READING GROUPS AND STUDY GROUPS

Reading groups and study groups were informal groups or occasions for friends to get together to talk, read, and sing. Evidence from interviews and memoirs suggests these groups existed wherever there were sent-down youth. In personal correspondence, one former sent-down youth compared them to "coral reefs scattered in the tropical ocean. . . . Some were small, some were bigger, with some overlapping connections among them."[55] In one case, three friends who had been sent to a small village in Inner Mongolia formed a group to study what they thought of as "practical and useful" knowledge. One of them took note of their discussions in his diary:

> Tonight, the three of us had an informal discussion in Qian's place. We mainly discussed the nature of our study group and the study methods. We decided to have our first meeting tomorrow. Yang Ke proposed that our main goal is to study the practical problems that we come across in our daily work. . . . Qian Bingqiang suggested that we should study everything: "I don't have a focus," he said, "I want to study everything, find the study methods and an analytic approach, and then go on to examine one specific issue. . . . " I agree with the latter mostly, though I have some different opinions of my own. It's true that we should study everything in the world in order to avoid limitations. However, at every stage there should be a focus. My temporary focus is philosophy. My life aim is literature.[56]

Another example was a poetry reading group in a village in Shanxi province. It happened that Guo Lusheng (pen named Shi Zhi, or Forefinger), one of the first and most powerful poetic voices of the Red Guard generation, had been sent down to the village in 1969. By then, he had already written his most famous poems, including one titled "This Is Beijing at 4:08," which captures the painful emotions of young people departing Beijing for the countryside.[57] One reminiscence well conveys the atmosphere of the poetry readings in the village:

> The readings usually took place after supper. Guo Lusheng would stand beside the kitchen range in his worn shirt and pants. He would stand with his back against the dark night outside the window. The small oil lamp on the top of the kitchen range would cast its dim light on his slim and tall figure. . . . Guo Lusheng often selected some of his old poems to read. Sometimes he also read his new poems. Our favorite was to listen to him read the poem "This Is Beijing at 4:08." We would ask him to read it to us again and again, because the poem presented a true picture of our life. It expressed our feelings.[58]

UNDERGROUND "SALONS"

Underground cultural activities existed in both rural and urban areas. Several such underground circles existed in Beijing and Shanghai, which have sometimes been called "salons" by scholars but were not necessarily called such in the Cultural Revolution. "The name 'salon' is an embellishment used by people today. There was no such a thing then," said Chen Suning. Both Chen and her husband Sun Hengzhi were of the Red Guard generation, and Sun was and is still known as the host of the famous Xiao Donglou underground salon in Shanghai. Said Sun Hengzhi, "It is just that a group of friends who shared common interests would get together to talk. Some wild talk." Chen added: "Mainly because at that time, during off-season, sent-down youth in various places would return to the cities. With nothing to do back in the cities, would they get stuck at home? They would naturally gather together to talk about books they had recently read, to share their personal thoughts, and to exchange news and information they had heard of."[59] Another sent-down youth, Ji Liqun, recalls similar gatherings during their holiday trips back to the cities: "Every year, around the lunar New Year, many of us returned to Beijing for a short period. During this period, we held social gatherings, and one salon after another was formed among sent-down youth. Through letters from distant places, ideas and thoughts were exchanged among sent-down youth. Through visiting and social gatherings, educated youth communicated their ideals and aspirations."[60]

"Salon" activities had already started among Red Guards in the latter stage of the Red Guard movement, when the movement was on the decline, school was open only half-heartedly, and there was time to kill. The better-known ones include the Baiyangdian poetry circles in rural Hebei Province, the poetry circles in Inner Mongolia, groups of sent-down youth sent from Nanjing to rural Jiangsu,[61] from Shanghai to Henan, from Xiamen to rural regions of Fujian Province, from Chengdu to the villages of Sichuan, and from Beijing to Jilin. Many others existed on an occasional basis. While most activities took place in the sent-down regions, they were not confined there. A few underground circles were active in Beijing, Shanghai, and Guizhou.[62] Table 5.2 shows a list of such groups and their main participants.

As Table 5.2 shows, the participants were most likely from the same city and even the same school. Some had been friends or been involved in salon activities before being sent down. One group had been friends in the Red Guard movement. In the village, they edited and published an underground magazine with skills learned in school as Red Guards. As one of them recalls, "First we talked about it among a few friends. Then we wrote to friends in

TABLE 5.2 SELECTED UNDERGROUND CULTURAL GROUPS IN THE SENT-DOWN PERIOD

LOCATION OF GROUP	KEY MEMBERS	ACTIVITIES	FORMER TIES
Yong'an and Sanming, Fujian Province	Shu Ting	Ran mimeographed magazine and published Shu Ting's poems	Natives from Xiamen city
Inner Mongolia	Wang Weiben, Li Sanyou, Li Datong	Wrote prose about grassland	Students in Beijing
Inner Mongolia	Yin Zhanhua, Li Xiangzhen, Zhao Bingzhi, Ye Xiaojing	Wrote, exchanged, and discussed poetry	Students in Beijing
Inner Mongolia	Xing Qi, Shi Xiaoming, Liu Yuping, Chen Dashi, Dong Yufang	Wrote poetry	Students in Beijing
Inner Mongolia	Yang Ke, Qian Bingqiang, and Mu Zhai	Reading, studying, discussion	Former friends
Shaanxi	Ji Liqun	Published underground magazine	Former friends and classmates in Beijing
Shanxi Province	Zheng Guangzhao, Gan Tiesheng	Reading, writing	Students in Beijing
Shanxi Province	Guo Lusheng, Ge Xiaoli	Poetry reading	Mostly students from Beijing
Anshun, Guizhou Province	Qian Liqun, Lan Zi	Reading, writing	Locals and students from Beijing
Guiyang, Guizhou Province	Leng Wei, Li Shuangbi, Han Jun	Reading, studying, discussion	Students in Guiyang
Yinchuan, Ningxia	Lu Zhili, Wu Shusen, Wu Shuzhang, Xu Zhaoping, Chen Tongming, Zhang Weizhi, Zhang Shaochen; this	Reading and writing. Ran mimeographed magazine	Students from Yinchuan, Ningxia

	group was declared a counterrevolutionary organization; the first three were executed; others were sentenced to many years in prison		
Zhumadian, Henan Province	Chen Yizi, Deng Yingtao, Wu Yan	Reading, writing, rural investigation	College and middle school students in Beijing
Tuquan, Jilin Province	Ren Gongwei, etc.	Ran mimeographed magazine	Magazine mainly distributed to former Red Guards in the same faction
Baiyangdian Lakes, Hebei Province	Rong Xuelan, Pan Qingping, Kong Lingyao (Girls' Middle School Attached to Beijing Teachers' University); Zhao Zhe and Zhou Chui (Middle School Attached to Peking University); Yue Zhong, Duo Duo, Lin Mang (No. 3 Middle School in Beijing); Mang Ke, Sun Kang, Song Haiquan, Bei Dao, Tao Luosong, Xia Liuyan	Wrote poetry, fiction, prose; reading, discussing, exchanging, and circulating manuscripts	Some from the same school; others had known one another in salon activities before being sent down
Sichuan Province	Chen Ziqiang, Du Jiusen, Deng Ken, Xu Pei	Wrote poetry and maintained correspondence	Students in Chengdu, Sichuan Province

SOURCES: YANG, *ZHONGGUO ZHI QING WEN XUE SHI*; JI, "CHA DUI SHENG YA"; LIAO, *CHEN LUN DE SHENG DIAN*; MU ZHAI, *HUANG RUO GE SHI—WO DE ZHIQ ING SUI YUE*; YIN, *SHI ZONG ZHE DE ZU JI*; LENG, "LENG WEI KOU SHU (III)."

other places to ask them to contribute. After receiving their contributions, we selected some articles and poems and mimeographed them into a magazine. Then we sent the magazines to other places—educated youth in the neighboring counties, in Beidahuang, in Northern Shaanxi and Inner Mongolia, etc."[63]

The best known of all were the previously mentioned poetry circles in the Baiyangdian Lakes region. These circles consisted of former schoolmates or fellow salon participants from Beijing, mostly sent down in early 1969. They included the major contributors to the future literary journal *Today* (*Jin tian*) in the Democracy Wall movement: Bei Dao, Mang Ke, Lin Mang, Duo Duo, and Jiang He. Their activities encompassed the whole range of underground activities found among sent-down youth in that period, from borrowing, copying, and circulating banned books and handwritten manuscripts to reading, writing, and discussing them. Lin Mang recalls that he often met with Duo Duo, Song Haiquan, and Gan Tiesheng in their lakeside village to talk about life experiences and poetry writing: "These kinds of conversations were frequent. Whenever we got together, these were the things we talked about. We also exchanged forbidden books."[64] According to Duo Duo's recollections, he wrote many poems in his six-year stay in the Baiyangdian Lakes region. Each year after 1972, he produced one notebook full of poems for exchange with Mang Ke. These poems went into underground circulation in the literary salons in Beijing.[65]

Strategically located in rural Hebei Province near Beijing, the young people in the Baiyangdian Lakes circles were both linked to sent-down youth in other parts of the country and to groups in Beijing (such as Zhao Yifan's salon). They functioned like communication hubs between China's rural areas and its political and cultural center. On the one hand, these circles of cultural activists—poets, essayists, and novelists—were large enough to provide audience and critics for the authors. On the other, the communication channels helped to circulate their works to a wider audience.

ARTICULATING A NEW SENSE OF SELF AND SOCIETY

What did the underground cultural movement accomplish? Certainly, in the aftermath of the Red Guard movement, the reading, copying, writing, and circulation of songs, stories, poems, books, and letters in small groups provided social support, intellectual stimulation, and psychological comfort for a generation in the doldrums. Equally important, these activities were forms of self-exploration following a movement that made the self the target of attack.

It is not hard to see why foreign works and hand-copied entertainment fiction appealed to sent-down youth. The interest in works by authors like Solzhenitsyn and Trotsky revealed a sustained engagement with problems concerning the past and future of the communist movement. The popularity of works by Beckett, Camus, Kerouac, Osborne, Salinger, and Sartre reflected the concerns of the modern individual—the antihero.

To varying degrees, sent-down youth experienced disillusionment and disenchantment. They were themselves antiheroes. That was why characters like Holden Caulfield (who was, incidentally, sixteen—roughly the same age level as sent-down youth in their first year of rustication) struck a chord in their hearts. The same concern with the conditions of the modern individual also explains the popularity of entertainment fiction. On the one hand, a sense of loss, disenchantment, banality, on the other, a passion for adventure, mystery, and romance. In the drabness of rural life, hand-copied entertainment fiction presented a world of adventure.

Poems written at the end of the Red Guard movement and at the beginning of the sent-down campaign expressed the pains of departure and separation, homesickness in the countryside, and the loss of friendship. They expressed a sense of self-doubt and a crisis of belief. Sent-down youth expressed painful disillusionment with their revolutionary ideals and the new realities of life. The moral frameworks that had supported their self-identity were on the verge of collapse. New values were in the throes of birth, but still inchoate. It was a time of death and rebirth, made tragically powerful by profound inner anxieties and contradictions. The poet Huang Xiang compared himself to a beast: "I am a wild beast hunted down / I am a captured wild beast."[66] Guo Lusheng described himself as a mad dog: "I no longer see myself as a human being, / It was as if I had turned into a mad dog."[67] In another famous poem, Guo expressed hope for the future, but in a sad and somber tone:

When spider webs relentlessly sealed my stove,
When wisps of smoke from the ashes sighed pitifully over poverty,
I stubbornly unfolded the ashes of disappointment,
And wrote in the beauty of snowflakes: Believe in the Future![68]

In a letter to a friend dated February 18, 1972, Zhao Zhenkai, who would become known as Bei Dao, expressed the loss of belief that the future poet in him would translate into powerful poetic images. He told the friend not to belive in "noble ideals," but to scrutinize the "base rock" upon which the ideals were built, to study the attributes of the "rock" and test its solidity. Without such scrutiny, he argued, "then you will not have that supporting point that is necessary for every aspiring person—a spirit of doubt." He wrote that he was not all against having beliefs: "I think that some day perhaps I will have a belief too, but before I stand on it, I will study it thoroughly, just as an archaeologiest would study a rock: knocking it here and there."[69]

There were cynical expressions too. An anonymous poem described how a young man who had returned to the city from the countryside rejected his political ideals and adopted what was then considered a "bourgeois" outlook. The young man in the poem said that for him life still had its "heroic style," except that it was a different kind of grandeur. The earlier heroic style derived from a sense of revolutionary mission and, with it, asceticism and self-sacrifice. Today's "heroic style" was about self-appreciation:

> This hair of mine
> Is carefully done by the best barber on Xidan Avenue.[70]
> This cashmere scarf
> Gives me a handsome look.[71]

And he declared that he no longer wanted a revolution, but "a worker's wage, a peasant's freedom, / A student's life, a petty bourgeoisie's ideas."[72]

This was a straightforward rejection of the heroic style of revolution, the moral framework that had defined the self-identity of the generation up to the Red Guard movement. This rejection signaled the weakening of the generation's identification with the party-state, its charismatic leaders, and its hallowed revolutionary tradition. A historically significant shift, it marked the starting point of a crisis of political confidence that would soon find its open expression in the Democracy Wall movement.[73]

Finally, with the old moral frameworks losing ground, new understandings of self and society surfaced. One central aspect of this new understanding was the affirmation of personal interests and the values of ordinary life that I discussed in the previous chapter. The growing concern with personal interests by no means implies that the generation had been unconcerned with personal interests before. Nevertheless, within the moral frameworks into which the generation had been socialized, the pursuits of self-interest had been condemned as morally wrong and politically reactionary. The core values had been collective goals and revolutionary causes.[74]

Affirmation for the values of ordinary life was evident in the diaries, letters, and poems produced by sent-down youth. Some poems contain vivid descriptions of the hardships of rural life as well as expressions of optimism, humor, love, joy, and friendship. A poem titled "Cold" describes the author's humorous attitude toward winter life in Inner Mongolia:

It was daylight. I huddled up under the sheets.
I counted numbers to force myself to get up,
And clenched my teeth.
"Shit!"—I cursed, the boots were freezing cold.
No hurry to clean the room. Start the fire first
And warm up—cow dung was the treasure of all treasures.

An anonymous poem titled "On the Road with the Ruts of a Tractor" combines the images of labor with love:

A bright red scarf
Flutters on the road with the ruts of a tractor . . .
My girl
Is coming closer and closer.[75]

Drawing on their newly gained knowledge, some of the sent-down youth analyzed China's official economic policies and political system. There were debates about how to reform agriculture as well as calls for democracy and the rule of law. In these exchanges, important ideas that were to dominate the reform era had already emerged. The now well-known essay "On Socialist Democracy and the Legal System," produced by the Li Yizhe group, for example, called for the protection of people's democratic rights.[76] There were even discussions about whether some form of market economy might not be a feasible approach to tackling China's agricultural problems.[77] These discussions foreshadowed the agricultural policy debates in the early years of the reform.[78]

In time, the underground writers, poets, and other "cultural activists" would emerge aboveground throughout the 1980s to redefine China's cultural landscape, introducing a new cultural politics that stretched all the way to the pro-democracy movement in 1989.[79]

6

NEW ENLIGHTENMENT

BEGINNING IN THE SPRING of 1976, a new wave of popular protest started in China. There had been many other protest activities in between, notably in 1974,[1] but 1976 marked the dawn of a new era. The generation that had thrown itself into the Red Guard movement had gone through another, more prolonged ordeal—the sent-down movement. By 1976, as the previous two chapters show, members of the Red Guard generation had had time to brood and meditate as well as to "temper" themselves in the "furnace" of another kind of revolution—rural development.[2] The self-proclaimed saviors of the Chinese and world communist revolution had learned to appreciate the values of an ordinary life in their new circumstances. Abandoning their revolutionary dreams in pursuit of a more livable material life, many had returned to their native cities through legitimate or illegitimate channels. It was an unhappy, restive, and lost generation. Lost were the political ideals of the Red Guard period, opportunities for education, career, and family, and, indeed, the best years of their lives. Yet, despite all the adversities, all hope was not lost. The wave of protest from 1976 to 1980 would not have happened without a persistent sense of hope for the future.

The April Fifth movement in 1976 was the first salvo of this new political wave, followed by the Democracy Wall movement and the sent-down youth protests in 1978–1979, and finally the agitation during the democratic election campaigns in major universities in 1980. This chapter studies this wave of political activism as a crucial turning point in the trajectory of the Red Guard generation and modern Chinese history. This new wave was both a radical reversal of the Red Guard movement and a precursor to the student protests in 1989. Indeed, were it not for the party-state's suppression of memories of the Democracy Wall movement, this movement and the protests in 1989 would have made up one uninterrupted cycle of post–Cultural Revolution protests.[3]

This chapter will show that the Red Guard generation is the vital linkage between these two historical eras. I will argue that among the three waves of protest from 1966–1968, 1976–1980, and 1989, there were both fundamental differences and striking similarities. The most important difference was between the goals and demands of the Red Guard movement and those of the 1976–1980 wave, a reversal as dramatic as one can imagine. This reversal was the unintended consequence of the Red Guard movement and the sent-down experiences.

I will also argue, however, that there are three important continuities among these three political waves. First, members of the Red Guard generation were involved in all three waves, though to varying degrees. Second, the repertoires of collective contention in the Cultural Revolution were , in part, inherited in the later waves of protest and net of violence. Third, a political romanticism, driven by visions of a strong Chinese nation, was discernible in all three waves.

I will start with an overview of the four sequences of political activism from 1976 and 1980 and then compare their similarities and differences.

THE APRIL FIFTH MOVEMENT, 1976

Political and natural earthquakes shook China in 1976. The first fatal hit was Zhou Enlai's death on January 8, 1976. Then Zhu De died on July 6. And on July 28, a catastrophic earthquake hit the city of Tangshan and killed a quarter-million of its population. Several weeks later, on September 9, Mao died. Mao had already installed Hua Guofeng as the premier back in February. Soon after Mao's death, joining forces with Ye Jianying and Li Xiannian, Hua crushed the radical leftist elements within the party, the so-called Gang of Four. Hua officially became the chairman of the Central Committee of the Chinese Communist Party and of the Central Military Commission on October 7, 1976.[4]

Amidst these epochal changes, the ephemeral April Fifth movement was almost negligible, but in fact it was a crucial transitional point. It was the most powerful explosion of popular protest since the end of the Red Guard movement. Two and a half years later, activists in the Democracy Wall movement would claim that "they were following and carrying on the spirit of the April Fifth Movement,"[5] as would the activists in the campus election period in 1980.

The April Fifth movement was ostensibly a response to the death of Zhou Enlai, but in effect a barely disguised protest against the ultraleftist regime and the policies of the Cultural Revolution.[6] As is often the case in Chinese history, the death of a national leader became an opportunity for mounting protest. April 4, 1976, would be the first Qingming Day after Zhou Enlai's death. Scattered memorial activities had appeared in late March in Beijing and Nanjing. Nanjing, the provincial capital of Zhou's native town, took the lead when four hundred students and teachers marched on March 24 to lay wreaths at Yuhuatai commemorating Zhou.[7] The largest public protest event was a demonstration on March 28 by students from Nanjing University and led by Li Xining, secretary of the Youth League in the Department of Mathematics.[8]

A former sent-down youth, Li Xining spoke publicly about how his experience in the countryside influenced his participation in the movement:

> At the beginning of the Cultural Revolution, we were quite young, about 14 or 15. We didn't really understand what this revolution was all about, and we didn't know what we were doing when we followed others in the fighting. I had no idea then what revolution was all about. After I went to the country to live, close to the people, I realized that this society was not as good as we had imagined it to be. Especially in the country, life was bitter. After working hard all day, we were able to earn only 20-odd cents a day, not even enough to feed ourselves. Then, although we could see all this, we didn't know what the cause was, why it was that after so long our socialist country couldn't even feed itself.[9]

The April Fifth movement in Beijing happened several days later. Indeed, the events in Nanjing acted as a catalyst to mobilize citizens in Beijing. One of the earliest slogans in Tiananmen Square expressed support for the people in Nanjing.[10] In Beijing, every day in the first few days of April, small groups of people went to Tiananmen Square to present wreaths at the Monument of People's Heroes. People in the crowd would pin scraps of paper onto the wreaths, usually with poems, sometimes with essays. In classical Chinese verse forms, most were elegiac poems in memory of Zhou, but many contained clever political puns, satires and barely concealed attacks on Jiang Qing and even Mao himself. One of the most famous poems to come out of the movement condemns those who secretly rejoice at Zhou's death and expresses the desire to fight to defend Zhou's honor.[11] As in many other public protest activities since the Cultural Revolution, there were public speeches and the chanting of slogans. Chen Ziming, one of the best known activists of the April Fifth movement, got tangled in it quite accidently because he was asked to read aloud a poster to crowds in Tiananmen Square. Born in 1952, Chen was sent down to Inner Mongolia in 1968 at a young age. In 1974 he was admitted into the Beijing University of Chemical Technology as a worker-peasant-soldier student. In August 1975 he was arrested because he had criticized party policies in his personal correspondence with other sent-down youth. Right before the April Fifth movement, he was officially charged with being a counterrevolutionary and expelled from college. He was given three days to go home to pack and then he would be sent to a labor camp on April 7. Thus he hit upon the April Fifth during his short home visit. Considering his situation, Chen did not want to get involved, but he could not help going to Tiananmen Square to read the posters. It was while he was reading the posters that he was sucked into the protest activities. On the eve of April 4 he found himself reading a poster that directly attacked Jiang Qing. There were large crowds around him, and because he was the closest to the poster, he was asked to read it aloud. What happened then was something that the Occupy Wall Street protesters did as well—the creation of a human microphone. Chen recalled the scene in his 2009 memoir: "When I read a sentence, the dozen people around me would repeat after me. This created a human microphone. This peculiar microphone system worked for a long time. Later on, I read from the newspaper that the person who took it over from me to continue the reading was arrested by plainclothesmen when he was leaving Tiananmen Square."[12]

April Fifth was a nationwide movement. Sebastian Heilmann estimates that commemorative activities took place in at least forty-one places across the country. In Beijing the commemorative activities reached their climax on April 4 with demonstrations and large gatherings in Tiananmen Square. On April 5 the regime sent in "worker militia" to crush the movement, calling it a "counterrevolutionary" incident. Arrests were made, followed by months of witch-hunting. Accused of being the backstage supporter of the protest, Deng Xiaoping was removed from his position as vice premier. Not surprisingly, after Mao died and Deng Xiaoping came back to power in 1977, the verdict on the April Fifth movement was quickly reversed in an editorial in the *People's Daily* published in November 1978. The verdict's reversal had a direct impact on the Democracy Wall movement.

THE DEMOCRACY WALL MOVEMENT

When Democracy Wall activists claimed they were acting on the spirit of the April Fifth, they had a good reason. On November 15, 1978, an editorial in *People's Daily* announced the decision of the Beijing municipal government to reverse the verdict on the April Fifth movement. It was declared an entirely revolutionary event, not a counterrevolutionary incident.[13] The reversal of the verdict led to the rehabilitation of hundreds of April Fifth activists who had been imprisoned or persecuted and provided an opportunity to voice new protests.

In the unofficial periodicals (or *min ban kan wu*) of the ensuing Democracy Wall movement,[14] many essays appeared about the April Fifth movement and activists, linking the new protest activities back to the just rehabilitated April Fifth. In fact, one of the first unofficial publications to appear in Beijing was called the *April Fifth Forum*.

The Democracy Wall movement literally started in front of a wall.[15] Seven or eight feet high and about a hundred yards long, it sat humbly at the intersection of Xidan Road and Changan Avenue. Several blocks to the east are Zhongnanhai, the government compound, and Tiananmen Square. It was as if by gathering and speaking out at this dilapidated section of a wall, people wanted to squeeze open the awesome gates of power that were literally close by—the compound that sheltered China's national leaders.

From November 1978 to December 1979, when the Beijing municipal government shut it down, the wall served as an informal center for public information and gatherings. People put up posters or went there to read or copy posters. Many of the "people's publications" were sold there. There were public speeches and discussions. Some discussions led to the founding of organizations.

In Beijing, posters had appeared on the wall before the reversal of the verdict on the April Fifth movement. Most of them were personal complaints and petition letters. Posters increased significantly after the reversal of the verdict and reached a climax on November 25 with American journalist Robert Novak's visit to the wall. Novak told the crowd there that he was going to see Deng Xiaoping the next day and would be happy to deliver questions to Deng and report back any responses that Deng might have. Novak did not show up the next day, but he did send a representative to tell the crowd that Deng Xiaoping thought putting up posters was a good thing.[16]

In this atmosphere, the first contingent of unofficial periodicals appeared in Beijing. Unveiled with a poster on Tiananmen Square on November 24, the Enlightenment Society of Guiyang laid claim to the first unofficial journal of the movement. The core members of Enlightenment were four workers from Guiyang city in Guizhou Province—Huang Xiang, Li Jiahua, Fang Jiahua, and Mo Jiangang. They had put up a poster of a long poem in Beijing's busy commercial center Wangfujing on October 11, 1978. They then went back to Guiyang, only to return to Beijing again on November 24, when they headed straight to Tiananmen Square to announce the inauguration of Enlightenment Society.[17]

Edited by Liu Qing, a small paper called *April Fifth News* (*si wu bao*) first appeared on November 26, 1978. It then merged with another small paper edited by Xu Wenli to form *April Fifth Forum* (*si wu lun tan*). In the next few months, such periodicals blossomed in Beijing and other cities. *Today* (*jin tian*) and *Mass Reference News* (*qun zhong can kao xiao xi*) were launched on December 23, 1978. *Beijing Spring* (*Beijing zhi chun*) and *Exploration* (*tan suo*) first appeared on January 8, 1979.[18] Nationwide, at least 182 people's journals appeared in 27 cities, with 45 on university campuses, making up a total of 227.[19] Besides Beijing, the largest number of unofficial periodicals appeared in Guangzhou, Shanghai, Tianjin, Hangzhou, Wuhan, Changsha, and Guiyang. The editorial boards of these journals usually also functioned as bases for organizing group activities such as meetings and public speeches. Some editorial boards were synonymous with their organizations. The Enlightenment Society in Guiyang, for example, published a journal called *Enlightenment* (*qi meng*); the China Human Rights League published *China Human Rights* (*zhong guo ren quan*).

While most of the publications were inaugurated in the first few months of 1979, new journals and organizations continued to appear even after the initial wave of repression in March 1979, often as a protest against the repression and in order to keep the movement alive. Thus in the first half of 1980, *Without a Name* (*wu ming*) appeared in Kaifeng, Henan, *New Era* (*xin shi dai*) in Anyang, Henan, and *Folks' Voice* (*shu sheng*) in Shaoguan, Guangdong. In late 1980 *Zhi River* (*Zhi jiang*) appeared in Hangzhou, *Flying Saucer* (*fei die*) in Ningbo, *Times* (*shi dai*) in Beijing, and *Responsibility* (*ze ren*) in Guangzhou. On September 15, 1980, an All China Unofficial Journals Association was established, with its organizer, He Qiu, still in jail. A Regional East China Unofficial Journals Association was formed in late 1980, launching the *East China Unofficial Journal* (*hua dong min kan*) on January 15, 1981. The first and only issue advocated the abolition of one-party rule. Another regional organization was the Beijing Unofficial Journals Association headed by He Depu, editor of *Beijing Youth* (*Beijing qing nian*).

Two central themes emerged from the wall posters and unofficial publications of this movement. One was the critique of the Cultural Revolution. The other was a call for democratic political reforms. The critique of the past was imbued with a sense of misplaced confidence in the party leadership, particularly Mao, while calls for democratic reforms were uttered with a sense of mission to modernize the nation and an optimistic attitude toward the future. The inaugural statement of *Enlightenment* announces, for example, "We want to sing a song for the future. We want to light the torch of enlightenment with our own lives." The fifth issue of *Explorations*, published on China's National Day in 1979, carries a cover poem that opens with an apostrophe to the nation:

Republic
Today
The day of your adulthood
Young explorers
Present
Our bleeding hearts
As
A birthday gift.[20]

Explorations is the same magazine that carried Wei Jingsheng's essay, "The Fifth Modernization." That the call for democracy and a devotion to the nation should go hand in hand is a historically important fact that I will come back to later. Suffice it to note here that the moral identification with the nation was the direct heir of Red Guards' devotion to the party-state articulated at the beginning of the Red Guard movement.

The state's repression of the Democracy Wall activists was quick and decisive. Wei Jingsheng was arrested on March 29, 1979, and sentenced to fifteen years of imprisonment on October 16. In September 1980 the article that protected individuals' rights to use wall posters was removed from the Chinese Constitution. Meanwhile, other core Democracy Wall activists were arrested. Lin Muchen, editor of *The Petrel*, was arrested in 1981 and imprisoned for four years. He Qiu, who was involved in publishing *People's Road* and *Responsibilities*, was arrested in 1981 and sentenced to ten years' imprisonment in 1982. Wang Xizhe was arrested in April 1981 and sentenced to fourteen years in prison in May 1982. All the members of the Enlightenment Society were also arrested.[21]

PROTESTS BY SENT-DOWN YOUTH

Although there were scattered protest activities among sent-down youth between 1968 and 1976, large-scale and relatively sustained sent-down youth
protests did not occur until 1978. The main demands in all these protests
were to be allowed to return to the cities and to be assigned city jobs. In
the lingering language of the Cultural Revolution, these might well be labeled as blatant economic, materialistic, bourgeois, and selfish demands. Yet
sent-down youth unabashedly voiced these demands. These protests thus ✓
signaled a rejection of the generation's earlier revolutionary ideals.

In April 1978, large numbers of married sent-down youth in Fushun city
of Liaoning Province petitioned for job assignments. Several months later,
on July 2, 1978, nearly a thousand married sent-down youth in Lüda city of
Liaoning Province petitioned the municipal government, again for job assignments. These were the prelude to the large-scale protests to follow at
the end of the year. But the rise of nationwide protests among sent-down
youth occurred with the opening of new political opportunities in late 1978.
The publication in August 1978 of a short story titled "Scars" provoked a national debate about the psychological "scars" left by the Cultural Revolution,
opening the door for public critiques of Cultural Revolution policies. From
October 31 to December 10, 1978, a national conference was held in Beijing
to reexamine the sent-down policy. Although the conference reaffirmed the
policy's "correct orientation," it also provided a realistic assessment of its
problems and made concrete recommendations to tackle the problems and
adjust the policy. On December 16 the Chinese and American governments
announced the establishment of formal diplomatic relations, to be effective
January 1, 1979. And from December 18 to 22, the CCP convened the Third
Plenum of its Eleventh Congress, announcing a historic shift from an ideology of class struggle to a policy of economic development, thus officially
opening the post-Mao economic reform era. The second half of 1978 was
thus a period of unprecedented policy shifts toward a more open China. For
the disgruntled sent-down youth and the Democracy Wall activists, this political context signaled new political opportunities for voicing protest, and
protest they did.[22]

In late October, while the national conference on sent-down youth was
in session, youth on the paramilitary production and construction farms in
Yunnan Province expressed their demand to return home in an open letter
to Deng Xiaoping.[23] The letter carried nearly a thousand signatures. With no

response forthcoming, a second open letter was issued in November with over ten thousand signatures. Still receiving no response, they composed a third letter, collected about forty thousand signatures, and announced a strike of indefinite duration. On December 16, forty representatives of the Yunnan sent-down youth set off for Beijing to petition their case, much as the Red Guards had done a decade earlier. Their first stop was the provincial capital Kunming, where they put up posters and made speeches in the streets to mobilize support and raise funds. Yet, after they boarded the Beijing-bound train, the train was canceled, and they were stopped from continuing their petition trip. Meanwhile, however, another petition delegation representing the same groups of Yunnan sent-down youth had made their way secretly to Beijing, where the first thing they did was to unveil a huge slogan in Tiananmen Square: "We want to go home!" On January 4, 1979, they were received by vice premier Wang Zhen, who expressed his sympathy and the government's willingness to resolve the crisis. Meanwhile, protest activities also took place in other areas of Yunnan. For example, two hundred sent-down youth called a hunger strike on January 6, 1979, and central government envoys were dispatched to deal with the situation. In late January, at a provincial conference on sent-down youth, the Yunnan provincial party secretary announced the decision to allow the youth to return to their cities.

The successful protests in Yunnan sent encouraging signals to sent-down youth across China. Throughout 1979, protests by sent-down youth took place in other cities including Hangzhou, Xi'an, Chongqing, Nanjing, Tianjin, Nanchang, Harbin, Urumqi, and Akesu in Xinjiang. While the basic demand in all these protests was to return to their native cities, in Shanghai protesters tied it to the issue of human rights. More than in other cities, the petitions of sent-down youth in Shanghai were intertwined with the Democracy Wall movement.

By 1979 the sent-down campaign that started in the middle of the Cultural Revolution had sent about one million middle school graduates in Shanghai to villages or state farms. Public petitions to return to Shanghai began to appear in November 1978. The first major rally took place on December 10. Demonstrators chanted slogans such as "We want work!," "We want food!," and "We demand human rights!"[24] The most radical action was an attempt to block the Shanghai Railway Station on February 5, much as Shanghai's rebel Red Guards did at the Anting Incident at the beginning of the Cultural Revolution. Another demonstration took place on March 15, 1979, organized by a group called Association of Sent-down Youth in Especially Dire Circumstances (te kun zhi qing hui). This was "their last major exercise," in Tom

election campaigns on university campuses around the country. This form of political activism aimed at producing change from within the political establishment rather than through extra-institutional channels of protest. In 1979 the revolutionary committees that had been set up in the Cultural Revolution as the new structures of state power were abolished and replaced by people's congresses. With the establishment of people's congresses, procedures were instituted to elect representatives to the township- and county-level people's congresses in the fall and winter of 1980. Such elections had taken place before the Cultural Revolution, but at that time voters could only vote on officially approved candidates. This was the first time in thirteen years that the government had allowed direct elections.[29] Popular passions about their democratic implications were strong. At that time, leading members of Democracy Wall journals or organizations had been arrested. Some had been sentenced to long prison terms. In September 1980 the article that protected individuals' rights to use wall posters was removed from China's Constitution. Under these circumstances, public protest became an increasingly dangerous form of political activism. While some persisted in protest, others saw the elections as a new opportunity to participate in politics through institutionalized channels. Thus Democracy Wall veterans took a special interest in the elections. In Peking University, three of the seventeen candidates had been editors of unofficial journals, namely Hu Ping of *Fertile Land*, Fang Zhiyuan of *People's Voice*, and Wang Juntao of *Beijing Spring*.[30] The debates among these candidates focused on the nature of socialist democracy,[31] the same theme in the Democracy Wall movement a year earlier.

Besides Peking University, there were about a dozen known cases of Democracy Wall activists participating in elections.[32] In other universities around the country, students showed similar enthusiasm toward the elections. If we broaden our lens beyond the Democracy Wall to include the April Fifth movement and the sent-down youth, then we would expect that many of the students involved in the 1980 campus elections were likely to have had experiences in the Red Guard movement and the rustication movement. This is because the majority of the college student population at that time had been enrolled in 1977 and 1978. Of the total number of 680,000 college students enrolled in 1977 and 1978, 350,000, or over 51 percent, were sent-down youth.[33]

While public debates on issues related to political reform were common during the election period, not all these debates evolved into protest activities. The elections in Fudan University, for example, were peaceful. Students at Guizhou University published collections of poems celebrating individual-

ism and democratic ideals, but no unrest was reported there. The most influential protest activities happened in Hunan Teachers' College in the city of
Changsha. The two leading candidates, Tao Sen and Liang Heng, were former
Red Guards. During their election campaigns, they organized forums and put
up posters, much as Red Guards had done earlier. Liang announced that he
no longer believed in Marxism-Leninism,[34] but rather favored democratic
socialism.[35] Tao advocated legal reform, the separation of the party from
the government, and "all rights to the people."[36] The vice president of the
college denounced these campaign activites as illegal. To protest official interference, Tao and Liang organized a hunger strike, launching what turned
out to be the strongest protest nation-wide during the campus election period. In a move that connected the protest activities of the election period
directly to the Democracy Wall movement and the Red Guard movement,
Tao Sen and a few others traveled to Guangzhou, in the fashion of the Great
Linkup popular during the Red Guard movement, to seek counsel with Wang
Xizhe and other Democracy Wall veterans.

No sooner had some of the most contentious elections taken place than
the party launched another crackdown on the democracy activists. In a
speech at a party conference on December 25, 1980, Deng Xiaoping accused
the activists of being "counterrevolutionaries," whereas they had been labeled as "disruptive elements" in 1979.[37] Document No. 9 of the Chinese
Communist Party, issued in early 1981, instructed that there be a crackdown
on democracy wall activists by firing any work unit members and expelling
party and youth members associated with the activities. Over the next few
months about fifty leaders of the movement were arrested.[38] The new wave
of protest had come to an end.

BIOGRAPHICAL CONTINUITIES AND DISRUPTIONS

The significance of this wave of protest can only be fully grasped by situ-
ating it between two world-historical events—the Red Guard movement in
1966–68 and the student movement in 1989. Coming just ten years after the
launching of the Cultural Revolution, the new wave of protest could not be
more different, and yet it essentially involved members of the same Red
Guard generation. Happening about ten years before the 1989 student movement, it shared fundamental similarities with the movement in 1989, despite
the fact that the core participants in 1989 were of a younger generation. In
other words, highlighting the significance of the new protest wave requires

an understanding of its relationship with the mass protests that came before and after it. I will start with the biographies of the participants.

There are two important features in the history of popular protest in China from 1966 to 1989. One is the presence of members of the Red Guard generation in all the major protest events in these twenty-three years, showing a degree of persistence and continuity in the biographies of protest. The other feature is the gradual funneling out of the radical activists of the generation through state suppression, which significantly limits the degree of movement continuity.

The sent-down protests in 1978 and 1979 evidently involved youth of the Red Guard generation. So did the April Fifth movement. Based on the information he collected of 182 activists in the April Fifth movement, Heilmann finds that a minimum of 92 of them, or more than half, were younger than 35 years of age. That was basically the Red Guard age cohort. This estimate was confirmed by the profiles of 22 activists who were imprisoned in Nanjing because of their involvement in the movement. He finds that at least 10 out of the 22 activists were sent-down youth and at least 11 of them were former Red Guards.[39] Heilmann thus concludes that the April Fifth movement shows that "the generation which had been used as the basis of mobilization at the beginning of the 'Cultural Revolution' openly turned against the radical Left in 1976."[40]

In scale the April Fifth movement and sent-down youth protests involved more people than the Democracy Wall and the democratic elections in 1980. In Beijing alone in the April Fifth movement, up to two thousand work units laid wreaths in Tiananmen Square,[41] a scale that was matched only by the mass demonstrations in 1989 (when participation was also organized by work units).

In my own database of 122 Democracy Wall activists, age information is available for 47 people. Of these 47, 7 were between ages 5 and 8 in 1966, presumably too young to be involved in the Red Guard movement. The other 40 activists were all old enough to have direct experiences. Their profile was similar to those involved in the April Fifth movement. Many of them had been sent down; some were workers.

According to sources I collected, about 27 magazines of the Democracy Wall period were unofficially published in Beijing alone. Of these 27 titles, about 12 were regularly produced. The editors or chief contributors of the most influential half-dozen of these magazines were all former Red Guards. If we count the key unofficial magazines produced in other cities, then

TABLE 6.1 UNOFFICIAL MAGAZINES OF THE DEMOCRACY WALL MOVEMENT EDITED BY FORMER RED GUARDS

MAGAZINE	EDITORS
Exploration	Wei Jingsheng, Yang Guang
Beijing Spring	Han Zhixiong, Li Zhousheng
Today	Bei Dao, Mang Ke
The Thaw Society	Li Jiahua, Lu Mang
The April Fifth Forum	Xu Wenli
Enlightenment (Beijing and Guiyang)	Huang Xiang
People's Road (Guangzhou)	He Qiu, Wang Xiang
The Future (Guangzhou)	Wang Min
People's Voice (Guangzhou)	Liu Guokai
The Petrel (Shanghai)	Lin Muchen

UNLESS OTHERWISE NOTED, ALL MAGAZINES WERE EDITED AND PRODUCED IN BEIJING.

close to a dozen of the most influential publications in the Democracy Wall movement were edited by former Red Guard activists. Table 6.1 shows the names of these magazines and the editors.

The activists in the campus elections in 1980 were also mainly drawn from former Red Guards and sent-down youth. They were clearly among the more "successful" members of the generation, given that only a tiny percentage of youth could enter college. Among the 22 election candidates in several universities in Beijing whose ages are known, only one was 6 years old in 1966 and another was 9. The others were mostly 16, 17, or 19 in 1966 and had sent-down experiences or experiences as workers.[42]

In all these cases, there were transmovement veterans who had experiences in more than one movement and who thus served as linkages across different movements, providing a much-needed reservoir of social memory.[43] There were, however, conspicuous absences and discontinuities. By 1976, the dissident voices of the Cultural Revolution, which we studied in chapter 3, had been crushed. Key figures, such as Yang Xiguang and Lu Li'an, had been sentenced to long years in prison or had even been sentenced to death, as in the case of Yu Luoke. Leading rebels of the Red Guard movement had also been subject to repression in the "cleansing of class ranks" campaign that immediately followed the Red Guard movement. The suppression of the Democracy Wall movement similarly led to the imprisonment of its core figures. They were missing in the democratic elections in 1980, although Wei Jingsheng, who had been imprisoned, was present as an issue of debate. One of the questions for candidates to debate about in Peking University was "Your views about the case of Wei Jingsheng."[44] By 1989 the Democracy Wall movement had all but disappeared from public memory, although, again, Wei Jingsheng, who was still in prison, served as a rallying point in the initial mobilizations in 1989 when a signature petition was launched to call for his release. Beginning with the end of the Red Guard movement in 1968, but then especially after the suppression of the April Fifth movement, the majority of the radical elements in political contention had been funneled out, while a small minority remained active.

This funneling out of political radicals disrupted the continuity of democratic protest in recent Chinese history, making it difficult for new entrants to learn from the past. Thus participants in the student movement in 1989 knew little about the Democracy Wall or even about the Cultural Revolution. Although they drew inspiration from the earlier histories of the May Fourth movement and the French Revolution, the disruptions of the history and memories of recent protests created a situation where each time a new movement started it seemed as if it had to start from the scratch.

Of course, each protest movement had its new entrants from younger generations, since both conditions internal and external to the movement may significantly influence what sociologists sometimes refer to as cohort replacement in social movement participation.[45] One consequence of the funneling out of radical activists in PRC history is that the social movement field in China has always remained decentralized and fragmented. Stable movement organizations have little chance of surviving repression. Paradoxically, this creates a space for new entrants to assume more prominent roles in new protest waves. That was precisely what happened in 1989, when younger students took a leading role while veteran activists served as backstage advisers.

CONTINUITY AND CHANGE IN REPERTOIRES OF ACTION

A comparison of the 1976–1980 wave of protest back and forth would be incomplete without a discussion of the most visible forms of differences and commonalities, those in the forms of protest or repertoires of collective contention.

The most important difference was a shift from violent to nonviolent forms of protest. Certainly, there were many nonviolent forms of protest in the Red Guard movement. But, as the case of Chongqing shows, violence was a distinct feature. In calling for the rule of law and democratic reform, the April Fifth and Democracy Wall protesters rejected the violence of the Cultural Revolution and embraced nonviolent forms of protest. Nonviolence was also the chosen method of protest in 1989.

Mass struggle meetings were a standard form of collective action during the Red Guard period. Passed down from the tradition of mass criticism in the Chinese communist revolution, these meetings often had specific targets to criticize and shame, such as a party leader denounced as a "capitalist roader." The concentration of large crowds in the same space heightened public emotions and made the denunciations especially overpowering. The grandeur of these occasions was a way of displaying organizational power.

An important continuity is that although mass struggle meetings were no longer used in the protests after the Cultural Revolution, a passion for grandeur persisted, most clearly in the Tiananmen demonstrations in 1989. To quote veteran of the movement turned dissident and Nobel Peace laureate Liu Xiaobo again:

> Although ten years of reform have attenuated the sacred quality of "revolution" and weakened the political culture built upon class struggle, we still worship "revolution" in our bones. We are still the "revolutionary successors." As soon as we meet with a large-scale political movement, our enthusiasm for "revolution" swells; as soon as the kindling of revolution is lit, it burns—the fire rapidly becoming flames that reach to heaven, consuming everything.[46]

Liu goes on to argue that the 1989 protest movement, in its sublime struggles for democracy, was also a revolution born out of the worship of "revolution": "It was an earthshaking opportunity. Everyone wanted to take advantage of this opportunity to perform a great deed, a great achievement to impress the generations that would follow."[47] Liu's words about the 1989 protest bring us back to the revolutionary performances of the Red Guard period, revealing an underlying continuity between 1966 and 1989, one that I have elsewhere called aspirations for the grand narratives of Chinese modernity.[48] It is not until the 1990s, I have argued in my analysis of Chinese online activism, that popular contention in China begin to take on post-apocalyptic stylistic features of playfulness or mundane realism.

There are other notable continuities. Perhaps most important, the Cultural Revolution established the big-character poster as a modular repertoire of contention in Chinese politics. Big-character posters were the most common method of mobilizing support and attacking opponents in all the major protest activities covered in this book, from the Red Guard movement to the campus elections in 1980. Although the student movement in 1989 was known better for its televised character,[49] big-character posters still played an important role in the crucial initial stage of the movement, when students on university campuses in Beijing used posters to express their condolences on the death of Hu Yaobang.

One reason why big-character posters were an all-time favorite method of protest is convenience. Posters could be put up wherever there are walls. Their authors could choose to remain anonymous or sign their names.[50] Another is their effectiveness. Posters usually appear in the most central public spaces of a community. All public institutions from schools and factories to government bureaucracies and hospitals have their centers of public activity, and these are the favored places for putting up posters, because to members of a community it is common knowledge where their communal centers may be found—where to go for news and gossip. The appearance of a wall poster in a busy location of a university campus, such as the triangle area in Peking University, will attract crowds and achieve the effect of instant dissemination. So it is not surprising that at Peking University all major protest activities started in the triangle area, until the bulletin boards in that area were all removed in November 2007 in an ostensible effort to forestall future contentious gatherings.[51]

For writers of wall posters, not only is the content of a poster important, but its form also matters. The size of the posters, the color of the paper and ink, and, most important, the calligraphy, may enhance the power and popularity of the poster and the personal reputation of the poster writers. Richard Kraus writes about the importance of calligraphy in the Red Guard period in the following terms, "Red Guard engaged in calligraphic warfare. The students with the best handwriting were selected to copy out manifestos and proclamations and to prepare forceful characters for armbands and newspaper masterheads."[52] In surveying the uses of calligraphy, Geremie Barmé writes:

> For over a century street politics saw calligraphy used as a cheap, convenient and popular means for communicating slogans, short messages and otherwise

banned ideas. Anonymous protest, calls to arms, revelations, exhortations and denunciations could all be written up using the traditional brush, ink and paper and posted with facility on walls in cities, towns or even villages. These slogans and exhortations could act as a form of public outcry; they were posted outside government offices; they could give expression to interrogations on the doors of publishers, direct accusations at miscreants, appeal for justice to the courts or the police, or just give voice, in written form, to personal grievances.[53]

Might calligraphy and Chinese characters lose their magic in the 21st-century culture of Internet expression? Certainly, sounds, images, and videos are easier to create and disseminate online. Yet the fascination with words has not weakened. But instead of calligraphy, which is an art of writing the same character in multiple ways, creative character making is especially popular in the online culture of protest, as evidenced by the grass-mud-horse lexicon compiled by the China Digital Times.[54] Today the art of making up characters, instead of the art of writing old characters, has become a new protest technique.

THE NEW ENLIGHTENMENT BETWEEN 1966 AND 1989

Comparing the three protest waves in 1966–1968, 1976–1980, and 1989 shows that the most striking differences were between the goals and demands of the Red Guard movement and the new wave of protest in 1976–1980. The wave of protest in 1976–1980 made Mao and the Cultural Revolution its targets. It is hard to imagine traveling the distance from total loyalty to doubting and even rejecting Mao and the CR in a matter of ten years. The main ideas advocated by activists in the Democracy Wall and the campus elections—of enlightenment, democracy, rule of law, human rights, political reform—were alien in the Red Guard period. I have tried to show throughout this book that this great reversal represents the transformation of both a political generation and Chinese political culture. It is the unintended consequence of the Red Guard movement and the sent-down campaign. Insofar as the 1976–1980 protest wave marked an emergence from a historical nonage and a farewell to idolatry, it inaugurated an era of "new enlightenment" in modern Chinese history, as the decade of the 1980s has come to be known.

The striking difference between the goals of the Red Guard movement and the 1976–1980 new wave is matched only by the new wave's equally striking similarity to the student movement in 1989. The April Fifth and Democracy Wall activists rejected the Cultural Revolution as much as student protesters did in 1989. In 1989, students were at pains to distinguish themselves from Red Guards while government authorities attempted to discredit them by comparing them to Red Guards.[55] And the same calls for democracy, enlightenment, human rights, and modernization put forward by activists in 1976–1980 remained central to student protesters in 1989. The ideals of the 1989 movement were crystallized in the "New May Fourth Manifesto" issued by student protesters on May 4, 1989: "Fellow students, fellow countrymen, the future and fate of the Chinese nation are intimately linked to each of our hearts. This student movement has but one goal, that is, to facilitate the process of modernization by raising high the banners of democracy and science, by liberating people from the constraints of feudal ideology, and by promoting freedom, human rights, and rule of law."[56]

The reference to the May Fourth movement raises an intriguing question. Historian Rana Mitter argues that the Cultural Revolution was in many ways a child of the May Fourth movement, however distorted a version of that earlier era it might have been.[57] The celebration of youth, violence, and iconoclasm characterized both the Cultural Revolution and the May Fourth. And yet May Fourth was and remains the fountainhead of China's enlightenment project. The ideals of democracy, science, and freedom embraced by the Democracy Wall and 1989 activists were the same ideals of the May Fourth generation at the beginning of the twentieth century.

Did the 1976–1980 wave of protest and the 1989 movement share some underlying commonality with the Cultural Revolution, despite their obvious differences? Was there a century-long lineage running from the May Fourth movement in 1919 through the Red Guard movement, the Democracy Wall, and the 1989 protest?

There was, but the lineage was not just an emphasis on youth, violence, and iconoclasm. Violence was rejected in the wake of the Cultural Revolution and the protest waves from 1976 to 1989 were anything but violent. On the contrary, nonviolence became the conscious method of popular struggle in the post-Mao era.

Viewing Mao as the heir of European romanticism, Mitter argues that this European romanticism runs through the May Fourth generation to the Cultural Revolution: "the mindset Mao revealed in setting the policy forward is heavily rooted in European romanticism, one of the most powerful cultural threads of May Fourth. . . . Romanticism encouraged the belief in a transcendent hero, in a figure who could drag an entire people into the future through the force of sheer will."[58] As I have shown in my analysis of the practices of violence and theorizing in the Red Guard movement, and as we see in the analysis of the new wave of protest in 1976–1978, while Mao was the arch-romanticist, generations of Chinese young people were romanticists as well. Indeed, members of the Red Guard generation were brought up as young romantics imagining themselves to be the heroes of a worldwide communist revolution. They had a sense of a mission to save the world from capitalism and imperialism and bring the communist utopia to earth. During the Red Guard period, Red Guards and rebels painstakingly emulated the young Mao in their relentless efforts to live up to their imagined ideals of true revolutionaries.

In other words, the genealogy from the May Fourth through the Cultural Revolution to 1989 is not just a matter of Mao's personal mindset, but the imaginations and sentiments of generations of young people throughout the twentieth century. The romantic mentalities of the Red Guard generation suffered profoundly in the sent-down period, yet, despite disillusionment and disenchantment, hope lived on. By the time of the 1976–1980 protest wave, the concrete ideals and goals pursued by the Red Guard generation had changed from loyalty to Mao to demands for freedom, democracy, and modernization, but a sense of hope persisted. If anything, hope was the keynote of the Democracy Wall movement. We see this already in the inaugural statements of unofficial publications such as *Enlightenment* and *Explorations*. Even the poems in the pages of *Today*, the only purely literary publication of the Democracy Wall period, carried words of great hope.

Called "misty" because of an alleged obscure quality in these works, "misty poetry" first appeared in the Democracy Wall movement in the unofficial magazine *Today*. Poetic obscurity, however, was only a thin veil for its political poignancy. Many of these poems were written in the early years of the 1970s while the authors were sent-down youth in the countryside. They lamented the material poverty and the spiritual crisis of the Chinese society, but still articulated an enduring sense of idealism and conviction in national rejuvenation. The following lines from Bei Dao's famous poem "The Answer" is now the well-known declaration of intellectual independence among this generation:

Let me tell you, world,
I-do-not-believe!
If a thousand challengers lie beneath your feet,
Count me as number one thousand and one.

. . .

A new conjunction and glimmering stars
Adorn the unobstructed sky now:
They are the pictographs from five thousand years.
They are the watchful eyes of future generations.[59]

The optimism conveyed here in millennium images are expressed more explicitly in a poem entitled "O Motherland, Dear Motherland" by Shu Ting,
another representative misty poet of the Red Guard generation:

I am poverty,
I'm sorrow,
I'm the bitterly painful hope
Of your generations. . . .
I'm your smiling dimple wet with tears;
Your newly drawn lime-white starting line.
I'm the scarlet dawn emerging with long shimmering rays
—O Motherland.[60]

It seems that the unifying thread running from 1919 through 1966 and
1976 to 1989 was what Calhoun and Wasserstrom see as the underlying connection between the Cultural Revolution and the 1989 student protests. As
they put it, "both movements were shaped in important ways by the much
broader modern Chinese project of affirming national identity and strength-
ening the nation. This is not something the Cultural Revolution brought to
the 1989 student movement, but rather a basic problematic of the last hundred years of China's history."[61] This basic problematic of twentieth-century
China was translated into passions for social change on a grand scale, cul-
minating in the grandiose protest rallies in Tiananmen Square in the spring
of 1989.

At this point, we may summarize the general social and political out-
comes of the historical experiences of the Red Guard generation through the
Red Guard movement to the protest wave of 1976–1980. In brief, the historical experiences of this generation created a generation that first embraced
and then rejected the Cultural Revolution and the Red Guard movement,
eventually providing the critical intellectual and social foundation for the
reform policies of the 1980s. Such rejection was a negation and a remaking
of the self, which began in the middle of the Red Guard movement and was
completed in the long years of the sent-down period. Thus the entire decade
of "new enlightenment" in the 1980s, to the extent that it was built on an

intellectual consensus about the directions of Chinese modernity,[62] was built on a negation. It was in the negation of the Cultural Revolution that the Red Guard generation, indeed intellectuals of the nation, found common ground in their vision for a new Chinese modernity, one based on economic reform. The negation was never total, however, because a common thread of political idealism ran from the May Fourth Movement to the Cultural Revolution and through the "new enlightenment" of the 1980s.

Rebecca Klatch's study of the 1960s-generation in the United States shows a clear generational divide between the New Left and the New Right emerging out of their years of political activism.[63] Despite the factional rivalry of the Red Guard movement, however, no clear generational divide appeared from within the Red Guard generation in the decade following the end of the Cultural Revolution. Surely, those who would most likely have dissented from the intellectual consensus of the "new enlightenment," such as rebel leaders from the Red Guard movement, had met with political repression. And surely, the intellectual discourse even in the relatively open 1980s was significantly shaped by politics. Yet still, a broad-based consensus for reform and change characterized the cultural discourse of the 1980s and that had to be viewed as a major unintended outcome of the Cultural Revolution. The Red Guard generation, especially the intellectual voices of the generation, did go through fragmentation in the 1990s, but that was no longer the result of their Cultural Revolution experiences, but of entirely new circumstances, the foremost being the conditions of a new marketized society.[64] By that time the "grand narratives" of twentieth-century China would give way to a radically different style of protest, prosaic rather than epic and grandiose, reflecting the conditions of a more fragmented society.[65]

7

FACTIONALIZED MEMORIES

IN THE FIFTY YEARS since its end, the Cultural Revolution has never been forgotten in China. But it is remembered selectively, and what is remembered depends on who does the remembering and when and is highly contested.[1] In broad terms, each decade since the 1980s has had a different memory politics. The general features of Cultural Revolution memories in each decade are significantly shaped by the politics of that period and the social conditions of specific units of the Red Guard generation as agents of memory.

As a result, contemporary memories of the Cultural Revolution are broken and fragmented. In some sense, they have fallen along the lines of factional divisions formed during the period of the Red Guard movement. This suggests that Deng Xiaoping's efforts to exorcise the ghost of factionalism in the political campaigns following the end of the Cultural Revolution were not entirely successful and that the factional conflicts in 1966–1968 continue to haunt Chinese society and politics in the twenty-first century.

The memory practices concerning the Cultural Revolution lend support to an interactive theoretical model that integrates two competing perspectives in theories of collective memory.[2] In the presentist model, what is remembered of the past and how it is remembered depend on present circumstances and the mediated practices of memory.[3] In the cultural model, "the present is rooted in the past" and the past "is in some respects, and under some conditions, highly resistant to efforts to make it over."[4] In an integrated model, memories of the past are the result of interactions between the deep-rooted character of past experiences and the conditioning of the present.

Consistent with an integrated perspective, we will see how broad shifts in the national trends of memory narratives in the decades since the Cultural Revolution are significantly influenced by contemporary politics, but we will also see how the liminal experiences of the Red Guard movement and the sent-down period have not only left deep memories but in fact continue to shape thoughts and behavior today.

DE-MAOIFICATION IN THE 1980S

The 1980s was a forward-looking decade, a period of consolidating a new regime of post-Mao leadership and jump-starting economic reform. Public memories of the Cultural Revolution were condemnatory and negative, reflecting the rising fortunes of party leaders who had been persecuted in the Cultural Revolution as well as general social discontent with the CR. The faction that emerged as the victors of the Cultural Revolution, represented by Deng Xiaoping at the top and by conservative Red Guards at the grassroots, dominated the narration of the history and memories of Mao and the Cultural Revolution. Most memory stories are told by intellectuals and party cadres who were victimized in the Cultural Revolution.

In the late 1970s, as the Mao era came to an end, its history and memory became arenas of intense political struggle, and retrospective views of the CR reflect "the factional balance of power at the top."[5] The fall of Mao's hand-picked successor, Hua Guofeng, and the rise of Deng Xiaoping were played out in these symbolic struggles. One of the first feats Hua accomplished in his six years as China's post-Mao leader (1976–1982) was the construction of the Chairman Mao Memorial in Tiananmen Square. In his maneuvers to undermine Hua, Deng similarly resorted to mnemonic struggles, though of a different kind. As Harry Harding puts it, Deng "encouraged popular pressure for a more explicit repudiation of the Cultural Revolution and a more rapid and thoroughgoing rehabilitation of its victims."[6]

Popular pressures for repudiating the Cultural Revolution took two concrete social forms. One was the "literature of the wounded" literary movement, the other was the Democracy Wall social movement discussed in chapter 6. Works of the "literature of the wounded" tell stories of the victims of the Cultural Revolution, where the culprit was invariably Lin Biao and the "Gang of Four" and their zaofanpai followers, while the Cultural Revolution was dismissed as "ten years of disaster." Although the term *literature of the wounded* applies mainly to works of art and literature, memoirs produced by party cadres and intellectuals who were persecuted in the Cultural Revolution fall under this category and were published in large numbers.

In comparison, the Democracy Wall movement was much more wide-ranging in its assessment and critiques of the CR. The wall posters and unofficial publications of the movement voiced alternative views. These alternative critiques were linked with demands for a democratic political reform, which could potentially undermine Deng's own position. Consequently, as Kleinman and Kleinman put it, "when these popular expressions began to coalesce into the early phase of a movement for democratization, they were attacked. Thus the social memory of the Cultural Revolution was silenced or reworked in an authorized version."[7]

In these two movements, then, mnemonic practices about the Cultural Revolution were appropriated as a means of winning political gains by the emerging Dengist regime. The CR was made to form a historical foil to the rise and moral rejuvenation of the post-Mao regime. Yet when popular grievances appeared to be going off political limits, Deng withdrew his support. Consequently, a more coercive regime of memory control shaped up.

Deng's regime shaped the history and memories of the CR through party policies and political campaigns. The historic communiqué of the Third Plenum of the CCP Central Committee in 1978 stated that the problems of the Cultural Revolution "should be summed up at the appropriate time,"[8] thus indicating that an official settling of accounts would take place sooner or later. Shortly afterward, a process of de-Maoification was initiated. In February 1979 an official party policy directive was issued to suspend distribution of the *Little Red Book* of Mao quotations.[9] Another party directive was issued in July 1980 to cut back on "propagating individuals," specifically minimizing the presence of Mao portraits and statues in public spaces. One month later, the National People's Congress removed article 45 from the PRC Constitution, thus stripping citizens of the four "great freedoms" to speak out freely, air views fully, hold great debates, and write big-character posters. These "four greats" were the officially endorsed "weapons of struggle" in the Cultural Revolution and had provided some degree of legitimacy to all forms of social protest.[10] Removing them from the constitution was another strike at the popular radicalism of the Cultural Revolution. A key document in the control of CR memory was the "Resolution on Certain Questions in the History of Our Party Since the Founding of the PRC." This document officially denounced the CR as a ten-year disaster for which Mao and a small handful of leftist radicals were held responsible. Mao, however, was partially absolved from his responsibility. His was not only "the error of a great proletarian revolutionary," but he personally "led the struggle to smash the counterrevolutionary Lin Biao clique" and "made major criticisms and exposures of Jiang Qing, Zhang Chunqiao, and others, frustrating their sinister ambition to seize supreme leadership."[11]

The rehabilitation of individuals who suffered persecution in the Cultural Revolution and the criminalizing of perpetrators were implemented through public spectacles. In 1978 and 1979 numerous funerals and memorial services were held all over China for government cadres and intellectuals persecuted to death in the Cultural Revolution. Following the rehabilitation program, the new regime turned its attention to criminalizing the CR radicals, both top leaders like the "Gang of Four" and leading rebel Red Guards. The nationally televised trial of the "Gang of Four" in January 1981 marked the climax of this criminalizing project.[12]

At the end of 1983, an inner-party rectification campaign was launched to remove "three types of people" (san zhong ren) from official positions.[13] Although the three types of people were identified as "followers of Lin Biao and the Gang of Four, those seriously affected by factional ideas, and the 'smashers and grabbers' of the Cultural Revolution,"[14] they were interpreted to refer broadly to Cultural Revolution zaofanpai rebels. Following the rectification, a nationwide campaign was launched in 1984 to "totally negate the Cultural Revolution."

Ostensibly to root out Cultural Revolution factionalism, the campaign to cleanse "three types of people" was an inversion of the factional politics of the CR. An article published in a 1983 issue of Academic Forum, the official organ of the Guangxi Social Sciences Academy, alludes to the resistance the campaign must have met in Guangxi: "At present, Guangxi is cleansing 'three types of people' and handling those who seriously violated laws and regulations in the Cultural Revolution. This work is a struggle to overcome factional spirit with party spirit. Yet some people are spreading the view that "in the past, it was this faction that struggled against that faction. Now it is that faction that is struggling against this faction."[15]

Despite some degree of resistance against the total rejection of the CR and despite the fact that leading rebel Red Guards such as Kuai Dafu, Nie Yuanzi and Han Aijing were imprisoned and their voices muted,[16] the top-down de-Maoification campaign in the early 1980s worked in a post-Mao era when Maoist Cultural Revolution policies and ideologies appeared increasingly out of sync with the popular mood for political relaxation and economic development. In that sense, de-Maoification was intertwined with the cultural movement for a "new enlightenment" and "liberation of the mind" in the 1980s.[17]

MAO FEVER IN THE 1990S

Reversing the cultural trends of the 1980s, the 1990s opened with a "Mao fever" and closed with a wave of *zhiqing* (sent-down youth) nostalgia, making it a backward-looking decade. In both these phenomena, strong nostalgic sentiments were expressed for certain aspects of the Cultural Revolution. Just a decade before, sent-down youth had protested vehemently for their right to return to the cities, while Deng Xiaoping launched a de-Maoification campaign. How to explain this reversal of public sentiments toward the Cultural Revolution?

Both Mao fever and zhiqing nostalgia reflected the social changes taking place in the 1990s and their impact on the psyche of the Red Guard generation. Since the two trends coincided with China's transformation from a planned to a market-based economy, it is crucial to examine how and why the market transformation has influenced memory production. The economic reform in the 1990s marked China's deeper entry into capitalism, the arch-enemy of the Cultural Revolution. The proliferation of Cultural Revolution memories was a critical response to the social consequences of the marketization of the Chinese economy.

The Mao fever is well documented in a volume edited by Geremie Barmé. Titled *Shades of Mao: The Posthumous Cult of the Great Leader* and published in 1996, the volume contains English translations of Chinese media stories that present various perspectives about the meaning of the Mao fever. Barmé views it as a new kind of Mao cult, which is markedly different from the Mao cult of the Cultural Revolution.

There are multiple versions of the origin myth of the Mao fever. Some believe it arose out of a disillusionment with Western cultural influences that had dominated the cultural scene of the 1980s, a sentiment certainly endorsed if not promoted by the post-June Fourth Chinese leadership. Others trace the origins to the late 1980s, when growing social problems of corruption brought back memories of Mao's crusade against bureaucrats. Perhaps the most fascinating origin story had to do with taxi drivers and is recounted by Barmé as follows:

According to a story that was to become one of China's most widely told urban myths, the driver of a vehicle involved in a serious traffic accident in Shenzhen that left a number of people dead survived unscathed because he had a picture of Mao on the dashboard. Another version of the story claims that the accident occurred in Guangzhou and a whole busload of people were protected by Mao's image. Shortly after the tale began spreading, laminated images of Mao appeared in vehicles in cities, towns and villages throughout China. These images were not unlike the St. Christopher medallions popular with European drivers or the Virgin Mary of the Highway images found, for example, in Brazil. Many of them showed Mao in the guise of a temple god or guardian spirit and were said to be capable of deflecting evil (pixie).[18]

The story allegedly happened in 1991. That would put it about one year later than another major event, a museum exhibition that opened on November 25, 1990, in Beijing dedicated to the history of the sent-down movement in the northernmost part of China. Titled "Our Spiritual Attachment to the Black Soil: A Retrospective Exhibition About the Sent-down Youth of Beidahuang," it featured the history of the sent-down movement through displays of not only documentary descriptions but also old photographs and mementos of ordinary life from that historical period. Attracting 150,000 visitors,[19] mostly former sent-down youth who had spent years in Beidahuang, the exhibition triggered the wave of zhiqing nostalgia that would sweep across China throughout the 1990s.

The Mao fever has two faces, a government-sanctioned propagandistic Mao craze and a nonofficial and spontaneous Mao cult.[20] The government-sanctioned Mao craze culminated with the centenary of Mao's birth in 1993, which was observed nationally with the issuance of Mao commemorative coins and stamps, movies about his life, the unveiling of his statue in his birthplace, a flourishing memorial literature, and reprints of Mao's works and portraits.[21] In 1989, 370,000 copies of the official portrait of Mao were printed. In 1990, 22.95 million Mao portraits were printed, of which 19.93 million were sold. Fifty million Mao portraits were printed in 1991.[22]

Government sponsorship of a Mao revival in the early 1990s reflected the political exigencies in 1989 and 1990, especially a counteroffensive led by Chen Yun and other conservative party elders against Deng Xiaoping's reform policy following the 1989 student protest. According to Suisheng Zhao, "Numerous articles published after June 1989 in *Renmin Ribao*, *Guangming Ribao*, *Xinwen Chuban Bao* (News and publication), and *Zhen Di* (Front) had simultaneously criticized the "cat theory" and sought to provide inspiration to a "Mao Zedong craze." These articles promoted the "struggle against peaceful evolution" in an attempt to restore Mao's ideas and discredit Deng's reform policy."[23]

If the government-sponsored Mao craze was rooted in an inner party factional struggle triggered by the political crisis of 1989, the populist Mao cult was a response to changing social conditions. That Mao became something of a guardian spirit reflected the growing sense of insecurity among the Chinese population at a time of accelerating change. It is for the same reason that a religious revival was taking place in Chinese society during the same period, with all kinds of qigong groups attracting large followings (from which Falun Gong would eventually emerge).[24]

The Mao fever coincided with the commercialization of the culture industry in the 1990s. From the beginning of the economic reform, CR-related cultural products had occupied a central place in the development of the culture industry. In the field of literature, some of the most influential literary movements focused on the representation of the Cultural Revolution. Besides the "literature of the wounded" mentioned earlier in this chapter, these literary movements include misty poetry, root-searching literature, zhiqing literature, self-reflexive literature (fan si wen xue), and prison literature (da qiang wen xue). In reportage literature (bao gao wen xue), celebrity figures from the CR period are the subjects of numerous shorter or longer stories. In music, rock star Cui Jian makes explicit references to images of the Maoist era in his songs, such as those in the album The Egg Under the Red Flag. In painting, the political pop represented by Wang Guangyi's parodies of Mao makes direct uses of CR images. In the filmmaking industry, major fifth-generation directors explored Cultural Revolution themes, from Chen Kaige's King of the Children (1988), Tian Zhuangzhuang's The Blue Kite (1993), and Zhang Yimou's To Live (1994), to Jiang Wen's In the Heat of the Sun (1995).[25] In television drama, the first great success, Aspirations (ke wang), was set during the Cultural Revolution, airing in 1990. It was so popular that it reportedly forced some factories to change their work schedules so that employees could go home to watch it.[26]

What about political control over the topic of the Cultural Revolution? In the late 1980s and throughout the 1990s, the CCP Central Propaganda Department and the State Press and Publication Administration issued several directives concerning the publication of CR-related materials. One set of regulations, issued in 1988, states that "from now on and for quite some time, publishing firms should not plan the publication of dictionaries or other handbooks about the 'Great Cultural Revolution'" and that "under normal circumstances, one should not plan to publish titles specifically researching the 'Great Cultural Revolution' or specifically telling the history of the 'Great Cultural Revolution.'"[27] A party circular issued in March 1992 concerning the commemoration of Mao's centenary required works published in conjunction with the centenary "be strictly reviewed and approved according to the stipulations and guidelines that have been set out."[28] In 1997 the State Press and Publication Administration issued more regulations about the reporting of "weighty and big" (*zhong da*) publication projects, including projects related to the CR.[29]

Despite these restrictions, CR-related cultural products multiplied in tandem with the rise of a consumer society. Historian Jay Winter has argued that affluence is a precondition of the "memory boom" in the West. "Dwelling on memory is a matter of both disposable income and leisure time."[30] He notes that economic growth and the expansion of the service sector after WWII increased the demand for cultural commodities such as those having to do with memory—books, films, television shows, and museum exhibitions about the past. Similarly, in China, growing affluence provides the disposable income and leisure time for people to dwell on the past.

ZHIQING NOSTALGIA

Zhiqing nostalgia started in the early 1990s and reached its apex in the late 1990s. The nostalgia is for a specific segment of the historical experience of the generation—namely, the sent-down movement. Although many former sent-down youth were involved in the Red Guard movement, that aspect of their lives provides relatively little of the "material" of zhiqing nostalgia. The Red Guard movement was officially denounced as a source of social chaos, and the label *Red Guards* took on negative connotations in the political discourse of the post–Cultural Revolution period. In contrast, the zhiqing identity does not have such politically negative resonance. If anything, the hardships of rural life gave the prolonged zhiqing experience a tinge of glory, making it the ideal material for nostalgia.

While elite writers published the zhiqing literature of the 1980s, ordinary members of the Red Guard generation produced the nostalgia of the 1990s by publishing personal memories, diaries, letters, and old photographs. One collection of essays, for example, was edited by a restaurant manager in Beijing. Among the contributors to the collection were four office employees, three accountants, three physicians, two associate professors, two journalists, two union officials, a newspaper editor, a nurse, a storage employee, a department store manager, a bus driver, an archivist, a laid-off worker, and a department store salesperson.[31] Because its authors are so diverse, the cultural production of the zhiqing nostalgia takes on a distinct social character.

Zhiqing nostalgia is a phenomenon of civic association and voluntary organizing. The museum exhibitions mentioned previously were organized by former sent-down youth. They then functioned to bring together long-separated friends. Editing a book brought people together, as did social gatherings. As one interviewee told me, social gatherings became a more or less regular part of the lives of many members of their generation in the 1990s. Sometimes informal support groups could emerge out of these activities. Members of one such association I came across in Beijing in 1999 raised funds to support the children of the poor families among them.[32] When the Internet became popular in the late 1990s, it became both a "virtual" gathering space for former sent-down youth and a digital archive for publishing and collecting their personal narratives.

Finally, the scope of the zhiqing nostalgia is matched by its emotional intensity. Documentary films of crowds at the museum exhibits captured the emotional encounters between old friends—tears were shed in abundance, hugs were long, photos were taken, conversations were endless.[33] The titles of the many published stories often refer to the past with such phrases as "emotional attachment," "deep love," "unforgettable joy," "years of suffering and joy," "yearning for the past," "reminiscences in tears," and so forth.

Why did all this happen? How to account for the rise of zhiqing nostalgia?

NOSTALGIA AND DESTABILIZED IDENTITIES

China in the 1990s saw unprecedented changes in all areas of social life. As the country shifted from a planned to a market economic system, its economy took off, but new social problems, such as unemployment and increasing social inequality, followed. These economic developments are accompanied by the rise of new cultural values, notably materialism. As a value system that reifies goods and possessions, materialism had fought a losing battle against revolutionary asceticism in the Maoist period, but the tide has turned. The contemporary culture of materialism appears in many forms, consumerism being its most conspicuous incarnation.

Rapid social change can disrupt the continuity of life and strain identities. Members of the Red Guard generation are among the most vulnerable to such change. By 1990, the average age of former sent-down youth was about forty. Most had been back in the cities for a decade or more, and they had not found the process of settling back to urban life easy.[34] When they first returned, many had difficulty finding jobs, housing, or marriage partners. Nevertheless, despite these challenges, members of the generation did not despair. Having returned from a difficult period of their lives, they looked forward with hope to a future of material prosperity. By the late 1980s and early 1990s, most of them had settled back to routine urban lives.

Into the 1990s, these lives began to come unsettled again as a result of new social transformations. One of the most serious problems facing this generation in the late 1990s was unemployment caused by the restructuring of state-own enterprises.[35] According to some estimates, former sent-down youth accounted for as much as 40 to 60 percent of the total laid-off workforce in 1998.[36] The depths of the psychological consequences of unemployment are hard to gauge. For many people, being laid off from work was an entirely new and unexpected experience in a socialist society that had at least nominally tried to provide job security. In 1999, at the height of the unemployment wave, an interviewee described to me how she felt after losing her job for the first time in her life:

Since I was a child, I have never had the feeling that there was no place for me to go. As a child, as soon as I woke up in the morning, I had to get up to hurry to kindergarten. Then elementary school, middle school. On the farm, I got up and went to work. At college, I got up and went to class. . . . There had never been a time in my life when, waking up in the morning, I had nowhere to go. In February last year, the company where I worked was disbanded. After that, there were days when I woke up in the morning and found I had no place to go. I had never had that kind of feeling [sobbing]. So I lay in bed and thought to myself: I have been a hardworking person since elementary school . . . this is not my fault, many other people have lost their jobs. . . . Yet despite such thoughts and self-comforting, I really felt bad, to be honest. From morning until night, there was nothing I could do. There are many books in my house, and I could read if I wanted to. Yet I always felt that my heart had lost its anchor, as if I were riding a bottomless boat. I felt empty in my heart, hollow and empty.[37]

Changes in cultural values also disoriented the zhiqing generation. Lu Xing'er, a zhiqing novelist whose works mostly concern the life experience of her generation, expresses this sense of disorientation in 1998 in the following words:

At that time [1986], I was still full of pride for our generation. My stories about our generation are optimistic and cheerful. . . . My characters have knowingly inherited the tradition, yet under the burden of history they still unequivocally yearn to accept and create a new life. For a generation that links the past, the present, and the future, the combination and conflict of the old and the new manifest themselves in thoughts of the most complicated and helpless kind. In 1986 and 1987, there still seemed to be various ways of resolving these problems. In the past year or two, however, rapid changes in the economy, consciousness, ideas, and human relations have exacerbated the problems to such an extent that they have become bewildering. Problems can be faced and solved. When they begin to bewilder, so that people are at a loss what to do about them, then they become the most profound predicaments. We find ourselves in such predicaments now.[38]

Lu sees her own career of novel writing as an endless search for a sense of self: "I often cannot see myself clearly. . . . Up to this day, it seems that I still have not formed a clear 'self.' . . . I'm still growing, struggling and wandering in the sea of life; I'm still searching all around me for a beacon. . . . I sometimes wonder: how much and how profoundly life has changed me. . . . I'm like a meteor unwilling to fall into oblivion and determined to plot my own orbit in the limitless expanse of the universe."[39] Through her creative sensibility, Lu articulates a generational phenomenon. More than any other social group in contemporary China, the Red Guard generation finds itself again in the vortex of social change and in renewed struggles against disruptions of identity. In these struggles, the past becomes a vital source for coping with the present.

CONNECTING THE PRESENT TO THE PAST

One way of managing identity crisis is to reestablish connections with the past. Among former sent-down youth, pilgrimages to the places to which they had been sent became common in the 1990s. In many cases, these are literally sentimental journeys in search of the self. One person explains the motives for such a visit:

Before I knew it, the bus had entered the region that was both familiar and strange to me. What was it that lured me back to this familiar land? . . . Because here were the traces of my past life that I was in search of. Here was the land that had a very special place in my heart. The people here had treated me like a member of their own families. In these hills I had left behind sparks of my life. Here I spent the unforgettable golden years of my life. Without the bygone days that I spent here, my current self would lose its meaning.[40]

The discoveries made on these sentimental journeys are mixed. A woman I interviewed in Beijing talked to me excitedly about one such trip, which she undertook in 1998 with dozens of other former educated youth. "Oh, the crowd," she said. "All the people were out in the streets to greet us. We couldn't hold back our tears at seeing our old friends."[41] She clearly felt great joy and excitement; the warm reception helped to validate her identity. In Beijing my interviewee worked as an accountant in a local hospital and faced uncertainty in her employment. Back where she once lived as a sent-down youth, she could at least temporarily leave behind her disciplined lifestyle and reexperience emotional solidarity among old friends and acquaintances.

Such journeys can also be frustrating. Some aspects of the past, once dear to the heart, may have changed beyond recognition or have been erased. Xiao Fuxing, a well-known writer of the Red Guard generation, describes his feelings upon finding that the grave he had traveled a long way to visit had disappeared:

Both the grave and the gravestone were gone. Only a patch of wild grass stood swaying in the lonesome wind. This was a female educated youth. I was once on the same team with her. At that time, she was not yet twenty years old. In front of her grave, we once held a solemn funeral. . . . We mourned the dead, held a memorial service for her, made her our model, and promised we would never forget her. We planted several poplar saplings to show that we would always stand by her. Alas, everything was gone now. The grave had been leveled, the trees cut. I had come to visit an old friend, only to find my heart broken. I lowered my head in shame.[42]

Here nostalgia took an unexpected twist, as yearning for the past was confronted by cold reality. Efforts to renew personal links to the past were thwarted by the discovery that the past had been literally erased. It dawned on the writer that his generation now faced the danger of being left out of history. At that point the sense of personal identity crisis characteristic of this generation in the 1990s turned into a generational identity crisis. As a writer, Xiao has devoted much of his life to writing stories about his generation in the hope that "when history gently turns its pages" it will not "casually omit us."[43]

The other way of connecting with the past is remembering. Remembering may take different forms, such as exhibitions and museums. Several museum exhibitions in China's major urban centers in the 1990s helped to build the national wave of zhiqing nostalgia. The power of these exhibitions derived from the connections they established between the present and the past, but also because, as David Davies shows, they created spaces for former zhiqing to talk about past experiences.[44]

Another form of remembering is the social gathering of former sent-down youth. A reencounter with old friends is a double meeting: it is an encounter with an old self as well as with the present self, as the following passage makes clear:

> At the time of our reunion, many pairs of eyes look into each other in search of something unspoken. Our past appearances and images . . . have become vague and hazy . . . we all look old now! The pretty faces of yesteryear are now mostly darkened with pigmentation. A sculptor named Time has jokingly and relentlessly carved stories into the faces of this generation. Some sad thought surges into my heart: we don't want old age, yet we cannnot sell it; we want youth, yet cannot buy it. Women are grieved to tears, as if they have lost their lovers; men also want to cry, but they have no tears.[45]

Writing and publishing personal narratives is also a form of remembering. In the zhiqing nostalgia of the 1990s, ordinary people, not cultural elites, became the authors of nostalgia narratives. Numerous collections of personal narratives were published by former zhiqing. Many more appeared in blogs and keep appearing until today. An analysis of three collections of zhiqing narratives I conducted shows that although the themes in these collections are quite wide-ranging (e.g., marriage and family life, love and death, conflict and friendship, hard labor, poverty, joy, loneliness, freedom, hunger, bravery, adventure), three are especially prominent, namely, suffering and misfortune, humanity, and meaning and purpose.[46] These experiences of the past are contrasted to the commercialism of the present. In this sense, the zhiqing nostalgia is less about the past and more about the present. Their narratives of past sufferings are often associated with a sense of pride in the ability of the generation to undergo these sufferings with courage or resignation and a mixed sense of sacrifice and achievement. The narratives of zhiqing nostalgia produce a collective critique of the dilemmas of a rapidly modernizing present.

A SECOND RED CULTURE REVIVAL

The first fifteen years of the twenty-first century in China was neither forward-looking nor backward-looking, but oriented to the present. The Chinese party-state was obsessed with maintaining social stability in a time of rising unrest. The wealthy middle class was preoccupied with consumerism if not hedonism. The disadvantaged segments of the population found their voices online and in the streets. Under these conditions, party leaders promoted a new red culture. Making a mockery of the militant red culture in the 1950s and 1960s, this new red culture celebrates not violence or revolution, but harmony and stability.

The official promotion of a red culture in the 2000s was paralleled by the appearance of an unofficial memory culture. Former rebels who were suppressed and scapegoated as the perpetrators of the violence of the Cultural Revolution by the post-Mao regime began to tell their side of the story by publishing memoirs and oral histories. This was due to the emergence of a network of Cultural Revolution "folk researchers" (min jian wen ge yan jiu zhe) and the opportunities of publishing online and outside China.

Insofar as the main supporters of the new red culture are the princelings and second-generation reds, who were likely to be among "old Red Guards" (lao bing) in the Red Guard movement, one might view the revival of red culture and the appearance of rebels' memoirs as the factionalized memories of two rival constituents of the Red Guard movement: the "old guards" and the rebels.

In a 2012 article, Willy Lam dates the beginning of the new wave of Mao fever to 2008 and its culmination to the festivities surrounding the ninetieth birthday of the CCP on July 1, 2011. Although a new red culture had been in the making before 2008, I agree with Lam that 2008 was an important turning point. From the vantage of 2016, however, the end point of Mao fever would not be the ninetieth birthday of the CCP in 2011. It turns out that after Xi Jinping took office in November 2012 as China's new top leader, the Mao fever heated up instead of cooling down. As of this writing, the new red culture is running strong, with no end in sight.

Compared with the Mao fever in the early 1990s, the one that started in 2008 has clear signs of a top-down political campaign. Soon after he became the party secretary of Chongqing in November 2007, Bo Xilai decided to make "red culture" a core element of his efforts to build a Chongqing model. Shortly afterward, he launched a campaign to "sing red songs" and "crack down on black [criminals]" (*chang hong da hei*). The campaign to "sing red songs" was supposed to revive China's revolutionary culture to counter the corrosive influences of contemporary commercialism and consumerism. Red culture was billed as the core of new socialist values, and inculcating these values was seen as necessary for building a harmonious and prosperous society, a new vision propounded under President Hu Jintao.

Bo's campaign used CR-style methods to mobilize Chongqing residents to join in the group singing of "red songs." According to one estimate, by the end of 2010, Chongqing had organized 155,000 red song–singing events. By per-head count, these activities involved almost all of Chongqing's adult population. In addition, 170 million text messages of "red classics" were reportedly sent to and by Chongqing residents on their mobile phones and the online texting service QQ.[47] In May 2009, 13 million mobile phone subscribers in Chongqing received Bo Xilai's personal texting, in which he shared a few of his favorite Mao quotations and commented, "These words are very concise, very true, and very elevating."[48] In its scale, the "red culture" campaign in Chongqing approached the proportions of the Cultural Revolution. Bo Xilai seemed to have tried to play the role of Mao in mobilizing participation through personal charisma and mass campaigns.

The red culture renaissance in the 2000s had complex social and political roots, but, as in the case of the Mao fever in the early 1990s, it was related to factional struggles within the Chinese communist party. According to Lam, "Implicit in the princelings' re-hoisting of the Maoist flag is a veiled critique of the policies undertaken by Hu and his CYL Faction, which seem to have exacerbated the polarisation of rich and poor and spawned a kind of crass commercialism that runs counter to Maoist spiritual values."[49] But, more important, Bo Xilai attempted to mobilize public support in his desperate bid for a top leadership position in the upcoming eighteenth CCP congress.

Bo Xilai met his downfall in a public scandal in 2012,[50] while Xi became the CCP leader late in the same year. Yet the ousting of Bo Xilai only ended the red culture campaign in Chongqing, not the national red culture renaissance. As CCP vice chairman, Xi Jinping had already shown his support for Bo Xilai's red culture campaign by touring Chongqing in December 2010 and speaking about "affirming the practice of singing red songs and studying [Maoist] classics . . . as a means of pursuing education in [Marxist] ideals and beliefs."[51] After Xi became China's supreme leader, he took the red culture campaign to a new level, going beyond the public fanfares of culture and red tourism and reaching into the realm of ideology, education, and the organization of the Chinese communist party. Xi's leadership style takes on a populist approach reminiscent of Mao in the Cultural Revolution. Called "more Maoist than reformer" by the *Los Angeles Times*,[52] Xi revived the Maoist practice of self-criticism as a method of curbing corruption among party officials.[53] Maoist political practices such as the "mass line" are brought back to official discourse, while the notion of civil society came under attack in the summer of 2013 as a Western import that ill fits Chinese reality. Indeed, by 2014 China's minister of education was publicly warning educational institutions against "allow[ing] into our classrooms material that propagates Western values.[54] Although nurtured in the shadows of the collapse of the former Soviet Union, this deep fear of Western values follows in a direct lineage with the Cultural Revolution. Similarly, Xi's promotion of the idea of a Chinese dream, especially the use of the language of a great national rejuvenation after a century of national shame and humiliation, follows after an earlier Maoist language of anti-imperialism and national independence.

There are complex reasons why red culture is being promoted in recent years. The reason most relevant to the theme of this book is that the proponents of this new wave of red culture, whether it is Bo Xilai or Xi Jinping, are themselves members of the Red Guard generation. Bo and Xi are not the only princelings to promote the new red culture, however. Many other second-generation reds have expressed explicit support of it. Although his father Marshall Chen Yi suffered persecution in the Cultural Revolution, Chen Xiaolu still considers Mao a great leader, as does the daughter of senior general Xu Haidong, who died in political exile in Zhengzhou during the CR.[55]

Why are they still adamant supporters of a political culture that brought misfortune and even disaster to their own families? One reason is that they have an emotional attachment to a culture in which they had come of age. This applies not just to the princelings but to other segments of the Red Guard generation as well. I personally know someone whose mother died of persecution in the Cultural Revolution but who continues to have a strong emotional attachment to those revolutionary years because he once felt a deep sense of freedom and exhilaration as a high school student freed from schoolwork and able to roam the country freely.

By promoting red culture, the princelings show support for a political regime to which they feel a sense of entitlement and ownership. Many members of the Red Guard generation experienced disillusionment and a sense of betrayal by the communist party they had pledged their loyalty to; when their parents came under attack, children of elite cadres resisted, as I have shown in chapter 3. Yet the sense of privilege and superiority derived from being children of elite families has never disappeared. When the "old guards" of the Red Guard movement were losing out toward the end of the Red Guard movement, they vowed to make a comeback, claiming, "In twenty years' time, we will know who the real winners are." "You may have pens (*bi gan zi*), but we have guns (*qiang gan zi*). Let's see who rules the *tianxia* in the future."[56]

It seems that this mentality persists among the princelings. If so, then the promotion of red culture is only a subtle way of promoting their own entitlement to the power of the regime.

THE REBELS ARE BACK

While red culture has become the "main melody" in the public memories of the Maoist past, the memories of former rebels have added discordant tunes to the main melody. In the Red Guard movement, rebels came onto the scene by challenging and thwarting "royalists," "conservatives," and "old guards." Today's former rebels and princelings would likely be opponents in the Red Guard movement period. In this sense, the factional rivalry of the past has persisted down to the present day.

Earlier in this chapter, I noted that rebel leaders were mostly criminalized toward the end of the Cultural Revolution and sentenced to many years in prison. The collective memories of the Cultural Revolution in the 1980s were dominated by narratives of trauma and condemnation. There were few memoirs from the "losers" of the Cultural Revolution—the rebels and alleged followers of the Lin Biao and Gang of Four "anti-party clique." Since the 1990s, but especially since the 2000s, many of these people have begun to accept interviews or publish memoirs. Because these narratives deviate from the official line, they are nonmainstream or alternative. They include mainly two types, those written by former zaofanpai and those by top party leaders accused of being followers of the Lin Biao and Gang of Four clique. I will discuss narratives by former rebels only, since they are the members of the Red Guard generation and not the party leaders.

Recently, many people who belonged to rebel organizations in the Red Guard movement have spoken out by publishing diaries, blogs, essays, and book-length memoirs. Among the nationally famous "five Red Guard leaders," one of them, Tan Houlan, died of cancer in 1982 and did not seem to have left behind any personal writing. Nor was Tan prosecuted due to her terminal illness. The other four were tried, convicted as "counterrevolutionaries," and sentenced in 1983. Because they had all been detained in or around 1970, their term of imprisonment was retroacted, so that with a fifteen- or seventeen-year term when they were sentenced in 1983, they only had several years left to serve in prison. Han Aijing was sentenced to fifteen years and released in 1986 upon serving his prison term.[57] Wang Dabin was sentenced to nine years and released in 1983. Kuai Dafu was sentenced to seventeen years and was released in 1987. Nie Yuanzi was sentenced to seventeen years and released on medical parole in 1984. All four of them have spoken out, Wang Dabin and Han Aijing through interviews and Nie Yuanzi and Kuai Dafu through their memoirs, published in Hong Kong.

Many other former rebels have also published memoirs. By my count, there are now book-length memoirs of former rebels in the following provinces or direct-governed municipalities: Anhui, Beijing, Guangzhou, Guangxi, Heilongjiang, Hubei, Hunan, Inner Mongolia, Jiangsu, Shandong, Shanghai, Shanxi, Sichuan, and Zhejiang. These narratives contain detailed accounts of the authors' experiences from childhood through the Cultural Revolution. Their views toward violence are, not surprisingly, critical and negative. Their assessments of the Cultural Revolution, Mao, and zaofanpai, however, are not all the same. Some are still believers in Mao and the legitimacy of the Cultural Revolution. They feel that as a group, zaofanpai has been wronged and made into the scapegoat for the horrors of the Cultural Revolution.

Zhou Lunzuo, a former rebel in Chengdu, Sichuan, has the following to say in the afterword to his book about zaofanpai in the Cultural Revolution:

> The main thing that motivated me to do this [write this memoir] is naturally not any utilitarian need, which has long died out. It is rather an inexpungible indignation. Since the 1980s, intellectuals within the establishment, on the margins of the establishment, and even outside of the establishment, have all distorted the popular dimensions of the Cultural Revolution and demonized the popular rebellion to such an extent that I felt the horror of a dirtied conscience. When people talk about the zaofanpai of the past, they are almost unanimously denunciatory, which makes me see even more clearly the seriousness of the nation's amnesia.[58]

Chen Yinan, a former rebel from Changsha, Hunan, writes in his preface to Yang Zengtai's memoir:

> The rebels' movement in the Cultural Revolution was a history of specific social circumstances of the time combining both passion and suffering. However, because of the authorities' deliberate suppression of the history of the Cultural

Revolution and the propaganda used to demonize the Cultural Revolution zaofanpai as a whole, even today, 38 years after the end of the Cultural Revolution,
many people, especially young people born after the Cultural Revolution, know
the Cultural Revolution zaofanpai only through the distorting propaganda, which
is far from historical truth, if they know anything at all.[59]

Liu Xigong writes in a review of Shi Minggang's book *Shanxi in the Cultural
Revolution*:

About fifty years have passed. Many of those who personally experienced the
Cultural Revolution are older than sixty years; some are in their seventies or
eighties. Those things of the past are carved in their bones and hearts. Yet young
people today know very little about that past; many people have forgotten about
it and official histories have distorted it. Those who personally experienced it
still remember it, understand it, and talk about it, but there is not much time
left. The urgency of time and the demand of history compel the contributors to
this book (who all experienced the CR) to write with an attitude of "salvageing"
[history] and with a strong sense of responsibility to try to leave behind a truthful
history of the Cultural Revolution in Shanxi. . . . The official history institutions
and research institutes in Shanxi, in accordance with the needs and intentions of
the authorities, distort history, cover up the evils, and magnify the "good deeds"
of some politicians who did evil in Shanxi. . . . Those who experienced the Cultural Revolution are witnesses to history. They must speak out without hesitation
in order to reveal the truth and correct the distortions.[60]

Others feel that they had gone through a ludicrous tragicomedy in which
they played the role of willing pawns, but, despite self-ridicule and critical
reflection, the detailed accounts of the passions, energies, and even sufferings of the past convey a subtle sense of pride that they had lived through
epoch-changing times.[61]

Given the political limits on Cultural Revolution discourse, how is it possible that the expression of alternative memories has taken on the scale of a
minor social movement in the past decade? Certainly, it attests to the depth
of the impact of the historical experience on the personal trajectories of the
authors involved. Another reason is that most of them have retired in recent
years. With retirement, there is more time on hand and less concern with
the political risks of writing—a retired person cannot be fired. The most important reason, however, is the appearance of networks of *minjian* Cultural
Revolution researchers inside China, minjian in the sense that they cannot

publish or discuss their research in open and mainstream channels in mainland China. He Shu and Wu Di are two of the most influential ones. The two of them have been long-term researchers on the Cultural Revolution. They have each developed an informal network of researchers, authors, and former participants who share an interest in collecting, preserving, and studying the histories and memories of the Cultural Revolution. In this sense, they are memory entrepreneurs of the Cultural Revolution.

A Chongqing resident, He Shu has devoted himself to the study of the Cultural Revolution in Chongqing and Sichuan. His book on armed fighting in Chongqing was published in Hong Kong in 2010. For many years he has not only encouraged former rebel leaders in Chongqing to write memoirs but has also edited many of them. Wu Di is a retired professor of film studies in Beijing. Wu became interested in researching the Cultural Revolution in Inner Mongolia when he was a sent-down youth there. He published a book on this topic in Hong Kong in 2010.

In 2008 He Shu and Wu Di launched *Ji Yi* (*Remembrance*), a "self-run, irregular, nonprofit electronic publication" (自办的不定期、非赢利的电子刊物) devoted to research on the Cultural Revolution. Michael Schoenhals characterizes it as "an electronic journal edited by Cultural Revolution historians in China in the May 4th tradition of the joint intellectual venture that does not so much put a premium on uniformity of opinion—and even less on common party political affiliation—as on a shared desire to explore a subject without prejudice in the pursuit of historical truth."[62] The semi-underground character of *Remembrance* puts it in the lineage of the unofficial journals during the Democracy Wall, though of course the production and distribution processes are very different now, with computerization and Internet connection.

In 2012 He Shu decided to produce his own journal, titled *Zuo Tian* (*Yesterday*), whose mission is to "save Cultural Revolution memories, collect Cultural Revolution material, exchange related information, and promote Cultural Revolution research."[63] Wu Di continues to produce *Remembrance*. As of this writing, the latest issue of *Remembrance* I received is no. 126, published on March 15, 2015. The latest issue of *Yesterday* is no. 48, published on March 30, 2015. With each of these 174 issues running from 60 to 90 pages, the two journals have together produced over 10,000 pages of documents. Although the contents cover a good variety (e.g., research reports, news items, conference notes, book reviews, and archival documents), the majority consists of "documents of life," such as oral histories, memoirs, diaries. Both *Remembrance* and *Yesterday* carry many special issues, such as on "The Cultural Revolution in Shanxi," "The Cultural Revolution in Guangxi,"

"The Cultural Revolution in Qingdao," "Armed Fighting in Chongqing," "Oral Histories of Students and Teachers in Nanjing University," "Marriage and Dating in the Cultural Revolution," and so forth. Some of these special issues feature the research output of local researchers who, like He Shu and Wu Di, began to study the Cultural Revolution in their own cities or provinces after retirement, suggesting that the networks of Cultural Revolution researchers are a national phenomenon. These researchers combine the hobby of collecting with research and writing and in this way have both discovered and preserved new historical documents and produced a reservoir of oral histories and memoirs. In some cases, as in Chongqing, small circles of researchers and authors were former comrades-in-arms during the Red Guard movement. Common experiences of the past and current interests and circumstances bring them together.

THE DIFFICULTIES OF APOLOGY

I cannot end this chapter without examining the politics of apology. Despite the horrendous consequences of the Cultural Revolution, the Chinese government has never made an official apology to the victims and their families. Instead, Lin Biao, the Gang of Four, and zaofanpai were turned into the scapegoat, with Mao being all but exonerated in the "30 percent bad and 70 percent good" assessment of his life's work.

Thus, when Chen Xiaolu, son of Marshall Chen Yi, issued a personal statement on August 20, 2013, to apologize to his former teachers and classmates for the harms he had done them in the Cultural Revolution, it made international news. Chen was a student leader in Beijing's No. 8 Middle School in the Red Guard movement period. He said that during his term as the head of his school's revolutionary committee some teachers and students were subject to mass criticism and labor reform. For that, he wrote, he was directly responsible and he offered his apologies.

Chen's apology was applauded by many as a good first step, but rebuked by others as opportunistic and insincere. The polarized responses to Chen's apology are symptomatic, as would become even clearer half a year later when an even more contested case of apology happened. On January 12, 2014, former students of the Experimental Middle School of Beijing Teachers University organized a meeting with their former teachers at their alma mater, whose school principal Bian Zhongyun was cruelly beaten to death by girl students on August 5, 1966 (the school was formerly a girls' school). Thirty-one former students, now in their sixties or seventies, attended the meeting, while twenty-three former teachers were present, the oldest among them ninety years of age. At the meeting, two former student leaders, Liu Jin and Song Binbin, read statements of apology for the violence in August 1966. Song Binbin's statement includes the following: "Please allow me to express my eternal condolences and apologies for the late Principal Bian and allow me to express my deep apologies to Hu Zhitao, Liu Zhiping, Mei Shumin, Wang Yubing, and other school leaders and their families for not giving them good protection. These are the pains and regrets of my entire life."[64]

Song Binbin had been embroiled in a long drawn out controversy implicating her as a key culprit of Bian Zhongyun's death, but she had refused to speak up until then. Like Chen Xiaolu, she apologized for failing to protect her teachers in her capacity as a student leader, but she did not plead guilty in the death of Bian. And, as in the case of Chen's apology, Song Binbin's apology prompted broad public response. Trying to sort out the numerous positions in these reactions, Wu Di, the editor of *Remembrance*, which published the transcript of the entire meeting on January 12, 2014, finds that there are five broad types of responses—those who approve of Song's apology, those who disapprove of it, those who condemn it, those who thought that Song's apology is not good enough, and those who use the occasion to promote their own agendas. Within each of the five categories, Wu identifies multiple subtypes.[65]

The public controversy prompted by these two prominent cases shows the difficulties of public apologies. The reason seems to be rooted in the factional conflicts of the past. The primary division in the responses to these public apologies is aligned with old factional politics. Those who disapprove of Chen's and Song's apologies, according to Wu Di, include second-generation reds like Chen and Song, who were likely to be members of the "old Red Guards" in the earlier period of the Red Guard movement. These people fear that Chen's and Song's apologies may implicate other former "old guards" who had committed violence in the Cultural Revolution and prompt a demand for public apologies on a bigger scale. Loyal Maoists, nowadays nicknamed *Mao zuo* (Maoist leftists), disapprove of their apologies, but for different reasons. They do not want such apologies to lead today's younger generation to reject Mao and the Cultural Revolution. But then liberals are also critical of Chen's and Song's apologies, contending that these

CONCLUSION

THIS BOOK OPENS WITH a chapter on factional violence in Chongqing. I showed that in a social world of enchantment and danger, and through the uncertain processes of the Cultural Revolution, a hallowed revolutionary culture became the currency of status and prestige and decisively shaped the behavior of the Red Guards and rebels. Factional violence in Chongqing was the result of youth striving to enact an imagined revolution.

From there, this book traces a history of two transformations, the transformation of the Red Guard generation and of Chinese political culture and popular protest.

As the first cohort socialized in the People's Republic, the Red Guard generation was cultivated as "flowers of the nation" and endowed with the mission of carrying on the Chinese Communist revolution. In 1966, when small groups of highschool students in Beijing launched the Red Guard movement pledging their loyalty to Mao and the revolutionary cause, and when Mao publicly supported these students in his own clarion call to launch the Great Proletarian Cultural Revolution, a political process was set in motion in which students competed to show who were the true revolutionaries. Death being the ultimate proof, the competitive process led inexorably to the radicalization of factionalism and eventually to violence and death.

Ironically, the same process of revolutionary competition also led to political dissent. The passions for revolutionary practice that led to violence were matched by passions for revolutionary theory. It was in the pursuit of revolutionary theory that small groups of youth expressed ideas of dissent, the most radical of which challenged the legitimacy of the Chinese political system by arguing that Chinese communist elites had formed a new privileged class to be overthrown. There began to appear a perceptual shift of the locus of social conflict from between the people and the bourgeoisie to between the people and the privileged class within the party.

The transformation of the Red Guard generation continued during the sent-down period, when the necessities of making a living under harsh rural conditions confronted and eroded their political idealism. In tandem with a growing disillusionment with their political idealism, they came to reaffirm the values of ordinary life and personal interest. They began to appreciate what they had attacked and to doubt what they had held sacred. The fundamental transformation came at the end of the Cultural Revolution and was expressed in the wave of protest from 1976 to 1980. It was a rejection of the sacred symbols of Mao and a hallowed revolutionary culture and with it the expression of aspirations for a new enlightenment.

Ultimately, the historical transformation of the Red Guard generation was full of paradoxes. Launched with a pledge of loyalty to Mao, the Red Guard movement caused untold violence and ended by shaking the beliefs of the true believers. The sent-down experiences tempered this generation further, creating many more skeptics and critics of Chinese politics and society.

For the individuals in these historical processes, a generational transformation was nothing less than a history of perpetual disruption of personal lives. It is hard to imagine what kind of social and psychological traumas individuals had to go through. The proliferation of memory narratives produced by members of the generation attests, perhaps only in a small way, to the depth of their historical experiences.[1]

Amidst these endless disruptions, however, members of the Red Guard generation retain a sense of optimism and hope. For some, the Maoist ideals of a socialist revolution still hold appeal at the beginning of the twenty-first century. Surely, the lingering appeal of past ideals may have a great deal to do with dissatisfactions with contemporary realities, but this does not negate the influences of the past. Generational change, like social change in general, is not a linear process, but is uneven, contradictory, and necessarily complicated by new social conditions.

THE RED GUARD GENERATION AND PROTEST CULTURES

The transformation of the Red Guard generation is intertwined with the transformation of Chinese political culture. As political culture molds people, so people change political culture. The chasm between the political culture at the beginning and end of the Cultural Revolution was the result of the mutual making of culture and people. The desacralization of the holy categories of revolution, class struggle, and Mao and the corresponding ascendance of new values of life, work, family, and the self took place as the Red Guard generation encountered fundamentally different life experiences after being sent down. These new values laid the foundation for new forms of protest from the end of the Cultural Revolution until 1989.

A distinct feature of the Red Guard generation's trajectory is its deep entanglement with political activism and protest. The Red Guard movement that gave its name to this generation was a decisive, liminal experience with long-term influences on the cultures of protest ever since. The spirit of rebellion, however destructive its consequences were, has been an inspiration to protesters at home and abroad in the decades after. Many of the repertoires of collective protest in the Red Guard movement continue to be used, in their original or adapted forms. Outside China, the Red Guard movement influenced the worldwide student radicalism of the 1960s and 1970s and the cultural politics of the new left more broadly.[2]

Yet there are clear disruptions to the history of this political culture. The history of political protest from 1966 to 1989 is like a long funnel. The funnel narrows gradually, screening out all but the most radical members of the Red Guard generation. Thus the number of protesters in 1976 was significantly smaller than in the Red Guard movement and smaller still in the Democracy Wall and democratic campus elections in 1980.

This funneling effect was the result of state suppression. At the end of the Cultural Revolution, zaofanpai leaders were prosecuted, imprisoned, and made the scapegoat of the violence and chaos of the Cultural Revolution. Even after their release from prison, they are watched by the police.[3] The most active members of the Democracy Wall movement were prosecuted too, while the student movement leaders in 1989 were put on the most wanted list and forced into exile if not arrested.

Because of state suppression, the history of political activism in the People's Republic is all but forgotten, if not totally denied. Among the younger cohorts, few know the social conditions of the Red Guard movement or the Tiananmen protests in 1989. Fewer would have even heard of the Democracy Wall movement, the sent-down youth protests in Yunnan, or the democratic elections in universities in 1980. These defining moments in the life course of the Red Guard generation are neither written into history books nor publicly discussed or debated. The result is the suppression and fragmentation of a protest tradition.[4] It is against this background that a study of the Red Guard generation assumes special importance, because this generation provides biographical continuity to a broken tradition.

MEDIATED ACTIVISM, REAL COMMUNITIES

Another important characteristic of the political trajectory of the Red Guard generation is the extent to which its generational identity was defined by media. The Red Guard movement was associated not only with violence but also with the explosion of wall posters and "small papers." In the underground cultural activities during the sent-down period, forbidden books and hand-copied manuscripts were sought after by sent-down youth who also produced large volumes of diaries, letters, verse, and notebooks of famous quotations. The wave of "new enlightenment" protest from 1976 to 1980 was defined first by verse on posters in the April Fifth movement and then by unofficial magazines in the Democracy Wall movement.

The explosion of activist alternative media was a characteristic of student radicalism in the global 1960s. The May Movement in 1968 France, for example, produced large volumes of media documents, as was the case with the American New Left.[5] The most influential research on the media of sixties student radicalism, however, has focused not on alternative media but on how mainstream news media covers social movements. A representative work of this scholarship is Todd Gitlin's landmark study of the "movement-media dance" between American news media and the student and antiwar movements from 1965 to the early 1970s. A key finding in Gitlin's study is that mass media dramatize and simplify social conflict by personifying causes and groups through highly visible leaders, thus compelling activists to seek the limelight of the mass media even when such media exposure and framing may harm the cause. Sociologists have since examined mass media-movement interactions in great detail.[6]

While the interactions between the mass media and social movements are relevant to the history of popular protest in China, and may be becoming increasingly important today,[7] the history of activism from the Red Guard movement to the "new enlightenment" wave was notable not for its interactions with the mainstream mass media but for its intensive use of alternative media forms. In China, if a protest movement is not recognized by the party-state, then the official media would simply ignore it until it can no longer pretend that no protest has happened. At that point, official media may shift to a mode of condemnation, which was what happened to the student movement in 1989.[8] If a movement is recognized as legitimate, as was the case with the Red Guard movement, then movement-media interactions would take on features similar to those in the United States, with the mass media framing the movement in ways consistent with mainstream ideologies and policies.

What was remarkable about the Red Guard press was that it created a parallel universe alongside the official press. In some cities, important newspapers run by Red Guard organizations, such as those run by organizations in Peking and Tsinghua Universities, were as influential as official newspapers. In many other ways, the Red Guard press was nothing but a galaxy of alternative activist media. As I showed in chapter 3, a key function of the Red Guard press was to serve as a weapon of factional warfare. In this respect, the militancy and violence of its language were equaled only by the militancy and violence of the factional battles of their affiliated organizations.

In other ways, however, the Red Guard press resembled the alternative movement media of the student radicals in the global 1960s. The underground press in the United States, according to John McMillian, fostered a sense of community among the radical youth in American society.[9] This was just as true of many Red Guard publications. The bustling editorial office of the *August Fifteenth Battle News* in Chongqing, as recounted by its editor Zhou Ziren, was full of comaraderie.[10] The study groups and theory circles that gathered around Lu Li'an in Wuhan and Yang Xiguang in Changsha, which produced some of the most subversive political pamphlets and posters of that period, similarly demonstrated a strong sense of community and solidarity. It was only within such a community that individuals could trust one another and engage in risky political activities.

Similarly, the cultural pursuits of sent-down youth were as much about community as about knowledge-seeking or politics, and in these they relied on media forms that would appear primitive by our contemporary standards. As I discussed in chapter 5, letter writing, note-taking, copying and circulating hand-copied manuscripts, borrowing books from friends, telling stories—all these seemingly "primitive" forms of media took on special meaning for a generation in the doldrums. The same may be said of the editorial collectives that produced unofficial journals and subversive commentaries in the Democracy Wall movement.[11] In these social practices, media was not just a bare technology. Each media form became a reservoir of historically specific meanings. A letter carried friendship and care, a shared notebook with a hand-copied version of a forbidden novel carried a sense of adventure and trust; singing a love song together was an act of transgression and emotional connection. There were elements of activism in all these acts, but there was also a longing for community and expression. The media forms in these actions were not just used to achieve some other goal, but were integral to a cluster of social practices that would not have existed in the first place without the various forms of media. One might call these practices the making of "real" communities, real in the sense that those involved were likely to know one another, as opposed to imagined communities, whose members can only imagine one another's existence. Yet even "real" communities are mediated, as much as imagined ones are. In short, the mediated activism of the Red Guard generation proves the one-sided nature of some common propositions about the character of face-to-face or mediated communities. For a community is mediated almost by definition. The mediated activism of the Red Guard generation also shows that activism itself cannot be separated from sociality. To the extent that activism is a collective endeavor, it is rooted in sociality and sometimes aims explicitly to build sociality.

POLITICAL CULTURE AND POLITICAL VIOLENCE

The study of factionalism in Chongqing shows the centrality of ideas and ideals to collective violence. The most important factor in influencing participation in the Red Guard movement was not class interests, nor manipulation of the masses by the party leaders, but the sacred culture of revolution that had formed prior to the Cultural Revolution, which had come into full play during it. The case demonstrates that human beings are capable of, and, indeed, may be attracted to, death to prove their devotion to an idea. And the more sacred the idea is made to be, the more deadly it may become.

In a way, the Chinese case merely proves an old theory, one that was articulated, for example, by theorists like Crane Brinton, Michael Walzer, and Barrington Moore in their studies of religious zealots and revolutionary radicals in modern world history.[12] It may be sobering to recall some long-forgotten insights from Brinton's analysis of revolutions, when he writes that "all these revolutions have at their crisis a quality unmistakably puritanical or ascetic or, to use an overworked word, idealistic."[13] He continues: "Our orthodox and successful extremists, then, are crusaders, fanatics, ascetics, men who seek to bring heaven to earth. No doubt many of them are hypocrites, career-seekers masquerading as believers, no doubt many of them climb on the bandwagon for selfish motives. Yet it is most unrealistic to hold that men may not be allowed to reconcile their interests with their ideas."[14]

In this respect, my study of violence in Chongqing may merely have reaffirmed the centrality of ideas to collective violence and collective action more broadly. It is a point, however, that cries out for attention. An earlier tradition of scholarship emphasizes values, ideologies, and beliefs in social movements and revolutions, yet that tradition has been sidelined in the scholarship on social movements and contentious politics in recent decades.[15] This is unfortunate. For the rampant violence in our contemporary world, committed by nation-states, ethnic groups, or terrorist organizations in one form or another, in the name of one sacred slogan or another, cannot be fully understood without understanding the ideas and passions that motivate them.

Naturally, my argument is not that ideas alone can kill. Without a context, even the most sacred ideas would be hollow, empty, and useless. Social and political context provides the soil for sacred ideas to thrive. It is context that makes ideas work. In the Chinese Cultural Revolution the context of domestic threat and international hostility during the cold war era gave the myth of revolution a reality. Across the uncertain and fluid atmospheres of the Cultural Revolution, that context provided Red Guards and rebels with the material for imagining a revolution.

Strangely, however, deadly ideas seem to seek out or create their own context, just as a social and political context seems to take shape precisely at the moment when deadly ideas begin to emerge. There is no shortage of such deadly "coincidences" in modern world history. The cold war was a perfect case, when everywhere there was violence committed in the name of sacred ideas, and when sacralized ideas, such as freedom in some countries and communism in others, had curiously powerful grips on the human imagination. But even the post–cold war era and our own world today remain hostage to such violent tendencies, and the social and political environments for the domination of certain deadly ideas continue to thrive.

The lesson for our contemporary world is twofold: on the one hand, a healthy suspicion of everything our own society holds sacred—indeed, an internal mechanism for the desacralization of our own sacred institutions; on the other, determined efforts to pluralize and diversify the values and experiences of members of our societies.

ORACLE TALES OF THE FUTURE

What is happening today to the revolutionary tradition and experiences that enchanted the Red Guard generation in the 1950s and 1960s? In chapter 7 I explored this question in my analysis of the red culture revival under Xi Jinping. Instead of recapitulating that analysis, let me conclude this book with two stories that I believe point to both the intransigence of past politics and a note of hope for the future.

One story was featured in the news. On February 3, 2015, about one thousand second- and third-generation children of China's communist revolutionary leaders gathered in Beijing to celebrate the Chinese New Year. According to a news story, "the 1,000-seat auditorium was completely full. All the people present at the New Year gathering share the same common identity, which is that they are all posterity of old revolutionaries. Every year, at the beginning of the New Year, they hold such a group gathering to exchange New Year's greetings. Several decades have passed, but they have maintained this fine style left behind by their fathers' generation."[16] This "common identity" of the children of the "old revolutionaries" of the Chinese communist revolution serves as a fitting, albeit troubling, endnote to my account of China's Red Guard generation. The only precedents for such massive public displays of an elite political status were the early Red Guard movement of the "old Red Guards" in 1966. It would not be surprising if, despite the time gap, many of the same individuals were present on both occasions. Considering that Xi Jinping, the representative par excellence of second-generation reds, now rules China with an ideology that is closer to Maoist than any of his predecessors, from Deng Xiaoping through Jiang Zemin and Hu Jintao, one cannot help but lament that, after all, the vows made by the "old Red Guards" in 1968 may have come true. Here again are their words, as remembered by the poet Bei Dao: "In twenty years' time, we will know who the real winners are. . . . Let's see who rules the *tianxia* [all under heaven] in the future."[17]

And we know who rules now.

My other story has different characters.

Ms. Wang is a former sent-down youth I interviewed in August 1999. After many years, we reconnected in 2014 by e-mail while she was visiting her daughter in the United States. When we finally met again in Beijing in March 2015, I was struck by how little she has changed after fifteen years. She is a person with a quiet demeanor and amiable appearance, but extraordinary inner strength. Wang was working for *People's Daily* in 1999. Since retirement, she has devoted herself to a project called Baoquan Tea House, named after the place where the founders of this tea house had been sent down during the Cultural Revolution. Not exactly a tea house, the project runs regular cultural events related to the history of the sent-down movement with a mission to "critically reflect on half a life's road of passion, loss, and hardship" (审视半生激情之路、迷茫之路、艰难之路). At our meeting on March 12, 2015, five of her former sent-down youth friends involved in the tea house project were with her. In the middle of our conversations, I was surprised and moved to hear that they have been conducting a survey of the current conditions of former sent-down youth in Beijing, and the questionnaire they used for their survey was based on the one I designed and used for my own research in 1999. They even gave me a copy of my original questionnaire!

Their project holds "tea parties" at which scholars and former sent-down youth give talks about the sent-down movement. The convening of each such meeting is called "pouring a pot of tea." Not long after I returned to Philadelphia, Ms. Wang e-mailed me to say that their tea house had just poured their twelfth pot of tea, meaning their twelfth gathering. This time, the theme was women's perspectives on the sent-down movement, and the speakers were seven female sent-down youth and one young woman called Liu Lili whose father had been sent down to Heilongjiang. Ms. Wang provided me with links to the video of the talks and the online comments people left on Baoquan Tea House's Internet forum. Especially thought-provoking was the talk given by Liu Lili. Growing up in Heilongjiang as the child of a sent-down father, Liu was seen as a Beijing girl by the locals. When she moved back to Beijing in 2000, however, she was surprised to find she was treated as an outsider. Now, at the age of thirty-five, Liu Lili still wonders where her home is and where her heart belongs. Liu's personal story captures the feeling of disorientation shared by many people from the Red Guard generation.

Ultimately, I was most deeply touched by Ms. Wang herself. Ms. Wang's mother was Bian Zhongyun. At the beginning of the Cultural Revolution, Bian was the vice principal of the elite girls' school attached to Beijing Teachers University. On August 5, 1966, she was beaten to death by Red Guard students in her own school. When I first interviewed Ms. Wang in 1999, she talked only briefly to me about her mother's death. After last year's controversy surrounding the public apologies given by Song Binbin and others, which I discussed in the previous chapter, I have sometimes wondered how she might have responded to those acts of apology. But I did not ask her anything. Seeing how committed she was to her Baoquan Tea House project and to the experiences and stories of her fellow sent-down youth, and realizing how carefully she must have kept my questionnaire from about fifteen years ago, I seem to get an inkling of the deeper meaning of their project. It is a project of preserving and understanding history and memory with a silent bravery, the kind of silent bravery that I have seen in Ms. Wang's attitude toward the history and memory of the traumatic experiences of her own family. Through their own example, Ms. Wang and her friends show how far they have come in the tumultuous journey of China's Red Guard generation, how closely connected to that history they still are, and how courageously they bear the burden of the passions and traumas of the past.

NOTES

NOTES ON DATA

1. On methodological issues in the use of personal narratives and documents of life, see Alwin et al. "The Life History Calendar"; Passerini, *Autobiography of a Generation*; Laslett, "Biography as Historical Sociology" and "Personal Narratives as Sociology"; and Sausmikat, "Resisting Current Stereotypes."

INTRODUCTION

1. He Shu, *Wei Mao zhu xi er zhan*, 349.
2. The English translation is mine, with a few adaptations from the translation published in Tony Barnstone's *Out of the Howling Storm*. See Gu Cheng, "Forever Parted." Unless otherwise noted, all quotations of original Chinese texts cited in this book are my translations into English.
3. It is important to differentiate violence among Red Guard factions from the mass killing studied in Yang Su's book. The mass killing in Guangxi, for example, happened mostly in rural areas and was organized by local authorities after the establishment of "revolutionary committees" as the new power structures. See Su, *Collective Killings in Rural China During the Cultural Revolution.*
4. Mannheim, *Essays on the Sociology of Knowledge*, 303.
5. Ibid. On important empirical studies of generational identities, see, for example, Schuman and Scott, "Generations and Collective Memories." On regional differences of generational identities, see Griffin, "'Generations and Collective Memory' Revisited." On a refinement of the theory of generations with a Bourdieusean perspective, see Eyerman and Turner, "Outline of a Theory of Generations."
6. See statistics on student population in Yang Dongping, *Jian nan de ri chu*, 164.

7. See also *Zhong guo bai ke nian jian,* 536. Michel Bonnin argues that what he refers to as the "Cultural Revolution" generation does not include the rural student population or the university students. Nevertheless, he considers those who experienced the sent-down period but not the Red Guard movement also as part of the Cultural Revolution generation. Thus, for him, the Cultural Revolution generation includes all urban people born approximately between 1947 and 1960, because some born in 1960 were still sent down at the end of the 1970s. See Bonnin, "The 'Lost Generation.'"

8. E.g., Leung, *Morning Sun.*

9. Li, and Schwarcz. "Six Generations of Modern Chinese Intellectuals."

10. Liu Xiaofeng. *Wo men zhe yi dai ren de ai yu pa* [The love and fears of our generation].

11. Liu Xiaomeng et al., *Zhong guo zhi qing shi* [A history of sent-down youths in China]. Bonnin, *The Lost Generation.*

12. Jin Dalu, *Ku nan yu feng liu.*

13. Chan, *Children of Mao.* Mi Hedu. *Hong wei bing zhe yi dai* Ashley and Jiang Mao's Children in the New China.

14. CCP Central Committee. "Resolution on Certain Questions."

15. Chan, "Dispelling Misconceptions About the Red Guard Movement." For the debate on periodization, also see Hao Ping, "Reassessing the Starting-Point of the Cultural Revolution."

16. On France, see Wolin, *The Wind from the East.* On the United States, see Frazier, *The East Is Black.* On Brazil, see Langland, *Speaking of Flowers.*

17. Wolin, *The Wind from the East,* 354, 355.

18. Turner, *The Ritual Process,* 94.

19. For example, see Pye, *The Spirit of Chinese Politics;* Solomon, *Mao's Revolution and the Chinese Political Culture;* Liu, *Political Culture and Group Conflicts in Communist China.*

20. Dittmer, "Thought Reform and Cultural Revolution," 69.

21. Schoenhals, "'Why Don't We Arm the Left?'" MacFarquhar and Schoenhals, *Mao's Last Revolution.*

22. Lee, *The Politics of the Chinese Cultural Revolution;* Chan, Rosen, and Unger, "Students and Class Warfare"; Rosen, *Red Guard Factionalism and the Cultural Revolution.*

23. Perry and Li Xun, *Proletarian Power.*

24. See Dittmer, "Thought Reform and Cultural Revolution"; Perry and Li Xun, "Revolutionary Rudeness"; Schoenhals, *Doing Things with Words in Chinese Politics* and "Proscription and Prescription of Political Terminology"; Lu, *Rhetoric of the Chinese Cultural Revolution.* Kerry Brown's study of the purge of the Inner Mongolian People's Party, however, emphasizes the role of language in the political struggles of the Cultural Revolution, showing how language was "intended to impact on and influence events in the negotiation and campaign to acquire power between various groups in the IMAR." See Brown, *The Purge of the Inner Mongolian People's Party,* 16.

25. Xu Youyou, *Xing xing se se de zao fan.*

26. Wu, *The Cultural Revolution at the Margins.*

27. Walder, *Fractured Rebellion;* Dong and Walder, "Factions in a Bureaucratic Setting."

28. Dutton, *Policing Chinese Politics,* 69.

29. Della Porta, "Violence and the New Left," 383.

30. Ibid.

31. Steinhoff and Zwerman, "Introduction to the Special Issue on Political Violence," 213.
32. Tilly, *The Politics of Collective Violence.*
33. Goodwin, "The Relational Approach to Terrorism," 393.
34. Della Porta, "Violence and the New Left," 390. Also see della Porta, *Social Movements, Political Violence, and the State.*
35. On cultural theories of revolutions and social movements, see Goldstone, "Ideology, Cultural Frameworks, and the Process of Revolution." Hunt, *Politics, Culture, and Class in the French Revolution.* Sewell, "Ideologies and Social Revolutions" and "A Theory of Structure." Polletta, *It Was Like a Fever.*
36. Drake, *The Revolutionary Mystique and Terrorism in Contemporary Italy,* 225.
37. Anderson, *Imagined Communities.*
38. Marvin and Ingle, *Blood Sacrifice and the Nation.*
39. Girard, *Violence and the Sacred.*
40. Hall, *Apocalypse.*
41. Juergensmeyer, *Terror in the Mind of God,* 124.
42. Kaufman, *Modern Hatreds,* 29.
43. Ibid., 28.
44. Tilly, *The Politics of Collective Violence,* 5; Bourdieu, *The Logic of Practice.*
45. Bonnell and Hunt, *Beyond the Cultural Turn.* Alexander, Giesen, and Mast, *Social Performance.*
46. On dramaturgical approaches to collective action, see Snow, Zurcher, and Peters, "Victory Celebrations as Theater"; and Benford and Hunt, "Dramaturgy and Social Movements."
47. Goffman, *The Presentation of Self in Everyday Life.*
48. Thus, as Giesen puts it, "In their most elementary form rituals do not just describe or imitate an order of the external world that is also available by other representations. Instead, the ritual performance is the poesis of order and this order exists only because it is performed. Rituals are constitutive performances in the Searleian sense." See Giesen, "Performing the Sacred," 340.
49. Benford and Hunt, "Dramaturgy and Social Movements."
50. Giesen, "Performing the Sacred," 349.
51. Apter, "Politics as Theatre," 227–28.
52. For sociological studies of the biographical consequences of political activism, see McAdam, *Freedom Summer* and "The Biographical Consequences of Activism." Whalen and Flacks, *Beyond the Barricades*; Klatch, *A Generation Divided.* A major difference in the case of the Red Guard generation is that it experienced more than one decisive historical experience.
53. Weber, *The Theory of Social and Economic Organization,* 367.
54. Ibid., 372.
55. Roth's study of charismatic communities provides support for viewing the Red Guard movement itself as involving an ideological charismatic community whose members, not just leaders, may be regarded as charismatic virtuosi. See Roth, "Socio-Historical Model and Developmental Theory."

56. Kiely, *The Compelling Ideal.*
57. Schwarcz, *The Chinese Enlightenment.*

1. VIOLENCE IN CHONGQING

1. September First Column of the Middle School Red Guards, "Wei you xi sheng duo zhuang zhi" [Death only strengthens the bold resolve], 3.
2. He, "Chongqing wen ge wu dou si nan zhe ming lu" [List of names of people killed in armed fighting in Chongqing].
3. Thus, in the same way that the Protestant ethic led individuals to rational, methodical moneymaking as a road to religious salvation, so a revolutionary ethic led China's Red Guards to factional violence as a means of achieving revolutionary nirvana.
4. Chongqing da xue xiao shi bian ji zu, *Chongqing da xue xiao shi* [History of Chongqing University], 2:126.
5. Ibid.
6. In 1949, with the founding of the PRC, the Central Committee of the Chinese Communist Party established six regional bureaus to provide regional leadership. Sichuan, Yunnan, Guizhou, Xikang, and Chongqing were under the leadership of the Southwest Regional Bureau. The bureau had its headquarters in Chongqing, which was then a direct-governed municipality (*zhi xia shi*).
7. The Sichuan provincial party secretary Liao Zhigao issued a "Decision on the Implementation of the Center's May 16 Circular" that "disclaimed any need to criticize the party generally. Instead, Liao's document borrowed the language and thrust of the prenatal Cultural Revolution and laid emphasis on rooting out incorrect thought among playwrights, scholars, novelists, and journalists." Mathews, "The Cultural Revolution in Szechwan," 98.
8. E.g., see "Sheng wei nei mu yi ban" [A glance at the inside story of the provincial party committee]. *Jinggangshan zhi sheng*, December 3, 1966, in Song, *Xin bian hong wei bing zi liao III*, 14093. Also see Ma, "Di tou ren zui, ge mian xi xin" [Lower my head, change my face and wash my heart].
9. Ma, "Di tou ren zui, ge mian xi xin."
10. Lu, *Sichuan sheng Chongqing Di liu zhong xue xiao xiao zhi* [History of No. 6 Middle School in Chongqing], 21.
11. Wei, "Ren Baige ji qi tong huo shi zen yang zhen ya shan cheng wen hua da ge ming de" [How Ren Baige and his followers suppressed the Cultural Revolution in the mountain city], 4.
12. Li, *Qin li Chongqing da wu dou* [My personal experiences of major armed fighting in Chongqing].
13. "Li Jingquan yan xing lu" [Words and deeds of Li Jingquan], *Jinggangshan zhi sheng*, November 26, 1966, 4. In Song, *Xin bian hong wei bing zi liao III*,14093.
14. Xin, "Chu bu jian cha" [Preliminary self-criticism].
15. "Chongqing da zhong xue xiao Mao Zedong zhu yi hong wei bing zong bu xuan gao cheng li" [Maoism Red Guard headquarters of the universities and middle schools in Chongqing inaugurated], 1. "Li ji xian qi yi ge gu li zi nü can jia Mao Zedong zhu yi

hong wei bing de re chao" [Immediately launch a hot tide to encourage children to join Maoism Red Guards], 1.

16. He, *Wei Mao zhu xi er zhan*, 25–30; Xin, "Chu bu jian cha"; Ma, "Di tou ren zui, ge mian xi xin."

17. This account about the June 18 incident is based on stories published in the anniversary issue of the incident in *August Fifteenth Battle News*, June 18, 1967. See Zhou, ed., *Xin bian hong wei bing zi liao*, 215–16.

18. Ibid. See also Chongqing da xue xiao shi bian ji zu, *Chongqing da xue xiao shi*, 2:127.

19. Ibid., 2:128.

20. Vice mayor Ma Li would later call this strategy "suppressing the revolution by promoting production" (*ya ge ming, cu sheng chan*). See Ma, "Di tou ren zui, ge mian xi xin."

21. On August 15, 1966, four thousand students from Chongqing University, forty students from the Sixth Middle School, and seventy students from the Middle School attached to CTJC gathered in CTJC for a mass meeting. See "815 shi hua" [History of August the Fifteenth], 2.

22. Ibid., 3.

23. Zhou, *Hong wei bing xiao bao zhu bian zi shu* [Personal story of an editor of a Red Guard newspaper], 41–45.

24. In reality, the petitioners would walk for some distance and then take the train to Beijing. Taking "long marches" in emulation of the famous long march of the Red Army was an ascetic practice during the period of *da chuan lian* (大串联) for the "exchange of revolutionary experiences." It became popular after national newspapers reported the feats of fifteen students from the Dalian Mercantile Marine Institute who walked over five hundred miles from Dalian to Beijing in October 1966. The story appears in English in the October 28 (1966) issue of *Peking Review* and has the following descriptions:

> The 15 young revolutionaries set out with a heroic spirit on the morning of August 25. Fearing neither wind nor rain and taking neither vehicles nor boats, they walked over mountains, swam across rivers, and travelled through 21 counties and cities and one reclamation region in Liaoning and Hopei Provinces. They faced the world and braved the storms as they marched over the vast land, they passed a severe test of their revolutionary will.
>
> When they encountered gales and downpours on their journey, they recited together Chairman Mao's poem: "The Red Army fears not the trials of a distant march; To them a thousand mountains, ten thousand rivers are nothing. . . . " In marching against wind and rain, they also loudly sang We Love Chairman Mao Most and other revolutionary songs. When big rivers cut across their route, they encouraged each other with the great examples of Chairman Mao swimming in the Yangtse and his majestic poem "I care not that the wind blows and the waves beat; It is better than idly strolling in a courtyard." They swam across the rivers, and said: "Chairman Mao swims in the Yangtse even at the age of 73. We are New China's future seamen who should all the more be tested in great storms.

25. "Wang Li, Qi Benyu jie jian Chongqing shi zhong xue sheng hong wei bing bei shang gao zhuang tuan de jiang hua" [Speeches given by Wang Li and Qi Benyu at the

meetings with the gao zhuang delegation of middle school students from Chongqing], in *Hong wei bing zi liao xu bian*, 1992, 4:2374.

26. Ibid.

27. Ibid., 2376.

28. Radio transmitters evoked the image of enemy agents secretly communicating with their commanders. According to *Chongqing shi zhi* (vol. 14), within two years after Chongqing was taken over in 1949 by the new PRC government, the Chongqing public security authorities cracked many cases of secret agents planted by the Jiang Jieshi regime and captured eight radio transmitters used by these agents. See *Chongqing shi zhi* [Gazette of Chongqing city], 14:29.

29. Tao, "Tao Zhu tong zhi jiang hua" [Comrade Tao Zhu's speech], 4:2294.

30. Zhou, *Hong wei bing xiao bao zhu bian zi shu*, 20.

31. Zhou Ziren's diary contains detailed descriptions of the street demonstrations on December 6 and the memorial service on the following day. See Zhou, *Hong wei bing xiao bao zhu bian zi shu*.

32. Ibid., 23.

33. White, *Policies of Chaos*.

34. Joint interview conducted by author and Sun Peidong, March 12, 2015, Beijing.

35. *August Fifteenth Battle News*, January 21, 1967, 1.

36. He, *Wei Mao zhu xi er zhan*, 150.

37. *August Fifteenth Battle News*, May 26, 1967. In Song, *Xin bian hong wei bing zi liao III*, 1625.

38. This was the pattern in border and frontier provinces like Tibet, Xinjiang, Inner Mongolia, Guangdong, and Guangxi. The reason for this, according to Xu Youyu, was that the central elites in Beijing did not want to see serious social disturbances in border regions. For reasons of national security, central leaders refrained from taking drastic steps to destroy the conservatives who were backed by local party and military leaders. See Xu, *Xing xing se se de zao fan*, 63.

39. Ibid., 101.

40. He, *Wei Mao zhu xi er zhan*, 110–13.

41. Xu, *Xing xing se se de zao fan*, 115–21.

42. "Jian jue an zhao Mao zhu xi de gan bu zheng ce ban shi" [Resolutely follow Chairman Mao's cadre policy], *August Fifteenth Battle News*, March 3, 1967, in Song, *Xin bian hong wei bing zi liao III*, 1584.

43. Huang, *Wo zen me cheng le Jiang Qing de gan nü er* [How did I become Jiang Qing's goddaughter], 133.

44. Li Zimao, "You guan wu dou de yi xie si kao" [Some thoughts on armed fighting].

45. *October 5 Storm*, February 20, 1967.

46. "Ge lian hui bi sheng" [The United Revolutionary Committee will surely triumph!].

47. Zhou, diary entry March 6, 1967, in *Hong wei bing xiao bao zhu bian zi shu*, 74.

48. From late February to the end of March 1967, however, a nationwide crackdown on radicals took place as a result of party policies from the top known as the "February suppression of counterrevolutionaries." With the support of the local military, the August Fifteenth in Chongqing went after the "Smashers" relentlessly, leading to

the arrest and persecution of individuals and the disbanding of organizations affiliated with the Smashers. By April 1, 1967, when this crackdown was finally halted,
again by fiat of a policy statement from the top leadership, 2,253 people had been
arrested, 36 organizations were disbanded by public security authorities, 82 organizations were "smashed" by other organizations, and 146 organizations had voluntarily terminated themselves. See He, *Wei Mao zhu xi er zhan*, 149–50. The halting
of the crackdown led to the release of the arrested personnel and the regrouping of
the disbanded organizations. Reborn from the suppression, the Smashers launched
counterattacks against the United Committee with new determination.

The experiences of suffering from suppression sealed the split between August
Fifteenth and the Smashers and exacerbated the violent confrontations that would
soon follow. But the split between the two camps continued to be defined by ideological differences. Indeed, the experiences of suffering deepened and magnified
these ideological differences. Thus the sacred code of revolution continued to be
a powerful influence on factionalism. In fact, it became more fatal and uncompro-
mising, as it was now given a new layer of reality by the experiences of political
oppression.

49. According to a story published on June 29, 1967, in *Angry Brows* (横眉), a tabloid edited by the August Fifteenth faction, its opposing faction, Fight to the End, had a
military division with the following units: 1. reconnaissance unit, 2. communication
unit, 3. explosion unit, 4. commando unit, 5. cover unit, 6. medical unit, and 7. security unit. See "Fan ge ming wu zhuang bao dong de zui e ji hua" [The evil plan for a
counterrevolutionary armed riot], in Zhou, *Xin bian hong wei bing zi liao*, 8574. August
Fifteenth had two military units, with the code names Unit 301 and Unit 302. Unit
301 was responsible for off-campus combat; Unit 302 was responsible for on-campus
combat and security.

50. He, *Wei Mao zhu xi er zhan*, 190.

51. Ibid., 197.

52. Ibid., 203.

53. Ibid., 206.

54. "Chongqing shi di fang zhi bian zuan wei yuan hui," 410.

55. Hung, *Mao's New World*.

56. Schoenhals, "'Why Don't We Arm the Left?,'" 286.

57. Based on a story published in the inaugural issue of *Shan cheng nu huo* on August 14, 1967.

58. The number of casualties is based on He, *Wei Mao zhu xi er zhan*, 197. He surmises that
the two deaths on the side of August Fifteenth might have been caused by friendly
fire due to the confusion of the situation.

59. Mao, *Quotations from Chairman Mao Tse-tung*, 182.

60. Ibid., 173–74.

61. On the history of the *Little Red Book*, see Leese, *Mao Cult*. On religious aspects of the
Mao cult, see Landsberger, "Mao as the Kitchen God" and "The Deification of Mao."

62. *August Fifteenth Battle News*, June 16, 1967, 2.

63. Apter and Saich, *Revolutionary Discourse in Mao's Republic*, 69.

64. Zhou, *Hong wei bing xiao bao zhu bian zi shu,* 141.

65. Ibid.,145.

66. "Li Shengpin lie shi gei yi wei peng you de yi shu" [A will left to a friend by martyr Li Shengpin], *August Fifteenth Battle News,* August 8, (1967), 3. In Song, *Xin bian hong wei bing zi liao III,* 1668.

67. Wu, *Wu Mi ri ji xu bian,* 8:173–74.

68. He, "Chongqing wen ge wu dou si nan zhe ming lu."

69. Qian, "The Way Our Generation Imagined the World."

2. FLOWERS OF THE NATION

1. Source omitted to protect anonymity.

2. Sang, "Memories for the Future."

3. Connerton, *How Societies Remember.*

4. Kleinman and Kleinman, "How Bodies Remember," 716–17.

5. There is a long-time debate about whether the present or the past has more influence on people's memories. A view that emphasizes the importance of the present is considered to be a presentist and constructionist perspective, whereas the view that stresses the persistent influence of past experiences is sometimes called the cultural perspective. For a review of the debate, see Schwartz and Kim, "Introduction."

6. For a historical analysis of Mao's concern with the dangers of revisionism, see Esherick, "The 'Restoration of Capitalism' in Mao's and Marxist Theory."

7. This is an incomplete but otherwise accurate recall of a text, not from the Nine Commentaries, but from the so-called Anterior Seven Commentaries. The Anterior Seven Commentaries were seven polemics against Soviet revisionism (but without naming the Soviet Union) published prior to the publication of the Nine Commentaries. See Cui, *Wo suo qin li de zhong su da lun zhan* [The Sino-Soviet Polemics I personally experienced]. The English translation quoted here is from "More on the Differences Between Comrade Togliatti and Us," *Peking Review* 6, nos. 10, 11 (March 15, 1963): 56–57. The complete original text, from the same translation in *Peking Review,* is as follows:

> Friends, comrades! If you are men enough, step forward! Let each side in the debate publish all the articles in which it is criticized by the other side, and let the people in our own countries and the whole world think over and judge who is right and who is wrong. That is what we are doing, and we hope you will follow our example. We are not afraid to publish everything of yours in full. We publish all the "masterpieces" in which you rail at us. Then, in reply we either refute them point by point, or refute their main points. Sometimes we publish your articles without a word in answer leaving the readers to judge for themselves. Isn't that fair and reasonable? You, modern revisionist masters! Do you dare to do the same? If you are men enough, you will. But having a guilty conscience and an unjust case, being fierce of visage but faint of heart, outwardly as tough as bulls but inwardly as timid as mice, you will not dare. We are sure you will not dare. Isn't that so? Please answer!

8. Qin, "Chen zhong de lang man" [Heavy-burdened romance], 286.

9. Xu, "Wo de wen ge jian wen" [What I saw and heard in the Cultural Revolution].

10. Jin Shan, "Wu shi nian qian ying xiang le yi dai ren de fan su jiu ping" [The anti-Soviet Nine Commentaries that influenced a generation of people fifty years ago].

11. Zhong, "'Long Live Youth' and the Ironies of Youth and Gender," 159. Also see Denton, "Model Drama as Myth."

12. Hong, "The Evolution of China's War Movie in Five Decades."

13. Zhang, Zhong guo shao nian er tong dian ying shi lun [A historical study of children's films in China], 37.

14. Hong, "The Evolution of China's War Movie in Five Decades."

15. Wang, The Sublime Figure of History, 125.

16. Ibid., 147–48.

17. Zhou, Hong wei bing xiao bao zhu bian zi shu, 162–63.

18. E-mail communication, December 22, 2014.

19. See Chen, "'Playing in the Dirt.'"

20. Source omitted to protect author anonymity.

21. He Shu, Wei Mao zhu xi er zhan.

22. Source: http://blog.sina.com.cn/s/blog_48fe5da801000mct.html (accessed December 28, 2014). Also see Hai Yan [Storm petrel], special issue in commemoration of the death of Martyr Zhu Qingfang, June 24, 1968.

23. Chen, "Growing up with Posters in the Maoist Era," 109.

24. Cai, "Shen sheng hui yi" [Sacred memory], 254.

25. Huang, "'Jie wa' de wu dou" [The armed fighting of street kids].

26. Both Little Soldier Zhang Gar and Li Xiangyang were popular heroes in the war films of the time. See Huang, "'Jie wa' de wu dou."

27. Xie, "Wo zai wen hua da ge ming zhong de jing li" [My experiences in the Cultural Revolution], 145.

28. Ibid., 148.

29. Liu, "That Holy Word, 'Revolution,'" 309.

30. Apter and Saich, Revolutionary Discourse in Mao's Republic.

31. Perry, Anyuan, 241.

32. Although I focus on the common core of this revolutionary tradition, this does not presume that the Chinese revolutionary tradition was uncontested in the process of its construction. Perry's work on the construction of the revolutionary tradition in Anyuan provides an illuminating example of the contestations in this process. See Perry, Anyuan.

33. Hung, Mao's New World.

34. Hobsbawm and Ranger, The Invention of Tradition, 9.

35. Wu, Remaking Beijing; Lee, "The Charisma of Power and the Military Sublime."

36. Cheng, Creating the New Man.

37. Townsend, The Revolutionization of Chinese Youth, 46.

38. Ridley, Godwin, and Doolin. The Making of a Model Citizen in Communist China; Cheng, Creating the New Man.

39. Cited in Scott, Chinese Popular Literature and the Child, 272.

40. Ibid.

41. Townsend, The Revolutionization of Chinese Youth, 49.

42. Ridley, Godwin, and Doolin, *The Making of a Model Citizen in Communist China,* 186.
43. There is no reason to assume that such an ideal person ever existed. However, interview data suggest that many youth had taken these values to heart. See Solomon, *Mao's Revolution and the Chinese Political Culture.*
44. Sheridan, "The Emulation of Heroes," 60, 61.
45. Ibid., 71.
46. See MacFarquhar, *The Origins of the Cultural Revolution,* vol. 2: *The Great Leap Forward* for a detailed study of one of these catastrophic projects.
47. Mi, *Hong wei bing zhe yi dai,* 76.
48. Qian, "The Way Our Generation Imagined the World," 525–26.
49. Ibid., 528.
50. Mao's theory of permanent revolution was spelled out in a speech delivered on January 28, 1958, and publicized by Liu Shaoqi in May 1958. The idea of permanent revolution had its origin in Marx and Trotsky. For Trotsky, who had the most elaborate formulation of the concept before Mao, the revolution would be "permanent" in two respects. As Meisner puts it, "First, a revolution in an economically backward land could not be confined to any distinct 'bourgeois-democratic' phase, but would proceed 'uninterrupted' to socialism. Second, a revolution could not be confined to a single nation; the survival of a revolution in a backward country was dependent on the timely outbreak of socialist revolutions in the advanced countries for only in an international revolutionary context could the permanence of the revolutionary process be maintained." See Meisner, *Mao's China and After,* 194.

Fundamentally different from Trotsky's view, Mao's theory of permanent revolution was that the whole revolutionary process, until the realization of communism, is characterized by an endless series of social contradictions and struggles. In his *Revolutionary Immortality,* Robert Lifton offers a psychohistorical explanation of Mao's theory and practice of permanent revolution. Commenting on the ongoing Cultural Revolution, Lifton wrote:

> much of what has been taking place in China recently can be understood as a quest for revolutionary immortality. By revolutionary immortality I mean a shared sense of participating in permanent revolutionary fermentation, and of transcending individual death by "living on" indefinitely within this continuing revolution. . . . Central to this point of view is the concept of symbolic immortality I have described in earlier work: of man's need, in the face of inevitable biological death, to maintain an inner sense of continuity with what has gone on before and what will go on after his own individual existence.

See Lifton, *Revolutionary Immortality,* 7.
51. MacFarquhar, *The Origins of the Cultural Revolution,* vol. 2: *The Great Leap Forward,* 17; Shen and Xia, "Hidden Currents During the Honeymoon."
52. Chen, *Mao's China and the Cold War,* 174.
53. MacFarquhar, *The Origins of the Cultural Revolution,* vol. 1: *Contradictions Among the People,* 314.
54. Ibid.
55. Mao, *Quotations from Chairman Mao Tse-Tung,* 165.

56. Shen and Xia, "Hidden Currents During the Honeymoon."
57. Perry, *Anyuan,* 157.
58. Chen, *Mao's China and the Cold War;* Tucker, *The China Threat.*
59. Bo, *Ruo gan zhong da jue ce yu shi jian de hui gu.*
60. MacFarquhar, *The Origins of the Cultural Revolution,* vol. 2: *The Great Leap Forward,* 264.
61. Ibid., 368.
62. MacFarquhar, *The Origins of the Cultural Revolution,* vol. 3: *The Coming of the Cataclysm,* 371.

3. THEORY AND DISSENT

1. Song and Sun, *Wen hua da ge ming he ta de yi duan si chao* [Heterodox thoughts during the cultural revolution].
2. Berlinerblau, "Toward a Sociology of Heresy, Orthodoxy, and Doxa."
3. For an English translation of the full text, see *Peking Review,* no. 33, August 12, 1966.
4. After Mao died and Deng came to power, Deng put forward "four basic principles" to uphold in 1979: "Uphold the socialist road, uphold proletarian dictatorship, uphold the leadership of the Communist Party, uphold Marxism–Leninism–Mao Zedong Thought." The similarity between these principles and the Cultural Revolution orthodoxy is only too clear. Although Deng was denounced as a capitalist roader during the Cultural Revolution, after he came back to power, he upheld basically the same orthodoxy as Mao. This "coincidence" is most ironic, because Deng completely rejected the Cultural Revolution. Yet it is most revealing about the nature of government in China: Those in power cannot reject China's political system without undermining their own position. Thus to strengthen their position, they will strengthen the system.
5. According to Lee, the Cultural Revolution followed a set of rules of the game, which could not be violated. He lists six of them, one of which being that no one should "openly challenge the raison d'être of the Cultural Revolution." See Lee, *The Politics of the Chinese Cultural Revolution,* 343–44.
6. Xu, "Yi duan si chao he hong wei bing de si xiang zhuan xiang" [Heterodox thoughts and changes in the thinking of Red Guards], 268.
7. Walder, "Cultural Revolution Radicalism," 59.
8. Wang, "'New Trends of Thought' on the Cultural Revolution," 198.
9. Ibid., 214.
10. Zheng, "'Wen hua da ge ming' de ba li gong she qing jie" [The Paris Commune Complex in the 'Great Cultural Revolution].
11. Jin Dalu, "Shanghai wen ge yun dong zhong de 'qun zhong bao kan'" ["Mass newspapers" in Shanghai's Cultural Revolution].
12. Zhong gong zhong yang guan yu bao zhi wen ti de tong zhi (Zhongfa 67, no. 9).
13. Song, *Xin bian hong wei bing zi liao II.*
14. Twenty volumes were published in 1975, eight volumes in 1980 and 1992 respectively, and twenty volumes in 1999. These fifty-six volumes contain 1,564 titles of Red Guard publications. In 2001, forty volumes of Red Guard newspapers in the

Beijing area were published, which contain 456 titles. In 2005, fifty-two new volumes were published, containing 1,135 titles. Altogether, these Red Guard publications contain a total of 3,155 titles. Different issues of the same title may appear in volumes published in different years. Thus some titles may have been counted more than once.

15. Chongqing xin wen zhi bian ji bu, n.d., 132.
16. Chengdu shi di fang zhi bian cuan wei yuan hui, ed., *Chengdu shi zhi*, 108.
17. Jin, "Shanghai wen ge yun dong zhong de 'qun zhong bao kan,'" 3.
18. "Decision of the Central Committee of the Chinese Communist Party Concerning the Great Proletarian Cultural Revolution," 8.
19. Wang, "Mao zhu xi zui zhu yi zaofanpai bao zhi."
20. Song, *Xin bian hong wei bing zi liao III*, 277.
21. Jin, "Shanghai wen ge yun dong zhong de 'qun zhong bao kan,'" 3.
22. *Dou pi zhan bao*, July 5, 1967, in Song, *Xin bian hong wei bing zi liao III*, 4062.
23. Xu, *Da yue jin yun dong zhong de zheng zhi chuan bo* [Political communication in the Great Leap Forward campaign].
24. Gao, *Hong tai yang shi zen yang sheng qi de* [How did the red sun rise].
25. Mao, *Selected Works of Mao Tse-Tung*, 485.
26. *Xin Nankai*, May 22, 1967, in Song, *Xin bian hong wei bing zi liao III*, 19559.
27. Ibid.
28. Yu, *Wei bei wei gan wang you guo* [Dare not forget worrying about the country even in a lowly position], 82.
29. Schoenhals, *China's Cultural Revolution*, 60.
30. Lee calls it the "December black winds." See Lee, *The Politics of the Chinese Cultural Revolution*, 125. In their *Wen hua da ge ming he ta de yi duan si chao*, Song and Sun call it the "November black winds."
31. Xin Beida 1210 zhan dou dui, "Chan chu Yilin-Dixi de da du cao" [Uproot Yilin-Dixi's big poisonous weed].
32. Pi pan "hu shan xing" lian luo zhan, "Che di qing suan Beijing da xue 'Jing Gang Shan,' 'Hong Lian Jun' de bie dong dui—'Hu Shan Xing' de fan ge ming zui xing." [Thoroughly settle account with the counterrevolutionary crime of "To the Tiger Mountain"—a special action team associated with Peking University's "Jinggang Mountain' and 'Red Alliance Army"]. *Xin Bei Da*, February 1, 1967, 1–4.
33. White, *Policies of Chaos*.
34. For a discussion of these class labels, see Unger, *Education Under Mao*.
35. Ya, "Out of the Conscience of an Intellectual"; Mu, "Si shui liu nian" [Years flowing by like water].
36. For more on the original essays written by Yu Luoke and recollections by his friends and family after the Cultural Revolution, see essays in Xu, Ding, and Xu, *Yu Luoke*.
37. My account of the founding of the April Third and April Fourth factions is based on Bu, "'Wen hua da ge ming' zhong Beijing de '4.3' he '4.4' pai" [The April Third and April Fourth factions in Beijing during the "Great Cultural Revolution"].
38. While two violent conflicts happened in April and May respectively, the violence got worse in the months of July, August, and September. See ibid.

39. Zhao Zhenkai. "Zou jin bao feng yu" [Walking into the storm], 251.
40. CCP Central Committee, "Decision of the Central Committee of the Chinese Communist Party Concerning the Great Proletarian Cultural Revolution," 8.
41. Song, *Xin bian hong wei bing zi liao III*, 19909.
42. Yang, "'Zhongguo xiang he chu qu?' da zi bao shi mo" [The story behind the big-character poster 'Whither China?'].
43. Yang, "Whither China?," 184.
44. Ibid., 194.
45. Unger, "Whither China?," 23–24.
46. Wu, *The Cultural Revolution at the Margins*.
47. Mao, *Selected Works of Mao Tse-Tung*, 1:26.
48. My own translation; original in Song and Sun, *Wen hua da ge ming he ta de yi duan si chao*.
49. Unger, "Whither China?," 27.
50. Ibid., 31.
51. Lu, *Yang tian chang xiao*, 202.
52. Ibid., 203.
53. Xu Xiao, *Ban sheng wei ren*, 147–48.

4. ORDINARY LIFE

1. Mao, "Dialogues with Responsible Persons"; also see Russo, "The Conclusive Scene."
2. Educated Youth Office of the State Council, "Er shi wu nian lai zhi qing gong zuo de hui gu yu zong jie" [A review and summary of the work on educated youth in the past twenty-five years].
3. London and London, "China's Lost Generation," 18.
4. Ibid. A sociological study conducted at about the same time makes a similar point, noting especially that sent-down youth "read with eagerness any underground literature they could lay hands on." See Chan, *Children of Mao*, 187.
5. Weber, *Economy and Society*, 2:1197.
6. Taylor, *Sources of the Self*, 211.
7. Ibid., 211–12.
8. Ibid., 213.
9. De Bary, *Self and Society in Ming Thought* and *Learning for One's Self*; Tu, *Humanity and Self-Cultivation*; Elvin, "Between the Earth and Heaven."
10. Lin, "The Suicide of Liang Chi"; Alitto, *The Last Confucian*; Chien, *Chiao Hung and the Restructuring of Neo-Confucianism in the Late Ming*; Chang, *Chinese Intellectuals in Crisis*.
11. Metzger, *Escape from Predicament*, 30–31.
12. Quoted in Lo, *K'ang Yu-wei*, 41.
13. Gao and Yan, *1966–1976*, 40.
14. According to Liu Xiaomeng, from 1950 to 1966 altogether 41.9 million elementary school graduates could not enter junior high, 8.01 million junior high students could not go on to senior high, and 1.37 million senior high students could not go on to college. The total number was 51.2 million. During the same period, employment

increased by 35.95 million. Thus there were about 15 million students waiting for employment. See Liu et al., *Zhong guo zhi qing shi,* 859.

15. The editorial drew criticisms from students, parents, and teachers. In several cases students even launched class strikes protesting against this policy. See Ding, *Zhong guo zhi qing shi,* 93–94.
16. Ding, *Zhong guo zhi qing shi,* 107.
17. Du, *Feng chao dang luo.*
18. Liu et al., *Zhong guo zhi qing shi,* 863.
19. For histories of the sent-down movement, see Du, *Feng chao dang luo;* Liu et al., *Zhong guo zhi qing shi.* For an early English-language analysis, see Bernstein, *Up to the Mountains and Down to the Villages.* For recent studies, see Pan, *Tempered in the Revolutionary Furnace;* and Bonnin, *The Lost Generation.*
20. Liu et al., *Zhong guo zhi qing shi.*
21. Mi, *Hong wei bing zhe yi dai* [A generation known as Red Guards], 153–54.
22. Ibid., 253.
23. Yang, "The Liminal Effects of Social Movements."
24. Hong, "Dujiashan shang de xin she yuan" [A new farmer in Dujiashan village].
25. Ding, *Zhong guo zhi qing shi,* 444.
26. Liu et al., *Zhong guo zhi qing shi,* 163.
27. Bernstein, *Up to the Mountains and Down to the Villages,* 50.
28. Bonnin, *The Lost Generation.*
29. Focus group interview, March 13, 2015, Beijing.
30. Liu et al., *Zhong guo zhi qing shi,* 287.
31. Ibid., 294.
32. Shi, *Zhi qing ri ji xuan bian* [Collected diaries by educated youth], 38.
33. Ibid., 45.
34. Ibid.
35. Mi, *Hong wei bing zhe yi dai,* 273.
36. Shi, *Zhi qing ri ji xuan bian,* 57.
37. Personal correspondence, March 30, 2000.
38. For example, a local Red Guard newspaper published on November 14, 1967 listed "20 crimes of being selfish," which claims that "selfishness" is the source of all evils. See Song, *Xin bian hong wei bing zi liao III,* 14612.
39. Jin, *Ku nan yu feng liu,* 117.
40. Ibid.
41. Shi, *Zhi qing shu xin xuan bian,* 61.
42. Jin, *Ku nan yu feng liu,* 123.
43. Mi, *Hong wei bing zhe yi dai,* 314–15.
44. Shi, *Zhi qing shu xin xuan bian,* 162.
45. Ibid., 91.
46. Xin, *Sui yue liu hen* [Remains of the day], 217.
47. Shi, *Zhi qing ri ji xuan bian,* 25.
48. Ibid., 185–86.
49. Ridley, Godwin and Doolin, *The Making of a Model Citizen in Communist China.*
50. Liu, *Political Culture and Group Conflicts in Communist China.*

51. Mi, *Hong wei bing zhe yi dai,* 297.
52. Interview, June 21, 1999, New York.
53. That the category of "the people" is always a stake of political struggle is of course well known and is not confined to Mao's China. For a sociological discussion, see Pierre Bourdieu, "The Uses of the 'People.'"
54. Interview, June 21, 1999, New York.
55. Mi, *Hong wei bing zhe yi dai,* 339–40.
56. *Ta lu ti hsia k'an wu hui pien* [Collection of mainland underground publications], 15:19.
57. For a general study of the reform, see Baum, *Burying Mao.* For studies of how state reform policies transformed urban life, see Ikels, *The Return of the God of Wealth.* For studies of bottom-up sources of economic reform, see Coase and Wang, *How China Became Capitalist;* and Tsai, *Capitalism Without Democracy.*
58. Parish, *Chinese Rural Development;* Kelliher, *Peasant Power in China;* Walder, *Zouping in Transition.*
59. White, *Unstately Power.*
60. Liu et al., *Zhong guo zhi qing shi,* 651.
61. Ibid., 680, 686.
62. Ibid., 728.
63. Ibid., 731.
64. Zhang, "1978."
65. Yang, "'We want to go home!'"
66. Gold, "Urban Private Business and Social Change."
67. Liu et al., *Zhong guo zhi qing shi,* 811.
68. By semiprivate business, I refer mainly to what is called the *min ban qi ye* (collective-run enterprises). Thomas Gold defines them as "cooperatives formed by young people waiting for work who raised their own funds." See Gold, "Urban Private Business and Social Change," 162. By private business, I refer to what Solinger calls practices of the "petty private sector." This sector consists of "the very small-scale commercial activity that individual peasants, peddlers, young people without state-sector jobs, and retired persons engage in at fairs, on city streets, or as itinerant hawkers in the rural areas." See Solinger, *China's Transition from Socialism,* 250.
69. E.g., see Hershkovitz, "The Fruits of Ambivalence"; Solinger, *China's Transition from Socialism,* 233.
70. Liu et al., *Zhong guo zhi qing shi,* 866.
71. Mi, *Hong wei bing zhe yi dai,* 362.
72. Solinger, *China's Transition from Socialism,* 250.
73. Tsai, *Capitalism Without Democracy.*
74. Interview, April 25, 1998, New York.

5. UNDERGROUND CULTURE

1. On the New Culture movement and the May Fourth movement, see Schwarcz, *The Chinese Enlightenment* and Mitter, *A Bitter Revolution.*
2. Interview, July 11, 1999, Beijing.

3. On the underground cultural activities during the Cultural Revolution, see Link, "Hand-copied Entertainment Fiction"; Crevel, "Underground Poetry in the 1960s and 1970s;" Emerson, "The Guizhou Undercurrent"; Clark, *The Chinese Cultural Revolution;* and Zhu, "Si xiang shi shang de shi zong zhe" [The missing thinkers in intellectual history].

4. See, for example, Shi, *Zhi qing shu xin xuan bian* [Collected letters by educated youth] and *Zhi qing ri ji xuan bian* [Collected diaries by educated youth]; and Xu, *Min jian shu xin* [Letters from among the people].

5. One letter collected in *Min jian shu xin* runs up to ten pages in print. See Xu, *Min jian shu xin*, 223–33.

6. See, for example, Bei Bao, *The August Sleepwalker;* Morin, *The Red Azalea;* and Barnstone, *Out of the Howling Storm.*

7. This includes the "misty poetry" of the late 1970s and 1980s as well as the less "artistic" amateur works that were published in the 1990s more as historical records than as works of art.

8. The CD album of sent-down youth songs, titled *Zhi qing lao ge* [Old sent-down youth songs], was issued in 1998 in Guangzhou.

9. Link, "Hand-copied Entertainment Fiction."

10. Zhou Lijing, "Zhang zai chuang ba shang de shu" [Trees growing out of scars].

11. Internal publications" (*nei bu shu ji*) were published for a limited readership, usually cadres and professional researchers. From 1949 to 1979, 18,301 titles of "internal publications" were published. See Zhong hua ban ben tu shu guan, *Quan guo nei bu fa xing tu shu zong mu.*

12. Zhang, "Wo liao jie de 'huang pi shu' chu ban shi mo."

13. See Ren, *Sheng si bei ge* [A song of life and death].

14. Yang, *Wen hua da ge ming zhong de di xia wen xue* [Underground literature during the Cultural Revolution].

15. Yin, *Shi zong zhe de zu ji* [Footprints of the missing].

16. Bakhtin, *Rabelais and His World;* Stallybrass and White, *The Politics and Poetics of Transgression.*

17. Scott, *Domination and the Arts of Resistance.*

18. Shi, *Zhi qing shu xin xuan bian* [Collected letters by educated youth], 114.

19. Zhang, " 'qing shu' yi jiu" [Memories of "affectionate letters"], 104.

20. Shu, "Sheng huo, shu ji yu shi" [Life, books, and poetry].

21. Xu, *Min jian shu xin.*

22. Shi, *Zhi qing shu xin xuan bian,* 337.

23. The three collections are: Shi, *Zhi qing shu xin xuan bian*; Lu, *Sheng shi zhen shi de* [Life is real]; and Xin, *Wu hui nian hua* [Years of no regret].

24. Shi, *Zhi qing shu xin xuan bian,* 18.

25. Ibid., 47.

26. Ibid., 38.

27. Dang dai zhong guo cong shu bian ji bu, *Dang dai zhong guo de chu ban shi ye* [The publishing industry in contemporary China], 2:400–2.

28. Ibid., 2:403.

29. Dang dai zhong guo cong shu bian ji bu, *Dang dai zhong guo de chu ban shi ye* [The publishing industry in contemporary China], 1:78.

30. Ibid., 1:429.

31. Ibid., 1:431.

32. Liu and Shi, *Xin zhong guo chu ban wu shi nian ji shi* [Chronicles of fifty years of publishing in new China], 140.

33. Stealing and borrowing were apparently not the only means of obtaining forbidden books. In some cities, especially in the 1970s, there were black markets where such books were traded, but the scale of these markets was small and, in any case, books on black markets were beyond the means of the poor youths. In Shanghai, for example, a copy of *Anna Karenina* with a cover price of 3.8 yuan sold for 10 yuan on the black market. See *Dang dai zhong guo de chu ban shi ye*, 2:429.

34. Zhu, *Lao san jie cai fang shou ji* [Notes on interviews with the old three classes], 216.

35. Ibid., 216.

36. Bei and Li, *Qi shi nian dai* [The seventies], 170.

37. Zhu, *Lao san jie cai fang shou ji,* 213.

38. Jin, *Dong fang shi ri tan,* 187.

39. Wang, "Qiu zhi qu shi," 97.

40. Hao, "*Liu dong de shu*" [Mobile books], 21.

41. Ibid., 22–23.

42. Several essays in a volume edited by Liao Yiwu recount stories about small circles of underground salons in Beijing. See Liao, *Chen lun de sheng dian* [The fallen altar]. The products (especially poems) of these underground circles are dealt with in Yang, *Wen hua da ge ming zhong de di xia wen xue;* and Yin, *Shi zong zhe de zu ji.*

43. Because access to internal publications was limited to high-level cadres, children of such families were more likely to have access.

44. Mi, *Hong wei bing zhe yi dai,* 297.

45. Wang, "Qiu zhi qu shi," 94.

46. Du, *Hun duan meng xing* [Broken hearts, awakened dreams], 126.

47. Liao and Chen, "Lin Mang fang tan lu" [Interview with Lin Mang].

48. Ibid., 286–87.

49. Han, "Man chang de jia qi" [A long vacation], 579.

50. Ah, "Ting di tai" [Listening to the enemy's radio station], 150.

51. Ren, *Sheng si bei ge,* 20.

52. Zhang, "Three-Horse Carriage," 202.

53. Wang, "Wo ai ni Beidahuang" [I love you, Beidahuang], 300.

54. Interview, July 28, 1999, Beijing.

55. Correspondence to author from Ji Liqun, May 12, 2000. Ji is the author of "Cha dui sheng ya" [Life in the countryside].

56. Mu, *Huang ruo ge shi* [Like another world], 121.

57. Shi, *Shi Zhi de Shi* [Forefinger's poems], 47.

58. Ge, "Guo Lusheng zai Xinghua cun" [Guo Lusheng in Xinghua Village], 63.

59. Unpublished interview with Sun Hengzhi and Chen Suning conducted by Sun Shuangyun, March 1, 2009.

60. Ji, "Cha dui sheng ya," 18.

61. The leading figure of these groups was Ren Yi, author of the famous "Zhi qing zhi ge" [A song of sent-down youth].

62. The most comprehensive account of the "salon" activities in Beijing and Shanghai as yet is found in Yang, *Wen hua da ge ming zhong de di xia wen xue*. While these salons emerged among Red Guards in the later stage of the Red Guard movement, they continued to exist intermittently through the rustication period and became more active when educated youths returned to Beijing for vacations. See Ji, "Cha dui sheng ya." For a study of similar activities in Guizhou, see Emerson, "The Guizhou Undercurrent."

63. Ji, "Cha dui sheng ya," 18.

64. Liao and Chen, "Lin Mang fang tan lu," 286.

65. Duo Duo, "Bei mai zang de zhong guo shi ren (1972–1978)" [The unknown Chinese poets (1972–1978)].

66. Huang, *A Bilingual Edition of Poetry Out of Communist China*, 47.

67. Shi, *Shi Zhi de Shi*, 88.

68. Ibid., 10.

69. Xu, *Min jian shu xin*, 162.

70. A well-known commercial area in Beijing, later to be the site of the Democracy Wall movement.

71. Yang, *Wen hua da ge ming zhong de di xia wen xue*, 157.

72. Ibid., 158.

73. Note again the class undertones of this poem. The bourgeois taste celebrated in the poem was surely the taste of youth from privileged families. The pride in a hairstyle done by a barber on Xidan Avenue could only come from someone who not only had the privilege to live in Beijing but also the luxury to enjoy Beijing's best in a period of material scarcity.

74. For an analysis of the core collective values promoted in socialist China, see Ridley, Godwin and Doolin, *The Making of a Model Citizen in Communist China*.

75. Yang, *Wen hua da ge ming zhong de di xia wen xue*, 424.

76. On the Li Yizhe poster, see Chan, Rosen, and Unger, *On Socialist Democracy and the Chinese Legal System*.

77. See letter written by a sent-down youth in 1969 in Xu, *Min jian shu xin*, 89–95.

78. The most influential document on agricultural reform, titled "Studies of Peasant Problems," was written by Zhang Musheng (张木生) as early as in 1968. He was sent down before the Cultural Revolution in 1965. In the countryside, he and a few friends started a farm to put into practice their ideas about scientific agriculture, but the experiment failed. Like many other youths that had been sent down, when the Cultural Revolution came, he left his village. When he returned, he was surprised to find that the village agricultural output had significantly increased, because the village leader had been bold enough to experiment with household economy when the entire country was busy with the Cultural Revolution. This inspired Zhang to ponder about agricultural reform. He argued in his essay that the fundamental cause of China's agricultural problems was the collective system of "people's commune." He

proposed that some form of household economy based on market principles might have its advantages. Zhang initially formulated his ideas in private conversations with friends and then wrote them down in a letter to a friend. Soon the essay went into underground circulation in hand-copied manuscripts and provoked discussions. The would-be reformist party leader Hu Yaobang allegedly read the document and held it in high regard. After the reform started, Zhang was among the first researchers to be recruited into the Institute of Agricultural Economy in the Chinese Academy of Social Sciences. On Zhang Musheng, see Liu et al., *Zhong guo zhi qing shi*, 637–43.

79. Chen and Jin, *From Youthful Manuscripts to River Elegy*.

6. NEW ENLIGHTENMENT

1. See, for example, Heilmann, *Turning Away from the Cultural Revolution in China*.
2. Pan, *Tempered in the Revolutionary Furnace*.
3. The most absorbing narrative and analysis of the student movement in 1989 remains Craig Calhoun's *Neither Gods nor Emperors*. On the concept of cycles of protest, see Tarrow, *Power in Movement*.
4. On Chinese politics at the end of the Mao era, see Teiwes and Sun, *The End of the Maoist Era*.
5. Chen, *Democracy Wall and the Unofficial Journals*, 5.
6. As in almost all cases of popular protest in China, the authorities being challenged by the protest claimed there were black hands behind the scene. This was the case with the April Fifth movement as well as the student movement in 1989. Following the repression of the protest, China's official media hinted at the possibility of a high-level plot with Deng Xiaoping as the backstage mastermind. The limited scholarly literature on this movement suggests that it was more of a case of popular protest with organizational structures rooted in informal social networks and China's work unit system. On the April Fifth movement, see Forster, "The 1976 Ch'ing-ming Incident in Hangchow"; Louie and Louie, "The Role of Nanjing University in the Nanjing Incident"; Dong and Walder, "Foreshocks." On 1989, see Black and Munro, *Black Hands of Beijing*.
7. Yuhuatai is a memorial site dedicated to China's revolutionary martyrs, much like the Monument of People's Heroes in Beijing.
8. Dong and Walder, "Foreshocks."
9. Cited in Louie and Louie, "The Role of Nanjing University in the Nanjing Incident," 347.
10. Ibid., 333.
11. The poem has four lines: "I feel sad, but hear the screams of a devilish ghost, / I want to cry, but hear the laughter of the wolves, / Shedding tears, I condole the death of a hero, / Raising my eyebrows, I pull my sword from its sheath."
12. Chen, *Jin ji lu, Du li lu* [A brambled road, an independent road]. Chen Ziming's memoir about this episode of his experience is also contained in Widor, *Documents on the Chinese Democratic Movement*, 115.

13. Ben bao ping lun yuan, "Shi shi qiu shi, you cuo bi jiu" [Follow the truth, correct mistakes].

14. Chen explains the changing meanings of these publications in the following words: "These mostly mimeographed journals were at first referred to by the government as *minjian chubanwu*, publications of the people, then termed *zifa chubanwu*, spontaneous publications, then changed to *dixia chubanwu*, underground publications. Finally, after the arrest of Wei Jingsheng . . . they were denounced as *fandong kanwu*, reactionary publications. Nevertheless, all the editors preferred to call their journals *minban kanwu*, publications by the people or unofficial journals, so as to indicate their difference from the official ones." See Chen, *Democracy Wall and the Unofficial Journals*, 2.

15. The term *min zhu qiang* (民主墙) was not an invention of the Democracy Wall movement, but had appeared in 1957 during the "Hundred Flowers" period. See Liu, "Beijing da xue 'min zhu qiang.'" For English studies of the Democracy Wall movement, see Nathan, *Chinese Democracy;* Seymour, *The Fifth Modernization;* Goldman, "Democracy Wall"; Finkel, *Splintered Mirror*. The most comprehensive collection of primary documents from the Democracy Wall movement is *Ta lu ti hsia k'an wu hui pien* [Collection of the mainland underground publications].

16. On November 29, American journalist Robert Novak told the crowd at the Tiananmen Square that Deng Xiaoping thought the democracy wall was a good thing. See Brodsgaard, "The Democracy Wall Movement in China." According to Ruoxi Chen, John Fraser of the *Toronto Globe and Mail* took American syndicated columnist Robert Novak to see the wall on November 26. People learned that Novak might see Deng the next day. Novak promised to return to tell of his interview with Deng. The next day, Novak went on his tour of China and Fraser showed up at the wall on his behalf. He told the people that Deng had declared the Xidan Democracy Wall to be "a good thing." See Chen, *Democracy Wall and the Unofficial Journals*, 12; also see Fraser, *The Chinese*, 245.

17. Chen, *Democracy Wall and the Unofficial Journals*, 15.

18. The inaugural issue of *Explorations* contains Wei Jingsheng's article "The Fifth Modernization," which had first appeared on December 5, 1978, on the Democracy Wall in the form of a poster.

19. Nathan, *Chinese Democracy*, 23–24.

20. *Ta lu ti hsia k'an wu hui pien*, 7:193.

21. Huang, "Awakening," 43.

22. This is not to deny that, in rising to power, Deng encouraged these popular protests as a way of delegitimizing his political opponents. Yet a conspiracy theory can only go so far. It is the interactions between elite politics and popular action that seemed to be central here.

23. This account is based on Liu et al., *Zhong guo zhi qing shi* [A history of the educated youth in China], 723–48.

24. Gold, "Back to the City"; Mclaren, "The Educated Youth Return"; Yang, "'We want to go home!'"

25. Gold, "Back to the City," 763.

26. While in Beijing the center of the Democracy Wall movement was the section of wall in the Xidan area, in Shanghai it was the People's Square.

27. Ya, "Ren quan yi shi zai zhong guo de jue xing" [The awakening of human rights consciousness in China].

28. Bin Yang argues that the success of the sent-down youth protests in Yunnan had to do with Yunnan's strategic location on the eve of the Sino-Vietnamese War, which would break out in mid-February of 1979. During this time of border crisis, Chinese leaders apparently did not want to see the aggravation of domestic trouble. See Yang, "'We want to go home!"

29. Nathan, *Chinese Democracy,* 196.

30. Ibid., 206–9.

31. Benton, *Wild Lilies, Poisonous Weeds,* 87.

32. Nathan, *Chinese Democracy,* 220.

33. Liu et al., *Zhong guo zhi qing shi.*

34. Nathan, *Chinese Democracy,* 212.

35. Benton, *Wild Lilies, Poisonous Weeds,* 106.

36. Tao, "Letter of Proposal."

37. Chen, *Democracy Wall and the Unofficial Journals,* 36.

38. Nathan, *Chinese Democracy,* 221.

39. Heilmann, "The Social Context of Mobilization in China," 11–12.

40. Ibid., 18.

41. Ibid., 7.

42. I compiled the information based on sources in Hu et al., *Kai tuo* [Exploration], 341.

43. On the continuity and its limits between the 1989 protest and earlier movements, see Calhoun, *Neither Gods nor Emperors,* 164–65.

44. Ibid., 299.

45. Whittier, "Political Generations, Micro-Cohorts, and the Transformation of Social Movements."

46. Liu, "That Holy Word, 'Revolution,'" 309.

47. Ibid., 310.

48. Yang, *The Power of the Internet in China,* chapter 4.

49. See Calhoun, *Neither Gods nor Emperors,* 201–11.

50. It is for this reason that when Internet discussion forums became popular, postings in these online forums were compared to wall posters.

51. Pan, "'San jiao di' de xian shi yu ji yi" [The reality and memories of the "Triangle"].

52. Kraus, *Brushes with Power,* 98.

53. Barmé, "History Writ Large."

54. See http://chinadigitaltimes.net/space/The_Grass-Mud_Horse_Lexicon (accessed August 17, 2015).

55. Calhoun and Wasserstrom, "Legacies of Radicalism."

56. Han, *Cries for Democracy,* 136.

57. Mitter, *A Bitter Revolution.*

58. Ibid., 232.

59. Bei Dao, *The August Sleepwalker,* 33.

60. Morin, *The Red Azalea*, 107.
61. Calhoun and Wasserstrom, "Legacies of Radicalism," 35.
62. See Xu, "Qi meng de zi wo wa jie."
63. Klatch, *A Generation Divided*.
64. See Xu, "Qi meng de zi wo wa jie."
65. These changes are examined in Yang, *The Power of the Internet in China*, chapter 4.

7. FACTIONALIZED MEMORIES

1. On the memory battles over the Cultural Revolution, see, among others, Gao, *The Battle for China's Past*. On how memory of the Mao era may vary with gender and locality, see Hershatter, *The Gender of Memory*.
2. Schwartz and Kim, "Introduction."
3. For example, see Zelizer's studies of photography as a shaping force of memory. Barbie Zelizer, *Remembering to Forget* and *About to Die*.
4. Schudson, "The Present in the Past Versus the Past in the Present."
5. Dittmer, "Rethinking China's Cultural Revolution Amid Reform."
6. Harding, *China's Second Revolution*, 61. On the repudiation of the Cultural Revolution in the early years after Mao's death, see Forster, "Repudiation of the Cultural Revolution in China"; Munro, "Settling Accounts with the Cultural Revolution at Beijing University."
7. Kleinman and Kleinman, "How Bodies Remember," 713.
8. Dittmer, "Rethinking China's Cultural Revolution Amid Reform," 7.
9. Barmé, *Shades of Mao*, 55.
10. See CCP Central Committee, "Decision Concerning the Great Proletarian Cultural Revolution," 6–11.
11. CCP Central Committee, "Resolution on Certain Questions in the History of Our Party." Harry Harding suggests that this "document marked the Party's formal acceptance of Deng's political and economic program. It repudiated the Cultural Revolution and the ideological tenets connected with the later years of Mao Zedong." See Harding, *China's Second Revolution*, 64–65.
12. See *A Great Trial in Chinese History*.
13. Citing official sources, Richard Baum notes that about forty thousand people were expelled from the Chinese Communist Party during the campaign, 25 percent of whom belonged to the "three kinds of people." See Baum, *Burying Mao*, 168.
14. Forster, "Repudiation of the Cultural Revolution in China," 6.
15. Shu, "Zeng qiang dang xing, gen chu pai xing" [Strengthen party spirit, eradicate factional spirit], 6.
16. Resistance may be seen from a circular issued by the Central Office of the CCP concerning the demolition of Mao status. An English translation of the directive is available in Barmé, *Shades of Mao*, 133. Han was sentenced to fifteen years in 1983; the other two each got seventeen years. See appropriate entries in Chao, *Wen hua da ge ming ci dian* [A dictionary of the Great Cultural Revolution].
17. On intellectual movements in the 1980s, see Wang, *High Culture Fever*; Calhoun, *Neither Gods Nor Emperors*; and Zhang, *Chinese Modernism in the Era of Reforms*.

18. Barmé, *Shades of Mao*, 22.
19. Jin, *Shi yun yu ming yun* [Social and personal destinies], 3.
20. Barmé, *Shades of Mao*, 4–5.
21. Scharping reviews twenty-eight works of the memorial literature on Mao and lists several Chinese-language bibliographies on the Mao literature. See Scharping, "The Man, the Myth, the Message."
22. Barmé, *Shades of Mao*, 9.
23. Zhao, "Deng Xiaoping's Southern Tour," 743–44.
24. Yang, *Religion in China*.
25. According to Xudong Zhang, *The Blue Kite* and *To Live*, among others, "mark and culminate a cultural and intellectual trend of pursuing cinematic narrative of a traumatic experience of the past or, more precisely, a visual reconstruction of the national memory through a post-revolutionary catharsis of trauma." See Zhang, "National Trauma, Global Allegory," 624.
26. Huang, *Dang dai zhong guo da zhong wen hua yan jiu* [Studies of popular culture in contemporary China], 58.
27. CCP Central Propaganda Department and State Press and Publication Administration, "Guan yu chu ban 'wen hua da ge ming' tu shu wen ti de ruo gan gui ding" [Regulations governing the publication of books about the 'Great Cultural Revolution.'" In PRC State Press and Publication Administration Policy Laws and Regulations Section, *Zhong hua ren min gong he guo xian xing xin wen chu ban fa gui hui bian (1949–1990)* [Operative press and publishing laws and regulations of the People's Republic of China, 1949–1990]. For an English translation, see Schoenhals, *China's Cultural Revolution*, 310–12.
28. The English translation of the document is reprinted in Barmé, *Shades of Mao*, 237.
29. Xin wen chu ban shu [State Press and Publishing Administration], "Tu shu, qi kan, yin xiang zhi pin, dian zi chu ban wu zhong da xuan ti bei an ban fa" [Measures for reporting major projects in the publication of books, magazines, audiovisual and digital publications]. In Zhongguo chu ban nian jian ed., *Zhongguo chu ban nian jian*. Beijing: Zhongguo chu ban nian jian she, 1998, 238.
30. Winter, "The Generation of Memory."
31. See chapters in Lee and Yang, *Re-Envisioning the Chinese Revolution*.
32. Wang, *Ke shu hui wang cheng gu xiang* [The temporary abode that we now call our hometown].
33. Interview, July 28, 1999, Beijing.
34. *Lao san jie* [The old three classes].
35. Chen, "Lost in Revolution and Reform."
36. Li, *Da dao chao tian* [The open road].
37. Interview, July 24, 1999, Beijing.
38. Lu, *Sheng shi zhen shi de* [Life is real], 201.
39. Ibid., 165.
40. Yan, "Ta zai shen qing de re tu shang" [Stepping onto the heart-warming land], 225.
41. Interview, July 29, 1999, Beijing.
42. Xiao, *Chu mo wang shi* [Gently touching the past], 359.
43. Ibid., 362.

44. Davies, "Visible Zhiqing."
45. An, *Zhi qing chen fu lu* [The rise and fall of sent-down youth], 194.
46. Sun, *Qing ji huang tu di* [Emotional attachment to the yellow earth]; Wang, *Ke shu hui wang cheng gu xiang;* and Xin, *Wu hui nian hua* [Years of no regret]. The stories in the first two collections focus on northern Shaanxi and Beidahuang in Heilongjiang Province. The third, *Years of no regret,* covers various regions, but most of the stories are about villages in Liaoning Province. I have also examined dozens of other similar collections, but found no significant differences among them in subject matter, theme, or style. Overall, these three collections are typical of this particular genre of nostalgic literature produced in China in the 1990s. For details of my content analysis, see Yang, "China's Zhiqing Generation."
47. Zhou, "Chongqing de 'chang, du, jiang, chuan' yu guo jia wen hua ruan shi li" [Sing, reading, storytelling, and disseminating red culture in Chongqing and national soft power], 92.
48. "Why Is Chongqing So Red?"
49. Lam, "The Maoist Revival," 12.
50. On media coverage of the scandal, see "Bo Xilai."
51. See Li, "Xi Jinping ken ding Chongqing chang hong ge xing wei" [Xi Jinping affirms singing red songs in Chongqing].
52. Demick, "China's Xi More Maoist Than Reformer Thus Far."
53. Roberts, "Xi Jinping Is No Fun."
54. Osnos, "Born Red."
55. Meng and Nan, "Loyal to Mao's Legacy."
56. Zhao, "Zou jin bao feng yu" [Walking into the storm], 263.
57. Song, "Lao san jie xiao you yu lao shi jian mian hui fa yan" [Speech at meeting of old three classes alum with their teachers].
58. Zhou, *Wen ge zao fan pai zhen xiang* [The historical truth about rebels during the Cultural Revolution], 329.
59. Chen, "Ji qing yu ku nan bing cun de li shi, duan bu hui mo ran wu hen" [A history combining passion and suffering will surely not be silent and traceless].
60. Liu, "Ju you li shi jia zhi de yi ben xin shu" [A new book with a historical value].
61. E.g., see Hong, *Mi mang* [Lost]; Huang, *Wo zen me cheng le Jiang Qing de gan nü er* [How did I become Jiang Qing's goddaughter]; Zhou, *Hong wei bing xiao bao zhu bian zi shu* [Personal story of an editor of a Red Guard newspaper]
62. Schoenhals, *Ji Yi* [Remembrance].
63. He, "Fa kan ci" [Inaugural statement].
64. Song, "Lao san jie xiao you yu lao shi jian mian hui fa yan."
65. Qi Zhi, "Song Binbin dao qian zhi hou."

CONCLUSION

1. Kleinman and Kleinman's study of embodied memory of the Cultural Revolution finds that their subjects' bodily complaints, such as dizziness, exhaustion, and pain, are expressions of social distress and suffering experienced during the Cultural Revolution. See Kleinman and Kleinman, "How Bodies Remember."

2. For example, see Calhoun and Wasserstrom, "Legacies of Radicalism"; O'Brien and Li, "Campaign Nostalgia in the Chinese Countryside"; Perry, "'To Rebel Is Justified'"; Lee, *Against the Law;* Calhoun, "The Cultural Revolution"; Frazier, *The East Is Black;* Ross, "Mao Zedong's Impact on Cultural Politics in the West"; Wolin, *The Wind from the East.*

3. Kuai Dafu had to move from place to place (Beijing, Shandong, Jiangsu) before he finally settled in Shenzhen. See Xu, *Qinghua Kuai Dafu.*

4. This is not to say that there are no other traditions to draw on. Students in 1989 drew on the traditions of the French Revolution and the May Fourth movement. The Democracy Wall activists drew on their immediate predecessors in the April Fifth movement in 1976. Activists in the twenty-first century learn the repertoires of contention from international NGOs and global activists. And earlier traditions of the Chinese communist revolution, such as Anyuan workers' strikes, continue to provide cultural resources. For a comprehensive treatment of the revolutionary tradition's relationship to protest, see Perry, *Anyuan.*

5. On the May movement in France, see Touraine, *May Movement.* On alternative activist media, see McMillian, *Smoking Typewriters.*

6. E.g., see Gamson and Wolfsfeld, "Movements and Media as Interacting Systems"; and Koopmans, "Movements and Media."

7. See, for example, discussions about the relationship between mainstream media and the Internet in the creation of online protest events in Yang, *The Power of the Internet in China.*

8. Calhoun, *Neither Gods nor Emperors.*

9. McMillian, *Smoking Typewriters.*

10. Zhou, *Hong wei bing xiao bao zhu bian zi shu.*

11. See, for example, Liu Qing's account of his encounter with Chen Erjin and how the April Fifth Forum published Chen Erjin's essay on class privileges. Liu, "Chen Erjin." Also see Xu Xiao's account of the editorial activities of the journal *Today:* Xu, *Ban sheng wei ren* [Half of my life].

12. Walzer, *The Revolution of Saints;* Moore, *Moral Purity and Persecution in History.*

13. Brinton, *The Anatomy of Revolution,* 217.

14. Ibid., 230.

15. Walder, "Political Sociology and Social Movements."

16. Li, "Jin qian ming ge ming hou dai xiang ju xin chun tuan bai hui" [Close to a thousand offspring of the revolution gather for New Year greetings].

17. Zhao, "Zou jin bao feng yu" [Walking into the storm], 263.

BIBLIOGRAPHY

Ah Cheng. "Ting di tai" [Listening to enemy's radio station]. In *Qi shi nian dai* [The seventies], ed. Bei Dao and Li Tuo, 147–54. Hong Kong: Oxford University Press, 2009.

Alexander, Jeffrey C. "Cultural Pragmatics: Social Performance Between Ritual and Strategy." *Sociological Theory* 22, no. 4 (2004): 527–73.

Alexander, Jeffrey C., Bernhard Giesen, and Jason L. Mast, eds. *Social Performance: Symbolic Action, Cultural Pragmatics, and Ritual.* Cambridge: Cambridge University Press, 2006.

Alitto, Guy S. *The Last Confucian: Liang Shu-ming and the Chinese Dilemma of Modernity.* Berkeley: University of California Press, 1979.

Alwin, Duanne, Deborah Freedman, Arland Thornton, Donald Camburn, and Linda Young-DeMarco. "The Life History Calendar: A Technique for Collection of Retrospective Data." In *Sociological Methodology*, vol. 18, ed. Clifford C. Clogg. Washington, DC: American Sociological Association, 1988.

Anderson, Benedict. *Imagined Communities: Reflections on the Origin and Spread of Nationalism.* New York: Verso, 1991.

Andreas, Joel. *Rise of the Red Engineers: The Cultural Revolution and the Origins of China's New Class.* Stanford: Stanford University Press, 2009.

An Zhi. *Zhiqing chen fu lu* [The rise and fall of sent-down youth]. Chengdu: Sichuan ren min chu ban she, 1988.

April 3 War Communique. "On the New Trend of Thought: The Declaration of the April 3 Faction." *Contemporary Chinese Thought* 32, no. 4, ed. Yongyi Song and Zehao Zhou, 47–55. Armonk, NY: M. E. Sharpe, 2001.

Apter, David E. "Politics as Theatre: An Alternative View of the Rationalities of Power." In *Social Performance: Symbolic Action, Cultural Pragmatics, and Ritual*, ed. Jeffrey C. Alexander, Bernhard Giesen, and Jason L. Mast, 218–56. Cambridge: Cambridge University Press, 2006.

Apter, David E., and Tony Saich. *Revolutionary Discourse in Mao's Republic.* Cambridge: Harvard University Press, 1994.

Ashley, Davis, and Yarong Jiang. *Mao's Children in the New China: Voices from the Red Guard Generation*. New York: Routledge, 2000.

Bakhtin, Mikhail. *Rabelais and His World*. Trans. Helene Iswolsky. Cambridge: MIT Press, 1968.

Barmé, Geremie. "History Writ Large: Big-character Posters, Red Logorrhoea, and the Art of Words." *PORTAL* 9, no. 3 (November 2012).

——. *In the Red: On Contemporary Chinese Culture*. New York: Columbia University Press, 1999.

——. *Shades of Mao: The Posthumous Cult of the Great Leader*. Armonk, NY: M. E. Sharpe, 1996.

Barnstone, Tony. *Out of the Howling Storm: The New Chinese Poetry*. Hanover: Wesleyan University Press, 1993.

Baum, Richard. *Burying Mao: Chinese Politics in the Age of Deng Xiaoping*. Princeton: Princeton University Press, 1994.

Bei Dao. *The August Sleepwalker*. Trans. Bonnie S. McDougall. New York: New Directions, 1988.

——. "The Birth of *Today*, a Literary Magazine." *China Rights Forum* (Fall 1998): 41.

Bei Dao and Li Tuo, ed. *Qi shi nian dai* [The seventies]. Hong Kong: Oxford University Press.

Ben bao ping lun yuan. "Shi shi qiu shi, you cuo bi jiu" [Follow the truth, correct mistakes]. *People's Daily*, November 15, 1978, 1.

Benford, Robert D., and Scott A. Hunt. "Dramaturgy and Social Movements: The Social Construction and Communication of Power." In *Social Movements: Critiques, Concepts, Case Studies*, ed. Stanford M. Lyman, 84–109. New York: New York University Press, 1995.

Benton, Gregor. *Wild Lilies, Poisonous Weeds: Dissident Voices from People's China*. London: Pluto, 1982.

Berlinerblau, Jacques. "Toward a Sociology of Heresy, Orthodoxy, and Doxa." *History of Religions* 40, no. 4 (2001): 327–51.

Bernstein, Thomas P. *Up to the Mountains and Down to the Villages: The Transfer of Youth from Urban to Rural China*. New Haven: Yale University Press, 1977.

"Bing chen qingming ji shi" [A documentation of Qingming 1976]. Beijing: Ren min chu ban she, 1980.

Black, George, and Robin Munro. *Black Hands of Beijing: Lives of Defiance in China's Democracy Movement*. New York: Wiley, 1993.

"Bo Xilai." "Times Topics," *New York Times*, http://topics.nytimes.com/top/reference/timestopics/people/b/bo_xilai/index.html. (accessed May 4, 2015).

Bo, Yibo. *Ruo gan zhong da jue ce yu shi jian de hui gu* [Retrospectives on a number of major decisions and events]. Beijing: Zhonggong dang shi chu ban she, 2008.

Bonnell, Victoria E., and Lynn Hunt, eds. *Beyond the Cultural Turn: New Directions in the Study of Society and Culture*. Berkeley: University of California Press, 1999.

Bonnin, Michel. "The 'Lost Generation': Its Definition and Its Role in Today's Chinese Elite Politics." *Social Research* 73, no. 1 (2006): 245–74.

——. *The Lost Generation: The Rustication of China's Educated Youth (1968-1980)*. Hong Kong: Chinese University Press, 2013.

Bourdieu, Pierre. *The Logic of Practice*. Stanford: Stanford University of Press, 1990.

———. "The Uses of the 'People.'" In *In Other Words*, 150–55. Stanford: Stanford University Press, 1990.

Braester, Yomi. "The Purloined Lantern: Maoist Semiotics and Public Discourse in Early PRC Film and Drama." In *Witness Against History: Literature, Film, and Public Discourse in Twentieth-Century China*, 106–27. Stanford: Stanford University Press, 2003.

Brinton, Crane. *The Anatomy of Revolution*. New York: Vintage, 1965.

Brodsgaard, Kjeld E. "The Democracy Wall Movement in China, 1978–1979: Opposition Movements, Wall Poster Campaigns, and Underground Journals." *Asian Survey* 21, no. 7 (1981): 747–74.

Brown, Kerry. *The Purge of the Inner Mongolian People's Party in the Chinese Cultural Revolution, 1967-69: A Function of Language, Power, and Violence*. Folkestone: Global Oriental, 2006.

Bu Weihua. "'Wen hua da ge ming' zhong Beijing de '4.3' he '4.4' pai" [The April Third and April Fourth factions in Beijing during the "Great Cultural Revolution"]. *Zhong guo dang shi zi liao* 2 (2008): 191–97.

Cai Xiang. "Shen sheng hui yi" [Sacred memory]. In *1966: Wo men na yi dai de hui yi* [1966: our generation's memories], ed. Xu Youyu, 253–66. Beijing: Zhong guo wen lian chu ban she, 1998.

Calhoun, Craig. "The Cultural Revolution: A Global Phenomenon." *Art and China's Revolution: A Guide to the Exhibition*, 8–25. New York: Asia Society Museum, 2008.

———. *Neither Gods nor Emperors: Students and the Struggle for Democracy in China*. Berkeley: University of California Press, 1994.

Calhoun, Craig, and Jeffrey Wasserstrom. "Legacies of Radicalism: China's Cultural Revolution and the Democracy Movement of 1989." *Thesis Eleven* 57 (1999): 33–52.

CCP Central Committee. "Decision of the Central Committee of the Chinese Communist Party Concerning the Great Proletarian Cultural Revolution." *Peking Review* 9, no. 33 (1966): 6–11.

———. "Resolution on Certain Questions in the History of Our Party Since the Founding of the People's Republic of China." *Beijing Review* 24, no. 27 (1981): 20–26.

Chan, Anita. *Children of Mao: Personality Development and Political Activism in the Red Guard Generation*. London: Macmillan, 1985.

———. "Dispelling Misconceptions About the Red Guard Movement: The Necessity to Reexamine Cultural Revolution Factionalism and Periodization." *Journal of Contemporary China* 1, no. 1 (1992): 61–85.

Chan, Anita, Stanley Rosen, and Jonathan Unger, eds. *On Socialist Democracy and the Chinese Legal System: The Li Yizhe Debates*. Armonk, NY: M. E. Sharpe, 1985.

———. "Students and Class Warfare: The Social Roots of the Red Guard Conflict in Guangzhou (Canton)." *China Quarterly* 83 (September 1980): 397–446.

Chang, Hao. *Chinese Intellectuals in Crisis: Search for Order and Meaning, 1890-1911*. Berkeley: University of California Press, 1987.

Chao, Feng. *Wen hua da ge ming ci dian* [A dictionary of the Great Cultural Revolution]. Hong Kong: Gang long chu ban she, 1993.

Chen, Fang-Cheng, and Jin Guantao. *From Youthful Manuscripts to River Elegy: The Chinese Popular Cultural Movement and Political Transformation, 1979-1989*. Hong Kong: Chinese University Press, 1997.

Chen, Feng. "Privatization and Its Discontents in Chinese Factories." *China Quarterly* 185 (2006): 42–60.

Chen, Jian. *Mao's China and the Cold War.* Chapel Hill: University of North Carolina Press, 2001.

Chen, Ruoxi. *Democracy Wall and the Unofficial Journals: Studies in Chinese Terminology* no. 20. Berkeley: Center for Chinese Studies, University of California, 1982.

Chen, Xiaomei. "Growing up with Posters in the Maoist Era." In *Picturing Power in the People's Republic: Posters of the Cultural Revolution*, ed. Harriet Evans and Stephanie Donald, 101–22. Boulder: Rowman and Littlefield, 1999.

——. "'Playing in the Dirt': Plays About Geologists and Memories of the Cultural Revolution and the Maoist Era." *China Review* 5, no. 2 (Fall 2005): 65–95.

Chen, Ya-ting. "Films on War Themes." *Chinese Literature* 11 (1965): 115–18.

Cheng, Tiejun, and Mark Selden. "The Origins and Consequences of China's Hukou System." *China Quarterly* 139 (1994): 644–68.

Cheng, Yinghong. *Creating the New Man: From Enlightenment Ideals to Socialist Realities.* Honolulu: University of Hawaii Press, 2009.

Chengdu shi di fang zhi bian cuan wei yuan hui, ed. *Chengdu shi zhi: Bao ye zhi.* [Chengdu City Annals—Annals on the Newspaper Industry] Chengdu: Sichuan Ci shu chu ban she, 2000.

Cheng Jiang, ed. *Lao zhiqing* [Former sent-down youth]. Beijing: Shi you gong ye chu ban she, 1998.

✓ Chenivesse, Sandrine. "For Us, Mao Was a First Love." *China Perspectives* 1 (1995): 70–74.

Chen Kaige. "Wo men du jing li guo de ri zi: shao nian Kaige" [The days we all experienced: the teenager Kaige]. *Zhong guo zuo jia* [Chinese writers] 5 (1993): 4–28.

Chen Xiaoya. "Beijing zhiqing li cheng hui mou" [A retrospective look at the trajectories of educated youth from Beijing]. In *Bei chuang qing chun: zhong guo zhi qing lei,* ed. Yu Fu and Wang Weihua, 1–21. Beijing: Tuan jie chu ban she, 1993.

Chen Yinan. "Ji qing yu ku nan bing cun de li shi, duan bu hui mo ran wu hen: Yang Zengtai hui yi lu xu" [A history combining passion and suffering will surely not be silent and traceless: preface to Yang Zengtai's memoir]. In *Xie gei li shi de jiao dai: Chongqing 815 wen gong wu wei si ling de zi shu* [A confession to history: the personal account of the commander-in-chief of the department of armed fighting of the August Fifteenth in Chongqing], ed. Yang Zengtai, 1–5. Hong Kong: Chinese Cultural Communication Press, 2014.

Chen Yixin. "Lost in Revolution and Reform: The Socioeconomic Pains of China's Red Guards Generation, 1966–1996." *Journal of Contemporary China* 8, no. 21 (1999): 219–23.

Chen Ziming. *Chen Ziming fan si shi nian gai ge* [Chen Ziming's reflects on ten years of reform]. Hong Kong: Dang dai yue kan, 1992.

——. *Jin ji lu, Du li lu: Chen Ziming zi shu* [A brambled road, an independent road: Chen Ziming's personal account]. Taipei: Xiu wei zi xun ke ji, 2009.

Chien, Edward T. *Chiao Hung and the Restructuring of Neo-Confucianism in the Late Ming.* New York: Columbia University Press, 1986.

Chongqing da xue xiao shi bian ji zu. *Chongqing da xue xiao shi* [History of Chongqing University]. 2 vols. Chongqing: Chongqing da xue chu ban she, 1994.

"Chongqing da zhong xue xiao Mao Zedong zhu yi hong wei bing zong bu xuan gao cheng li" [Maoism Red Guard headquarters of the universities and middle schools in Chongqing inaugurated]. *Chongqing Daily,* September 9, 1966, 1.

"Chongqing shi di fang zhi bian zuan wei yuan hui." *Chongqing shi zhi, di 14 juan* [Chongqing city annals, vol. 14]. Chongqing: Xi nan shi fan da xue chu ban she, 2005.

Chow, Gregory C. *Understanding China's Economy.* Singapore: World Scientific, 1994.

Chu, Godwin C., Philip H. Cheng, and Leonard L. Chu. *The Role of Tatzepao in the Cultural Revolution: A Structural Functional Analysis.* Carbondale: Southern Illinois University, 1972.

Clark, Paul. *The Chinese Cultural Revolution: A History.* Cambridge: Cambridge University Press, 2008.

Coase, Ronald, and Ning Wang. *How China Became Capitalist.* New York: Palgrave, 2013.

Collins, Randall. *Violence: A Micro-Sociological Theory.* Princeton: Princeton University Press, 2008.

Connerton, Paul. *How Societies Remember.* Cambridge: Cambridge University Press, 1989.

Crevel, Maghiel van. "Underground Poetry in the 1960s and 1970s." *Modern Chinese Literature* 9, no. 2 (Fall 1996): 169–219.

Cui Qi. "More on the Differences Between Comrade Togliatti and Us." *Peking Review* 6, nos. 10, 11 (March 15, 1963): 56–57.

——. *Wo suo qin li de zhong su da lun zhan* [The Sino-Soviet Polemics I personally experienced]. Beijing: Ren min ri bao chu ban she, 2009.

Dang dai zhong guo cong shu bian ji bu. *Dang dai zhong guo de chu ban shi ye,* 2 vols. [The publishing industry in contemporary China], 2:400–2. Beijing: Dang dai zhong guo chu ban she, 1993.

Davies, David. "Visible Zhiqing: The Visual Culture of Nostalgia Among China's Zhiqing Generation." In *Re-envisioning the Chinese Revolution: The Politics and Poetics of Collective Memory in Reform China,* ed. Ching Kwan Lee and Guobin Yang, 166–92. Stanford: Stanford University Press, 2007.

Davis, Fred. *Yearning for Yesterday: A Sociology of Nostalgia.* New York: Free Press, 1979.

Davis, Natalie Z. "The Rites of Violence: Religious Riot in Sixteenth-Century France." *Past and Present* 59 (1973): 51–91.

——. *Society and Culture in Early Modern France.* Stanford: Stanford University Press, 1975.

de Bary, William T. *Learning for One's Self: Essays on the Individual in Neo-Confucian Thought.* New York: Columbia University Press, 1991.

——. *Self and Society in Ming Thought.* New York: Columbia University Press, 1970.

della Porta, Donatella. "Life Histories in the Analysis of Social Movements Activists." In *Studying Collective Action,* ed. Mario Diani and Ron Eyerman. London: Sage, 1992.

——. "Research on Social Movements and Political Violence." *Qualitative Sociology* 31 (2008): 221–30.

——. "Social Movements and Violence: Participation in Underground Organisations." In *International Social Movement Research,* 4:3–28. London: JAI, 1992.

——. *Social Movements, Political Violence, and the State: A Comparative Analysis of Italy and Germany.* Cambridge: Cambridge University Press, 1995.

———. "Violence and the New Left." In *The International Handbook of Violence Research*, ed. Wilhelm Heitmeyer and John Hagan, 383–98. Dordrecht: Kluwer Academic Publishers, 2003.

della Porta, Donatella, and Sidney Tarrow. "Unwanted Children: Political Violence and the Cycle of Protest in Italy: 1966–1973." *European Journal of Political Research* 14 (1986): 607–32.

Demick, Barbara. "China's Xi More Maoist Than Reformer Thus Far." *Los Angeles Times,* June 8, 2013. Available online at http://articles.latimes.com/2013/jun/08/world/la-fg -china-xi-20130608 (accessed May 4, 2015).

Denton, Kirk. "Model Drama as Myth: A Semiotic Analysis of Taking Tiger Mountain by Strategy." In *Drama in the People's Republic of China*, ed. Constantine Tung, 119–36. Albany: SUNY Press, 1987.

Ding Yizhuang. *Zhong guo zhi qing shi: chu lan 1953-1958* [History of Chinese sent-down youth: The earlier wave, 1953–1958]. Beijing: Zhong guo she hui ke xue chu ban she, 1998.

Dirlik, Arif. "The Politics of the Cultural Revolution in Historical Perspective." In *The Chinese Cultural Revolution Reconsidered: Beyond Purge and Holocaust*, ed. Kam-Yee Law, 158–83. Houndmills: Palgrave Macmillan, 2003.

Dittmer, Lowell. "Radical Ideology and Chinese Political Culture: An Analysis of the Revolutionary Yangbanxi." In *Moral Behaviour in Chinese Society*, ed. Richard Wilson, Sidney Greenblatt, and Amy Wilson, 126–51. New York: Praeger, 1981

———. "Rethinking China's Cultural Revolution Amid Reform." In *China's Great Proletarian Cultural Revolution: Master Narratives and Post-Mao Counternarratives*, ed. Woei Lien Chong, 3–26. Lanham: Rowman snf Littlefield, 2002.

———. "Thought Reform and Cultural Revolution: An Analysis of the Symbolism of Chinese Polemics." *American Political Science Review* 71 (1977): 67–85.

Dittmer, Lowell, and Chen Ruoxi. *Ethics and Rhetoric of the Chinese Cultural Revolution*. Berkeley: University of California Center for Chinese Studies, 1981.

Documents of the Democracy Movement in Communist China, 1978-1981. Stanford University: East Asian Collection, Hoover Institution Library and Archives.

Dong Guoqiang and Andrew G. Walder. "Factions in a Bureaucratic Setting: The Origins of Cultural Revolution Conflict in Nanjing." *China Journal*, no. 65 (January 2011): 1–25.

———. "Foreshocks: Local Origins of Nanjing's Qingming Demonstrations of 1976." *China Quarterly* 220 (2014): 1092–110.

Downton, James, Jr., and Paul Wehr. *The Persistent Activist: How Peace Commitment Develops and Survives*. Boulder: Westview, 1997.

Drake, Richard. *The Revolutionary Mystique and Terrorism in Contemporary Italy*. Bloomington: Indiana University Press, 1989.

Du Honglin. *Feng chao dang luo: Zhong guo zhi shi qing nian shang shan xia xiang yun dong shi* [The rise and fall of a movement: a history of the "Up to the Mountains and Down to the Countryside" movement of the sent-down youth in China]. Shenzhen: Hai tian chu ban she, 1993.

———. *Hun duan meng xing—Zhong guo zhi qing shang shan xia xiang feng yun ji shi* [Broken hearts, bestirred dreams: a factual account of China's educated youth in the winds and storms of the Up to the Mountains and Down to the Countryside movement]. Ningbo: Ningbo chu ban she, 1996.

Duo Duo. "Bei mai zang de zhong guo shi ren (1972–1978)" [The unknown Chinese poets (1972–1978)]. In *Chen lun de sheng dian* [The fallen altar], ed. Liao Yiwu, 195–202. Urumqi: Xinjiang qing shao nian chu ban she, 1999.

Dutton, Michael. *Policing Chinese Politics: A History.* Durham: Duke University Press, 2005.

Edelman, Murray. *Politics as Symbolic Action: Mass Arousal and Quiescence.* New York: Academic Press, 1971.

Educated Youth Office of the State Council. "Er shi wu nian lai zhiqing gong zuo de hui gu yu zong jie" [A review and summary of the work on educated youth in the past twenty-five years]. Beijing: State Council, 1981.

"815 shi hua" [History of August the Fifteenth]. *815 feng bao,* no. 1, August 8, 1967, 2.

Elvin, Mark. "Between the Earth and Heaven: Conceptions of the Self in China." In *The Category of the Person,* ed. Michael Carrithers, Steven Collins and Steven Lukes, 156–89. Cambridge: Cambridge University Press, 1985.

Emerson, Andrew G. "The Guizhou Undercurrent." *Modern Chinese Literature and Culture* 13, no. 2 (2001): 111–33.

Esherick, Joseph W. "The 'Restoration of Capitalism' in Mao's and Marxist Theory." *Modern China* 5, no. 1 (January 1979): 41–78.

Evans, Harriet, and Stephanie Donald. "Introducing Posters of China's Cultural Revolution." In *Picturing Power in the People's Republic of China: Posters of the Cultural Revolution,* ed. Harriet Evans and Stephanie Donald, 1–27. London: Rowman and Littlefield, 1999.

Eyerman, Ron, and Bryan S. Turner. "Outline of a Theory of Generations." *European Journal of Social Theory* 1, no. 1 (1998): 91–106.

Fan Wenfa. *Bai shan hei shui: yige Shanghai zhiqing chen feng de ri ji* [White mountains, black rivers: a dust-covered diary of a Shanghai educated youth]. Zhuhai: Zhuhai chu ban she, 1998.

Fan Xing. "Wen ge ji yi: 'Dang dai si xiang shi' pian duan'" [Memories of the Cultural Revolution: fragments of "contemporary history of thought"]. *Wen yi ping lun* 1 (1996): 29–38.

Finkel, Donald, trans. *Splintered Mirror: Chinese Poetry from the Democracy Movement.* San Francisco: North Point, 1991.

Forster, Keith. "The 1976 Ch'ing-ming Incident in Hangchow." *Issues and Studies* 22 (1986): 13–33.

——. "Repudiation of the Cultural Revolution in China: The Case of Zhejiang." *Pacific Affairs* 59, no. 1 (1986): 5–27.

Foucault, Michel. "Self Writing." In *Ethics, Subjectivity and Truth,* ed. Paul Rabinow, 207–22. New York: New Press, 1997.

Fraser, John. *The Chinese: Portrait of a People.* New York: Summit, 1980.

Frazier, Roberson Tej. *The East Is Black. Cold War China in the Black Radical Imagination.* Durham: Duke University Press, 2015.

Galik, Marian. "Foreign Literature in the People's Republic of China Between 1970–1979." *Asian and African Studies* 19 (1983): 55–95.

———. "Some Remarks on 'Literature of the Scars' in the People's Republic of China (1977–1979)." *Asian and African Studies* 18 (1982): 53–74.

Gamson, William A., and Gadi Wolfsfeld. "Movements and Media as Interacting Systems." *Annals of the American Academy of Political and Social Science: Citizens, Protest, and Democracy* 528 (July 1993): 114–25.

Gao, Mobo C. F. *The Battle for China's Past: Mao and the Cultural Revolution.* Ann Arbor: Pluto, 2008.

Gao Hua. *Hong tai yang shi zen yang sheng qi de* [How did the red sun rise]. Hong Kong: Chinese University of Hong Kong Press, 2000.

Gao Mu and Yan Jiaqi. *1966-1976: Wen hua da ge ming shi nian shi* [1966–1976: a ten-year history of the cultural revolution]. Tianjin: Tianjin ren min chu ban she, 1986.

"Ge lian hui bi sheng" [The United Revolutionary Committee will surely triumph!]. *August Fifteenth Battle News,* February 25, 1967. In Yongyi Song, ed., *Xin bian hong wei bing zi liao III* [A new collection of Red Guard publications, part 3, a comprehensive compilation of tabloids in the provinces], 1578. 52 vols. Oakton, VA: Center for Chinese Research Materials, 2005.

Ge Xiaoli. "Guo Lusheng zai Xinghua cun" [Guo Lusheng in Xinghua Village]. In *Chen lun de sheng dian* [The fallen altar], ed. Liao Yiwu, 61–70. Urumqi: Xinjiang qing shao nian chu ban she, 1999.

Giesen, Bernhard. "Performing the Sacred: A Durkheimian Perspective on the Performative Turn in the Social Sciences." In *Social Performance: Symbolic Action, Cultural Pragmatics, and Ritual,* ed. Jeffrey C. Alexander, Bernhard Giesen, and Jason L. Mast, 325–67. Cambridge: Cambridge University Press, 2006.

Girard, René. *Violence and the Sacred.* Baltimore: Johns Hopkins University Press, 1977.

Gitlin, Todd. *The Whole World Is Watching.* Berkeley: University of California Press, 1980.

Goffman, Erving. *The Presentation of Self in Everyday Life.* New York: Doubleday, 1959.

Gold, Thomas B. "Back to the City: The Return of Shanghai's Educated Youth." *China Quarterly* 84 (1980): 55–70.

———. "Urban Private Business and Social Change." In *Chinese Society on the Eve of Tiananmen: The Impact of Reform,* ed. Deborah Davis and Ezra F. Vogel, 157–78. Cambridge: Harvard University Press, 1990.

Goldman, Merle. "Democracy Wall: The First Assertion of Political Rights in the Post-Mao Era." In *From Comrade to Citizen,* 25–50. Cambridge: Harvard University Press, 2007.

———. *Sowing the Seeds of Democracy in China: Political Reform in the Deng Xiaoping Era.* Cambridge: Harvard University Press, 1994.

Goldstone, Jack. "Ideology, Cultural Frameworks, and the Process of Revolution." *Theory and Society* 20 (1991): 405–53.

Goodman, David S. G. *Beijing Street Voices: The Poetry and Politics of China's Democracy Movement.* London: Marion Boyars, 1981.

Goodwin, Jeff. "The Relational Approach to Terrorism." *Swiss Political Science Review* 15 (2009): 387–94.

A Great Trial in Chinese History: The Trial of the Lin Biao and Jiang Qing Counter-revolutionary Cliques, Nov. 1980-Jan. 1981. Oxford: Pergamon, 1981.

Griffin, Larry. "'Generations and Collective Memory' Revisited: Race, Region and Memory of Civil Rights." *American Sociological Review* 69 (2004): 544–57.

Gu Cheng. "Forever Parted: Graveyard." Trans. J. P. Seaton and Mu Yi. In *Out of the Howling Storm: The New Chinese Poetry*, ed. Tony Barnstone, 76–82. Middletown, CT: Wesleyan University Press, 1993.

Gullestad, Marianne. *Everyday Life Philosophers: Modernity, Morality, and Autobiography in Norway*. Oslo: Scandinavian University Press, 1996.

Hall, John R. *Apocalypse: From Antiquity to the Empire of Modernity*. Cambridge: Polity, 2009.

Han Minzhu (pseudonym), ed. *Cries for Democracy: Writings and Speeches from the 1989 Chinese Democracy Movement*. Princeton: Princeton University Press, 1990.

Han Shaogong. "Man chang de jia qi" [A long vacation]. In *Qi shi nian dai*, ed. Bei Dao and Li Tuo, 563–85. Hong Kong: Oxford University Press, 2009.

Hao Li. "Liu dong de shu" [Mobile books]. *Qun Yan*, no. 11 (1998): 21.

Hao Ping. "Reassessing the Starting-Point of the Cultural Revolution." *China Review International* 3, no. 1 (1996): 66–86.

Harding, Harry. *China's Second Revolution: Reform After Mao*. Washington, DC: Brookings Institution, 1987.

Heilmann, Sebastian. "The Social Context of Mobilization in China: Factions, Work Units, and Activists During the 1976 April Fifth Movement." *China Information* 8, no. 3 (1993): 1–19.

——. "The Suppression of the April Fifth Movement and the Persecution of 'Counterrevolutionaries' in 1976." *Issues and Studies* 30, no. 1 (1994): 37–64.

——. *Turning Away from the Cultural Revolution in China: Political Grass-Roots Activism in the Mid-Seventies*. Stockholm: Center for Pacific Asia Studies, Stockholm University, 1996.

Hershatter, Gail. *Rural Women and China's Collective Past*. Berkeley: University of California Press, 2011.

Hershkovitz, Linda. "The Fruits of Ambivalence: China's Urban Individual Economy." *Pacific Affairs* 58 (1985): 427–50.

He Shu. "Chongqing wen ge wu dou si nan zhe ming lu" [List of names of those killed in armed fighting in Chongqing]. *Zuo Tian* [Yesterday], no. 36 (supplement), June 30, 2014.

——. "Fa kan ci" [Inaugural statement], *Zuo Tian* [Yesterday], no. 1, January 31, 2012.

——. *Wei Mao zhu xi er zhan: Wen ge Chongqing da wu dou shi lu* [Fighting for Chairman Mao: historical records of the armed fighting in Chongqing during the Cultural Revolution]. Hong Kong: San Lian Shu Dian, 2010.

Hobsbawm, Eric, and Terence Ranger, eds. *The Invention of Tradition*. Cambridge: Cambridge University Press, 1983.

Hoffer, Eric. *The True Believer: Thoughts on the Nature of Mass Movements*. New York: Harper and Row, 1951.

Hong Jinzhong. "Dujiashan shang de xin she yuan—ji Beijing zhi shi qing nian Cai Lijian dao nong cun luo hu" [A new farmer in Dujiashan village—Beijing educated youth Cai Lijian settles in the countryside]. *Ren min ri bao*, July 4, 1968, 4.

Hong, Junhao. "The Evolution of China's War Movie in Five Decades: Factors Contributing to Changes, Limits and Implications." *Asian Cinema* 10, no. 1 (1988): 93–106.

Hong Ou. *Mi mang: Shi nian hao jie qin li* [Lost: my personal experience of ten years of disaster]. Hong Kong: Shi dai zuo jia chu ban she, 2013.

Hong wei bing zi liao [Red Guard publications]. 20 vols. Washington, DC: Center for Chinese Research Materials, 1975.

Hong wei bing zi liao xu bian [Red Guard publications supplement]. 8 vols. Washington, DC: Center for Chinese Research Materials, 1980.

Honig, Emily. "Maoist Mappings of Gender: Reassessing the Red Guards." In *Chinese Fimininities/Chinese Masculinities: A Reader*, ed. Jeffrey N. Wasserstrom and Susan Brownell, 255–268. Berkeley: University of California Press, 2002.

Hsin pien hung wei ping tsu liao. Ti 1 pu: Hsiao pao [A new collection of Red Guard publications, part 1: newspapers]. Oakton, VA: Center for Chinese Research Materials, 1999.

Huang, Cary. "Leading Leftist Academic Mocked Over 'Maoist' Op-ed." *South China Morning Post* (July 20, 2013). Available online at http://www.scmp.com/news/china/article/1286519/leading-leftist-academic-mocked-over-maoist-op-ed (accessed July 25, 2013).

Huang Huilin, ed. *Dang dai zhong guo da zhong wen hua yan jiu* [Studies of popular culture in contemporary China]. Beijing: Beijing shi fan da xue chu ban she, 1998.

Huang Ronghua. *Wo zen me cheng le Jiang Qing de gan nü er* [How did I become Jiang Qing's goddaughter]. Hong Kong: Chinese Cultural Communication Press, 2013.

Huang Xiang. "Awakening." *China Rights Forum* (Fall 1998): 43.

——. *A Bilingual Edition of Poetry Out of Communist China*. Trans. Andrew G. Emerson. Lewiston: Mellen, 2004.

Huang Yibing. *Contemporary Chinese Literature: From the Cultural Revolution to the Future*. New York: Palgrave Macmillan, 2007.

Huang Zhenhai. "'Jie wa' de wu dou" [The armed fighting of street kids]. *Zuo Tian* [Yesterday] 3 (March 31, 2012).

Hua Sheng. 1990. "Big Character Posters in China: A Historical Survey." *Journal of Asian Law* 4, no. 2 (1990): 234–56.

Hung, Chang-Tai. *Mao's New World: Political Culture in the Early People's Republic*. Ithaca, NY: Cornell University Press, 2011.

Hunt, Lynn. *Politics, Culture, and Class in the French Revolution*. Berkeley: University of California Press, 2004.

Hu Ping. *Zhong guo min yun fan si* [Reflections on China's democratic movement]. Hong Kong: Oxford University Press, 1992.

Hu Ping, Wang Juntao et al., eds. *Kai tuo: Beida xue yun wen xian* [Exploration: Peking University student movement materials]. Hong Kong: Tian yuan shu wu, 1990.

Ikels, Charlotte. *The Return of the God of Wealth: The Transition to a Market Economy in Urban China*. Stanford: Stanford University Press, 1996.

Ji Liqun. "Cha dui sheng ya" [Life in the countryside]. In *Wu hui nian hua—bai ming zhiqing hua dang nian* [Years of no regret: one hundred educated youth on their past], ed. Xin Qun, 12–21. Shenyang: Shenyang chu ban she, 1998.

Jin, Chunming. "Si wu yun dong shu ping [A review of the April Fifth movement]." *Dang shi yan jiu* [Studies in party history, Beijing] 5 (1984).

Jin Dalu, ed. *Ku nan yu feng liu: lao san jie ren de dao lu* [Tribulations and courage: the lives of the old three classes]. Shanghai: Shanghai ren min chu ban she, 1994.

——. "Shanghai wen ge yun dong zhong de 'qun zhong bao kan'" ["Mass newspapers" in Shanghai's Cultural Revolution]. *Shi Lin* 6 (2005): 1–13.

——. *Shi yun yu ming yun: guan yu lao san jie ren de sheng cun yu fa zhan* [Social and personal destinies: on the existence and development of people of the old three classes]. Shanghai: Shanghai ren min chu ban she, 1998.

Jin Shan. "Wu shi nian qian ying xiang le yi dai ren de fan su jiu ping" [The anti-Soviet Nine Commentaries that influenced a generation of people fifty years ago]. February 24, 2012. Available online at http://blog.sina.com.cn/s/blog_4eddf60c0102du2m. html. Accessed December 19, 2014.

Jin Yonghua, ed. *Dong fang shi ri tan-lao san jie ren de gu shi* [An Oriental decameron: stories of the old three classes]. Shanghai: Shanghai ren min chu ban she, 1995.

Joseph, A. William, Christine P. W. Wong, and David Zweig, eds. *New Perspectives on the Cultural Revolution.* Cambridge: Harvard University, Council on East Asian Studies, 1991.

Juergensmeyer, Mark. *Terror in the Mind of God: The Global Rise of Religious Violence.* Berkeley: University of California Press, 2000.

Juris, Jeffrey S. "Violence Performed and Imagined: Militant Action, the Black Bloc, and the Mass Media in Genoa." *Critique of Anthropology* 25, no. 4 (2005): 413–32.

Kaufman, Stuart J. *Modern Hatreds: The Symbolic Politics of Ethnic War.* Ithaca, NY: Cornell University Press, 2001.

Kelliher, Daniel. *Peasant Power in China.* New Haven: Yale University Press, 1992.

Kiely, Jan. *The Compelling Ideal: Thought Reform and the Prison in China, 1904–1956.* New Haven: Yale University Press, 2014.

Klatch, Rebecca E. *A Generation Divided: The New Left, the New Right, and the 1960s.* Berkeley: University of California Press, 1999.

——. *The Cultural Revolution: A Very Short Introduction.* Oxford: Oxford University Press, 2010.

Kleinman, Arthur, and Joan Kleinman. "How Bodies Remember: Social Memory and Bodily Experience of Criticism, Resistance, and Delegitimation Following China's Cultural Revolution." *New Literary History* 25, no. 3 (1994): 707–23.

Kong, Shuyu. "Swan and Spider Eater in Problematic Memoirs of Cultural Revolution." *positions: east asia cultures critique* 7, no. 1 (1999): 239–52.

Kong Huiyun, ed. *Zhi qing sheng huo hui yi* [Recollections of life as sent-down youth]. Jinan: Shandong hua bao chu ban she, 1999.

Koopmans, Ruud. "Movements and Media: Selection Processes and Evolutionary Dynamics in the Public Sphere." *Theory and Society* 33 (2004): 367–91.

Kraus, Richard C. *Brushes with Power: Modern Politics and the Chinese Art of Calligraphy.* Berkeley: University of California Press, 1991.

——. *Class Conflict in Chinese Socialism.* New York: Columbia University Press, 1981.

——. *The Cultural Revolution: A Very Short Introduction.* Oxford: Oxford University Press, 2012.

Lam, Willy. "The Maoist Revival and the Conservative Turn in Chinese Politics." *China Perspectives* 2 (2012): 5–15.

Landsberger, Stefan R. "The Deification of Mao: Religious Imagery and Practices During the Cultural Revolution and Beyond." In *China's Great Proletarian Cultural Revolution: Master Narratives and Post-Mao Counternarratives*, ed. Woei Lien Chong, 139–84. Lanham: Rowman and Littlefield, 2002.

——. "Mao as the Kitchen God: Religious Aspects of the Mao Cult During the Cultural Revolution." *China Information* 11, no. 2–3 (1996): 196.

Langland, Victoria. *Speaking of Flowers: Student Movements and the Making and Remembering of 1968 in Military Brazil*. Duke: Duke University Press, 2013.

Lao san jie: yu gong he guo tong xing [The old three classes: cohort of the republic]. 600 min. 20 parts. Nanjing: Nanjing yin xiang chu ban she, 1999.

Laslett, Barbara. "Biography as Historical Sociology: The Case of William Fielding Ogburn." *Theory and Society* 20 (1991): 511–38.

——. "Personal Narratives as Sociology." *Contemporary Sociology* 28, no. 4 (1999): 391–401.

Lee, Ching Kwan. *Against the Law: Labor Protests in China's Rustbelt and Sunbelt*. Berkeley: University of California Press, 2007.

Lee, Ching Kwan, and Guobin Yang, eds. *Re-envisioning the Chinese Revolution: The Politics and Poetics of Collective Memories in Reform China*. Washington, D.C.: Woodrow Wilson Center Press and Stanford University Press, 2007.

Lee, Haiyan. "The Charisma of Power and the Military Sublime in Tiananmen Square." *Journal of Asian Studies* 70, no. 2 (2011): 397–424.

Lee, Hong Yung. *The Politics of the Chinese Cultural Revolution: A Case Study*. Berkeley: University of California Press, 1978.

Leese, Daniel. *Mao Cult: Rhetoric and Ritual in China's Cultural Revolution*. Cambridge: Cambridge University Press, 2011.

Leijonhufvud, Goran. *Going Against the Tide: On Dissent and Big-Character Posters in China*. London: Curzon, 1990.

Lei Yi. "Nan wang de 1968 nian" [The unforgettable 1968]. *Zhong guo qing nian yan jiu* [China youth study] 42, no. 2 (1996): 6–7.

Leng Wei. "Leng Wei kou shu (III)" [Leng Wei's oral history, part 3]. Conducted and written by Dai Weiwei. *Ji Yi* [Remembrance], no. 127 (March 31, 2015): 43–52.

Lenin, V. I. *What Is to Be Done: Burning Questions of Our Movement*. New York: International, 1969 [1902].

Leung, Laifong. *Morning Sun: Interviews with Chinese Writers of the Lost Generation*. Armonk, NY: M. E. Sharpe, 1994.

Li, Haobo. "A Journey Back to Mao's Birthplace." *Beijing Review* 36, no. 49 (1993): 17–22.

Li, Xueye. "Jin qian ming ge ming hou dai xiang ju xin chun tuan bai hui" [Close to a thousand offspring of the revolution gather for New Year greetings]. China Red Tourism Net, February 2, 2015. http://www.crt.com.cn/news2007/news/HStop/15241918111FG 7A835A4B0CAK655DF.html (accessed March 14, 2015).

Li, Yajie. "Xi Jinping ken ding Chongqing chang hong ge xing wei" [Xi Jinping affirms singing red songs in Chongqing]. *Xinhua News Agency*, August 12, 2011, http://china .huanqiu.com/roll/2010–12/1327317.html (accessed on April 7, 2015).

Li, Zehou, and Vera Schwarcz. "Six Generations of Modern Chinese Intellectuals." *Chinese Studies in History* 17, no. 2 (1984): 42–57.

Li, Zimao. "You guan wu dou de yi xie si kao" [Some thoughts on armed fighting]. *Yesterday*, no. 39 (September 30, 2014): 28–35.

Liang Xiaosheng. *Yi ge hong wei bing de zi bai* [The confessions of a Red Guard]. Chengdu: Sichuan wen yi chu ban she, 1988.

Liao Yiwu, ed. *Chen lun de sheng dian* [The fallen altar], ed. Liao Yiwu. Urumqi: Xinjiang qing shao nian chu ban she, 1999.

Liao Yiwu and Chen Yong. "Lin Mang fang tan lu" [Interview with Lin Mang]. In *Chen lun de sheng dian* [The fallen altar], ed. Liao Yiwu. Urumqi: Xinjiang qing shao nian chu ban she, 1999.

Lifton, Robert J. *Revolutionary Immortality: Mao Tse-tung and the Chinese Cultural Revolution*. New York: Vintage, 1968.

Li Guangping. *Zhong guo zhi qing bei huan lu* [Stories of joy and sorrow of China's educated youth]. Beijing: Hua cheng chu ban she, 1995.

"Li ji xian qi yi ge gu li zi nü can jia Mao Zedong zhu yi hong wei bing de re chao" [Immediately launch a hot tide to encourage children to join Maoism Red Guards]. *Chongqing Daily*, September 10, 1966, 1.

Li Musen. *Qin li Chongqing da wu dou* [My personal experiences of major armed fighting in Chongqing]. Hong Kong: China Cultural Communication Press, 2011.

Lin, Min, and Maria Galikowski. *The Search for Modernity: Chinese Intellectuals and Cultural Discourse in the Post-Mao Era*. New York: St. Martin's, 1999.

Ling Wei. "Wen hua da ge ming he di san dai ren" [The Cultural Revolution and the third generation]. *Zhi shi fen zi* (Spring 1986): 50–55.

Link, Perry. "Hand-copied Entertainment Fiction from the Cultural Revolution." In *Unofficial China: Popular Culture and Thought in the People's Republic*, ed. Perry Link, Richard P. Madsen, and Paul G. Pickowicz, 17–36. Boulder: Westview, 1989.

Lin Muchen. "Shanghai min yun hui yi lu" [Memoirs of the democratic movement in Shanghai]. *Zhong guo zhi chun* [China Spring] 133 (1994): 64–65.

Lin Yu-sheng. "The Suicide of Liang Chi: An Ambiguous Case of Moral Conservatism." In *The Limits of Change: Essays on Conservative Alternatives in Republican China*, ed. Charlotte Furth. Cambridge: Harvard University Press, 1976.

Liu, Alan P. L. *Political Culture and Group Conflicts in Communist China*. Santa Barbara, CA: American Bibliographical Center, 1976.

Liu Gao and Shi Feng, eds. *Xin zhong guo chu ban wu shi nian ji shi* [Chronicles of fifty years of publishing in New China]. Beijing: Xin hua chu ban she, 1999.

Liu Guanghua, "Beijing da xue 'min zhu qiang." *Wen hui ri bao*, May 26, 1957.

Liu Guokai. *A Brief Analysis of the Cultural Revolution*. Trans. Anita Chan. Armonk, NY: M. E. Sharpe, 1987.

Liu Qing. "Chen Erjin: Min zhu qiang qian nan fei yan" [The southern goose at the Democracy Wall]. Available online at http://blog.boxun.com/hero/chenyc/2_1.shtml (accessed May 10, 2015).

——. "Prison Memoirs." *Chinese Sociology and Anthropology* 15, nos. 1–2 (Fall-Winter 1982–1983).

Liu Tao, ed. *Da chuan lian* [The great linkup]. Beijing: Zhi shi chu ban she, 1993.

Liu Xiaobo. "That Holy Word, 'Revolution.'" In *Popular Protest and Political Culture in Modern China*, ed. Jeffrey N. Wasserstrom and Elizabeth J. Perry, 309–24. Boulder: Westview, 1994.

Liu Xiaofeng. *Wo men zhe yi dai ren de ai yu pa* [The love and fears of our generation]. Hong Kong: San lian shu ju, 1993.

Liu Xiaomeng, Ding Yizhuang, Shi Weimin, and He Lan. *Zhong guo zhi qing shi: da chao 1966–1980* [A history of sent-down youth in China: high tide 1966–1980]. Beijing: Zhong guo she hui ke xue chu ban she, 1998.

——. *Zhong guo zhi qing shi dian* [A dictionary of China's sent-down youth]. Chengdu: Sichuan ren min chu ban she, 1995.

Liu Xigong. "Ju you li shi jia zhi de yi ben xin shu" [A new book with a historical value]. *Zuo Tian* [Yesterday], no. 48 (March 30, 2015).

Liu Yingjie, ed. *Zhong guo jiao yu da shi dian 1949–1990* [Annals of education in China, 1949–1990]. Zhejiang: Zhejiang jiao yu chu ban she, 1993.

Liu Zhonglu. *Qing chun fang cheng shi: wu shi ge Beijing nü zhiqing hua dang nian* [The equations of youth: 50 female sent-down youth in Beijing on their past]. Beijing: Beijing University Press, 1995.

Li Xinhua. "Shi dai de jian zheng: jie ban ren yu 'di san dai ren'" [Witness to an era: successors and the 'third generation']. *Zhong guo qing nian yan jiu* [China youth study] 2 (1995): 4–16.

Li Yan. *Da dao chao tian—zhong guo xia gang zhi gong sheng cun bao gao* [The open road: a report on the living conditions of China's unemployed population]. Beijing: Zhong guo cheng shi chu ban she, 1998.

Li Yizhe. "On Socialist Democracy and Legal System." In *On Socialist Democracy and the Chinese Legal System*, ed. Anita Chan, Stanley Rosen, and Jonathan Unger, 31–86. Armonk, NY: M. E. Sharpe, 1985.

Li Zimao, "You guan wu dou de yi xie si kao" [Some thoughts on armed fighting] *Yesterday*, no. 39 (September 30, 2014): 28–35.

Lo, Jung-pang, ed. *K'ang Yu-wei: A Biography and a Symposium*. Tucson: University of Arizona Press, 1967.

London, Miriam, and Ivan D. London. "China's Lost Generation: The Fate of the Red Guards Since 1968." *Saturday Review*, November 30, 1974, 12–19.

Louie, Genny, and Kam Louie. "The Role of Nanjing University in the Nanjing Incident." *China Quarterly*, no. 86 (1981): 332–48.

Louie, Kam. "Discussions of Exposure Literature in the Chinese Press, 1978–1979." In *Between Fact and Fiction: Essays on Post-Mao Chinese Literature and Society*, 1–13. Sydney: Wild Peony, 1989.

——. "Educated Youth Literature: Self Discovery in the Chinese Village." In *Between Fact and Fiction: Essays on Post-Mao Chinese Literature and Society*, 91–102. Sydney: Wild Peony, 1989.

Lu, Li'an. *Yang tian chang xiao* [Outcry from a Red Guard imprisoned during the Cultural Revolution]. Hong Kong: Chinese University of Hong Kong, 2005.

Lu, Xing. *Rhetoric of the Chinese Cultural Revolution: The Impact on Chinese Thought, Culture, and Communication*. Columbia: University of South Carolina Press, 2004.

Lu Xing'er. *Sheng shi zhen shi de* [Life is real]. Jilin: Jilin ren min chu ban she, 1998.

Lu Xinhua and Liu Xinwu. *The Wounded: New Stories of the Cultural Revolution 77-78.* Trans. Geremie Barmé and Bennett Lee. Hong Kong: Joint, 1979.

Lu, Zhixuan, ed. *Sichuan sheng Chongqing di liu zhong xue xiao xiao zhi* [History of No. 6 Middle School in Chongqing]. Chongqing, 1991.

MacFarquhar, Roderick. *The Origins of the Cultural Revolution,* vol. 1: *Contradictions Among the People, 1956-1957.* New York: Columbia University Press, 1974.

———. *The Origins of the Cultural Revolution,* vol. 2: *The Great Leap Forward.* New York: Columbia University Press, 1983.

———. *The Origins of the Cultural Revolution,* vol. 3: *The Coming of the Cataclysm, 1961-1966.* New York: Columbia University Press, 1997.

MacFarquhar, Roderick, and Michael Schoenhals. *Mao's Last Revolution.* Cambridge: Belknap Press of Harvard University Press, 2008.

Ma Li. "Di tou ren zui, ge mian xi xin: wo de jiao dai he jian cha" [Lower my head, change my face, and wash my heart: my confession and self-criticism]. March 7, 1967. Insert in *Xin Chongqing bao,* March 13, 1967.

Mannheim, Karl. *Essays on the Sociology of Knowledge.* London: Routledge and K. Paul, 1952.

Mao Tse-Tung. "Dialogues with Responsible Persons of Capital Red Guards Congress." July 28, 1968. Available online at https://www.marxists.org/reference/archive/mao/selected-works/volume-9/mswv9_81.htm (accessed May 5, 2015).

———. *Quotations from Chairman Mao Tse-Tung.* Ed., with an introductory essay and notes, Stuart R. Schram. New York: Praeger, 1967.

———. *Selected Works of Mao Tse-Tung.* Vol. 1. Peking: Foreign Language Press, 1965.

———. *Selected Works of Mao Tse-Tung.* Vol. 4. Peking: Foreign Languages Press, 1977.

Marvin, Carolyn, and David W. Ingle. *Blood Sacrifice and the Nation.* Cambridge: Cambridge University Press, 1999.

Mathews, Thomas Jay. "The Cultural Revolution in Szechwan." In *The Cultural Revolution in the Provinces.* Cambridge: Harvard University Press, 1971.

McAdam, Doug. "The Biographical Consequences of Activism." *American Sociological Review* 54 (1989): 744–60.

———. *Freedom Summer.* New York: Oxford University Press, 1988.

McDougall, Bonnie S. "Dissent Literature: Official and Nonofficial Literature in and About China in the Seventies." *Contemporary China* 3, no. 4 (1979): 49–79.

———. "Poems, Poets, and Poetry 1976: An Exercise in the Typology of Modern Chinese Literature." *Contemporary China* 2, no. 4 (1978): 76–124.

Mclaren, Anne. "The Educated Youth Return." *Australian Journal of Chinese Affairs* 2 (1979): 1–20.

McMillian, John. *Smoking Typewriters: The Sixties Underground Press and the Rise of Alternative Media in America.* New York: Oxford University Press, 2011.

Meisner, Maurice. "The Cult of Mao Tse-tung." In *Marxism, Maoism and Utopianism,* 155–83. Madison: University of Wisconsin Press, 1982.

———. *Mao's China and After: A History of the People's Republic.* 3d ed. New York: Free Press, 1999.

Melucci, Alberto. *Nomads of the Present: Social Movements and Individual Needs in Contemporary Society.* Philadelphia: Temple University Press, 1989.

Meng, Angela and Wu Nan, "Loyal to Mao's Legacy, China's Princelings Have High Hopes for Fellow 'Red Descendant' Xi: Children of Revolutionary Leaders Persecuted Under Rule of Communist Party Head Say His Legacy Outweighs Violence and Political Turmoil." *South China Morning Post*, December 23, 2013. Available online at http://www.scmp.com/news/china/article/1388861/loyal-maos-legacy-chinas-princelings-have-high-hopes-fellow-red?page=all (accessed April 7, 2015).

Metzger, Thomas A. *Escape from Predicament: Neo-Confucianism and China's Evolving Political Culture.* New York: Columbia University Press, 1977.

Mi Hedu. *Hong wei bing zhe yi dai* [A generation known as Red Guards]. Hong Kong: San lian shu dian, 1993.

Milton, David, and Nancy Dall Milton. *The Wind Will Not Subside: Years in Revolutionary China, 1964-1969.* New York: Pantheon, 1976.

Mitter, Rana. *A Bitter Revolution: China's Struggle with the Modern World.* Oxford: Oxford University Press, 2004.

Mittler, Barbara. *A Continuous Revolution: Making Sense of Cultural Revolution Culture.* Cambridge: Harvard University Press, 2013.

Moore, Barrington. *Moral Purity and Persecution in History.* Princeton: Princeton University Press, 2000.

Morin, Edward, ed. *The Red Azalea: Chinese Poetry Since the Cultural Revolution.* Trans. Fang Dai, Dennis Ding, and Edward Morin. Honolulu: University of Hawaii Press, 1990.

Munro, Donald J. *The Concept of Man in Contemporary China.* Ann Arbor: University of Michigan Press, 1977.

Munro, Robin. "Settling Accounts with the Cultural Revolution at Beijing University, 1977–78." *China Quarterly* 82 (1980): 308–34.

Mu Zhai (Pseudonym). *Huang ruo ge shi—wo de zhiqing sui yue* [Like another world: my days as an educated youth]. Beijing: Zuo jia chu ban she, 1998.

Mu Zhijing. "Si shui liu nian" [Years flowing by like water]. In *Bao feng yu de ji yi: 1965-1970 nian de Beijing si zhong* [Memories of the storm: Beijing's No. 4 Middle School, 1965–1970], ed. Bei Dao, Cao Yifan, and Wei Yi, 1–52. Beijing: San lian shu dian, 2012.

Nathan, Andrew. *Chinese Democracy.* New York: Knopf, 1985.

O'Brien, Kevin J. and Lianjiang Li. "Campaign Nostalgia in the Chinese Countryside." *Asian Survey* 39, no. 3 (1999): 376–91.

Osnos, Evan. "Born Red: How Xi Jinping, a Unremarkable Provincial Administrator, Became China's Most Authoritarian Leader Since Mao." *New Yorker,* April 6, 2015. Available online at http://www.newyorker.com/magazine/2015/04/06/born-red (accessed April 7, 2015).

Pan, Yihong. *Tempered in the Revolutionary Furnace: China's Youth in the Rustication Movement.* Lanham, MD: Lexington, 2009.

Pan Xiaoling. "'San jiao di' de xian shi yu ji yi" [The reality and memories of the "Triangle"]. *Southern Weekend,* December 18, 2007. Available online at http://www.infzm.com/content/1784 (accessed March 28, 2015).

Parish, William, ed. *Chinese Rural Development: The Great Transformation.* Armonk, NY: M. E. Sharpe, 1984.

Passerini, Luisa. *Autobiography of a Generation: Italy, 1968*. Hanover, NH: University Press of New England, 1996.

Perry, Elizabeth J. *Anyuan: Mining China's Revolutionary Tradition*. Berkeley: University of California Press, 2012.

——. "'To Rebel Is Justified': Cultural Revolution Influences on Contemporary Chinese Protest." In *The Chinese Cultural Revolution Reconsidered: Beyond Purge and Holocaust*, ed. Kam-yee Law. New York: Palgrave MacMillan, 2003.

Perry, Elizabeth J., and Li Xun. *Proletarian Power: Shanghai Workers in the Cultural Revolution*. Boulder: Westview, 1997.

——. "Revolutionary Rudeness: The Language of Red Guard and Rebel Worker in China's Cultural Revolution." In *Twentieth-Century China: New Approaches*, ed. Jeffrey N. Wasserstrom, 221–36. New York: Routledge, 2002.

Peterson, Willard J. *Bitter Gourd: Fang I-Chih and the Impetus for Intellectual Change*. New Haven: Yale University Press, 1979.

Pi pan "hu shan xing" lian luo zhan. "Che di qing suan Beijing da xue 'Jing Gang Shan,' 'Hong Lian Jun' de bie dong dui—'Hu Shan Xing' de fan ge ming zui xing." [Thoroughly settle account with the counterrevolutionary crime of "To the Tiger Mountain"—a special action team associated with Peking University's "Jinggang Mountain' and 'Red Alliance Army"]. *Xin Bei Da*, February 1, 1967, 1–4.

Polletta, Francesca. *It Was Like a Fever: Storytelling in Protest and Politics*. Chicago: University of Chicago Press.

PRC State Press and Publication Administration Policy Laws and Regulations Section, ed. *Zhong hua ren min gong he guo xian xing xin wen chu ban fa gui hui bian (1949–1990)* [Operative press and publishing laws and regulations of the People's Republic of China, 1949–1990], 231–32. Beijing: Ren min chu ban she, 1991.

Pye, Lucian W. "Reassessing the Cultural Revolution." *China Quarterly* 108 (1986): 597–612.

——. *The Spirit of Chinese Politics: A Psychological Study of the Authority Crisis in Political Development*. Cambridge: MIT Press, 1968.

Qi Zhi. "Song Binbin dao qian zhi hou: Wu zhong sheng yin, yi ge bei jing" [After Song Binbin's apology: five voices, one background]. *Ji Yi* [Remembrance], no. 7 (2014): 19–26.

Qian Liqun. "The Way Our Generation Imagined the World." *Inter-Asia Cultural Studies* 6, no. 4 (2005): 524–34.

Qin Hui. "Chen zhong de lang man: Wo de hong wei bing shi dai" [Heavy-burdened romance: my Red Guard days]. In *1966: Wo men na yi dai de hui yi* [1966: Our generation's memories], ed. Xu Youyu, 285–306. Beijing: Zhong guo wen lian chu ban she, 1998.

Qin Xiaoying. "Hong wei bing zhi qi [Red Guards as a banner]." In *Hong wei bing mi lu* [Secret records about Red Guards], ed. Yu Hui, 1–29. Beijing: Tuan jie chu ban she, 1993.

Qun Zhong. *Ming yun lie che: zhiqing fan cheng chen fu lu* [A train called destiny: sent-down youth return to the city]. Chengdu: Sichuan wen yi chu ban she, 1994.

Raddock, David M. *Political Behavior in Adolescents in China: The Cultural Revolution in Kwangchow*. Tucson: University of Arizona Press, 1977.

Ren Wanding, "Reflections on the Historical Character of the Democracy Movement." In *Voices from Tiananmen Square: Beijing Spring and The Democracy Movement*, ed. Mok Chiu Yu and J. Frank Harrison, 47–53. New York: Black Rose, 1990.

Ren Yi. *Sheng si bei ge: "zhiqing zhi ge" yuan yu shi mo* [A song of life and death: the story of an unjust verdict for the author of "Song of Sent-down Youth"]. Beijing: Zhong guo she hui ke xue chu ban she, 1998.

Ridley, Charles P., Paul H. B. Godwin, and Dennis J. Doolin. *The Making of a Model Citizen in Communist China*. Stanford: Hoover Institution Press, 1971.

Roberts, Dexter. "Xi Jinping Is No Fun. Business Week." *Businessweek.* October 3, 2013. Available online at http://www.businessweek.com/articles/2013–10–03/china-president -xi-jinping-revives-self-criticism-sessions-in-maoism-lite. (accessed May 4, 2015).

Rosen, Stanley. "Guangzhou's Democracy Movement in Cultural Revolution Perspective." *China Quarterly* 101 (March 1985): 1–31.

——. *Red Guard Factionalism and the Cultural Revolution in Guangzhou (Canton)*. Boulder: Westview, 1982.

Ross, Andrew. "Mao Zedong's Impact on Cultural Politics in the West." *Cultural Politics* 1, no. 1 (2005): 5–25.

Roth, Guenther. "Socio-Historical Model and Developmental Theory: Charismatic Community, Charisma of Reason and the Counterculture." *American Sociological Review* 40 (1975): 148–57.

Russo, Alessandro. "The Conclusive Scene: Mao and the Red Guards in July 1968." *positions: east asia cultures critique* 13, no. 3 (2005): 535–74.

Sang Ye. "Memories for the Future." In *Yang Zhichao: Chinese Bible*, ed. Claire Roberts, 27–31. Sydney: Sherman Contemporary Art Foundation.

Sausmikat, Nora. "Resisting Current Stereotypes: Private Narrative Strategies in the Autobiographies of Former Rusticated Women." In *China's Great Cultural Revolution: Master Narratives and Post-Mao Counternarratives*, ed. Woei Lien Chong, 255–84. Lanham, MD: Rowman and Littlefield, 2002.

Scharping, Thomas. "The Man, the Myth, the Message—New Trends in Mao-Literature from China." *China Quarterly* 137 (1994): 168–79.

Schoenhals, Michael, ed. *China's Cultural Revolution, 1966-1969: Not a Dinner Party*. Armonk, NY: M. E. Sharpe, 1996.

——. *Doing Things with Words in Chinese Politics: Five Studies*. Berkeley: University of California Center for East Asian Studies, 1992.

——. "Jiyi [Remembrance]," ed. Wu Di and He Shu. *China Quarterly* 197 (March 2009): 204–6.

——. "Proscription and Prescription of Political Terminology by the Central Authorities, 1949–1989." In *Norms and the State in China*, ed. Chun-chieh Huang and Erik Zurcher, 337–59. Leiden: Brill, 1993.

——. "'Why Don't We Arm the Left?' Mao's Culpability for the Cultural Revolution's 'Great Chaos' of 1967." *China Quarterly* 182 (June 2005): 277–300.

Schram, Stuart R. "Introduction." In *Chairman Mao Talks to the People: Talks and Letters, 1956-1971*, ed. Stuart Schram, 7–57. New York: Pantheon, 1974.

Schudson, Michael. "The Present in the Past Versus the Past in the Present." In *The Collective Memory Reader*, ed. Jeffrey Olick, Vered Vinitzky-Seroussi, and Daniel Levy, 287–90. Oxford: Oxford University Press, 2011.

Schuman, Howard, and Jacqueline Scott. "Generations and Collective Memories." *American Sociological Review* 54 (1989): 359–81.

Schwarcz, Vera. *The Chinese Enlightenment: Intellectuals and the Legacy of the May Fourth Movement of 1919.* Berkeley: University of California Press, 1986.

Schwartz, Barry, and Mikyoung Kim. "Introduction: Northeast Asia's Memory Problem." In *Northeast Asia's Difficult Past: Essays in Collective Memory,* ed. Mikyoung Kim and Barry Schwartz, 1–30. New York: Palgrave Macmillan.

Schwartz, Benjamin. *In Search of Wealth and Power: Yen Fu and the West.* Cambridge: Harvard University Press, 1964.

Scott, Dorothea H. *Chinese Popular Literature and the Child.* Chicago: American Library Association, 1980.

Scott, James C. *Domination and the Arts of Resistance: Hidden Transcripts.* New Haven: Yale University Press, 1990.

September First Column of the Middle School Red Guards. "Wei you xi sheng duo zhuang zhi: Zhong xue sheng hong wei bing jiu yi zong dui yi shu" [Death only strengthens the bold resolve: testament of September First Column of the Middle School Red Guards]. *October Fifth Storm,* June 9, 1967.

Sewell, William H. Jr. "Historical Events as Transformations of Structures: Inventing Revolution at the Bastille." *Theory and Society* 25 (1996): 841–81.

——. "Ideologies and Social Revolutions: Reflections on the French Case." *Journal of Modern History* 57, no.1 (March 1985): 57–85.

——. "A Theory of Structure: Duality, Agency, and Transformation." *American Journal of Sociology* 98, no. 1 (1992): 1–29.

Seymour, James D. *The Fifth Modernization: China's Human Rights Movement, 1978-1979.* Stanfordville, NY: Human Rights, 1980.

Shen, Zhihua, and Yafeng Xia. "Hidden Currents During the Honeymoon: Mao, Khrushchev, and the 1957 Moscow Conference." *Journal of Cold War Studies* 11, no. 4 (Fall 2009): 74–117.

Sheridan, Mary. "The Emulation of Heroes." *China Quarterly* 33 (1968): 47–72.

Shi, Weimin, ed. *Zhiqing ri ji xuan bian* [Collected diaries by educated youth]. Beijing: Zhong guo she hui ke xue chu ban she, 1996.

——, ed. *Zhiqing shu xin xuan bian* [Collected letters by educated youth]. Beijing: Zhong guo she hui ke xue chu ban she, 1996.

Shi, Weimin and He Lan. *Zhiqing bei wang lu: shang shan xia xiang yun dong zhong de sheng chan jian she bing tuan* [Memorandum on educated youth]. Beijing: Zhong guo she hui ke xue chu ban she, 1996.

Shi Zhi. *Shi Zhi de Shi* [Forefinger's poems]. Beijing: Ren min wen xue chu ban she, 2000.

Shu Jun. "Zeng qiang dang xing, gen chu pai xing: Lun Guangxi qing li wen ge yi liu wen ti zhong de yi ge guan jian xing wen ti [Strengthen party spirit, eradicate factional spirit: on a key question in resolving issues left behind from the Cultural Revolution in Guangxi]." *Xue shu lun tan* [Academic forum] 4 (1983).

Shu Ting. "Sheng huo, shu ji yu shi" [Life, books, and poetry]. In *Chen lun de sheng dian* [The fallen altar], ed. Liao Yiwu, 297–307. Urumqi: Xinjiang qing shao nian chu ban she, 1999.

Snow, David A., Louis A. Zurcher, and Robert Peters. "Victory Celebrations as Theater: A Dramaturgical Approach to Crowd Behavior." *Symbolic Interaction* 4, no. 1 (1981): 21–42.

Solinger, Dorothy J. *China's Transition from Socialism: Statist Legacies and Market Reforms, 1980–1990.* Armonk, NY: M. E. Sharpe, 1993.

Solomon, Richard. *Mao's Revolution and the Chinese Political Culture.* Berkeley: University of California Press, 1971.

Song, Binbin. "Lao san jie xiao you yu lao shi jian mian hui fa yan [Speech at meeting of old three classes alum with their teachers]." *Ji Yi* [Remembrance] 108, February 15, 2015.

Song, Yongyi, ed. Zhong guo wen hua da ge ming wen ku [*Chinese Cultural Revolution Database.*] Hong Kong: Universities Service Centre for China Studies, the Chinese University of Hong Kong, 2002.

——, ed. *Xin bian hong wei bing zi liao II* [A new collection of Red Guard publications, part 2: a special compilation of newspapers in Beijing area]. 40 vols. Oakton, VA: Center for Chinese Research Materials, 2001.

——, ed. *Xin bian hong wei bing zi liao III* [A new collection of Red Guard publications, part 3, a comprehensive compilation of tabloids in the provinces]. 52 vols. Oakton, VA: Center for Chinese Research Materials, 2005.

——. "Zong lun: yi duan chu lu, si chao die qi de zhong guo wen hua da ge ming" [Introduction: the rise of heretical thoughts in China's Cultural Revolution]. In *Wen hua da ge ming he ta di yi duan si chao,* ed. Song Yongyi and Sun Dajin. Hong Kong: Tian Yuan Shu Wu, 1997.

Song, Yongyi and Sun Dajin, ed. *Wen hua da ge ming he ta di yi duan si chao* [Heterodox thoughts during the Cultural Revolution]. Jiulong: Tian yuan shu wu, 1997.

Stallybrass, Peter, and Allon White. *The Politics and Poetics of Transgression.* Ithaca: Cornell University Press, 1986.

Steinhoff, Patricia, and Zwerman, Gilda. "Introduction to the Special Issue on Political Violence." *Qualitative Sociology* 31 (2008): 213–20.

Su, Yang. *Collective Killings in Rural China During the Cultural Revolution.* Cambridge: Cambridge University Press, 2011.

Sun, Lizhe, ed. *Qing ji huang tu di* [Emotional attachment to the yellow earth]. Beijing: Zhong guo guo ji guang bo chu ban she, 1996.

Ta lu ti hsia k'an wu hui pien [Collection of mainland underground publications]. 20 vols. Taipei: Institute of the Study of Chinese Communist Problems, 1980–1984.

Tao, Sen. "Letter of Proposal." In *Documents of the Democracy Movement in Communist China, 1978-1981.* Stanford University: East Asian Collection, Hoover Institution Library and Archives, 1980.

Tao, Zheng. "Zi you de tu di" [The soil of freedom]. In *Qing ji huang tu di* [Emotional attachment to the yellow earth], ed. Lizhe Sun, 26–34. Beijing: Zhong guo guo ji guang bo chu ban she, 1996.

Tao, Zhu. "Tao Zhu tong zhi jiang hua" [Comrade Tao Zhu's speech]. In *Hong wei bing zi liao: xu bian* [Red Guard publications: supplement 2], 4:2294. Okaton, VA: Center for Chinese Research Materials, 1992.

Tarrow, Sidney. *Power in Movement: Social Movements and Contentious Politics.* 3rd ed. Cambridge: Cambridge University Press, 2011.

Taylor, Charles. *Sources of the Self*. Cambridge: Harvard University Press, 1989.

Teiwes, Frederick C., and Warren Sun. *The End of the Maoist Era: Chinese Politics During the Twilight of the Cultural Revolution, 1972–1976*. Armonk, NY: M. E. Sharpe, 2007.

Tian, Fan. "Yi wei jiao shi de 'chuan lian' ri ji" [Diary of a teacher on a linkup trip]. In *Da chuan lian* [The great linkup], ed. Liu Tao, 344–80. Beijing: Zhi shi chu ban she, 1993.

Tilly, Charles. *The Politics of Collective Violence*. Cambridge: Cambridge University Press, 2003.

Tong Huaizhou group. *Wei da de si wu yun dong* [The great April Fifth movement]. Beijing: Beijing chu ban she, 1979.

Touraine, Alain. *May Movement*. Trans. Leonard F. X. Mayhew. New York: Random House, 1971.

Townsend, James R. *The Revolutionization of Chinese Youth: A Study of Chungkuo Ch'ing-nien*. Berkeley: University of California Center for Chinese Studies, 1967.

Tsai, Kellee. *Capitalism Without Democracy: The Private Sector in Contemporary China*. Ithaca, NY: Cornell University Press, 2007.

Tu, Wei-ming. *Humanity and Self-Cultivation: Essays in Confucian Thought*. Berkeley: Asian Humanities Press, 1979.

Tucker, Nancy Bernkopf. *The China Threat: Memories, Myths, and Realities in the 1950s*. New York: Columbia University Press, 2012.

Turner, Victor. *Process, Performance and Pilgrimage: A Study in Comparative Symbology*. New Delhi: Concept, 1979.

——. *The Ritual Process: Structure and Anti-Structure*. New York: Aldine, 1969.

Unger, Jonathan. *Education Under Mao: Class and Competition in Canton Schools, 1960–1980*. New York: Columbia University Press, 1982.

——. "Foreword." In *Captive Spirits: Prisoners of the Cultural Revolution*, ed. Yang Xiguang and Susan McFadden, vii–xviii. Hong Kong: Oxford University Press, 1997.

——. "Whither China? Yang Xiguang, Red Capitalists, and the Social Turmoil of the Cultural Revolution." *Modern China* 17, no. 1 (1991): 3–37.

Vidor, Claude, ed. *Documents on the Chinese Democracy Movement, 1978–1980*. Hong Kong: Observer, 1981.

Walder, Andrew G. "Beijing Red Guard Factionalism: Social Interpretations Reconsidered." *Journal of Asian Studies* 61 (2002): 437–71.

——. *China Under Mao: A Revolution Derailed*. Cambridge: Harvard University Press, 2015.

——. "Cultural Revolution Radicalism: Variations on a Stalinist Theme." In *New Perspectives on the Cultural Revolution*, ed. William A. Joseph, Christine P. W. Wong, and David Zweig, 41–61. Cambridge: Council on East Asian Studies, Harvard University, 1991.

——. *Fractured Rebellion: The Beijing Red Guard Movement*. Cambridge: Harvard University Press, 2009.

——. "Political Sociology and Social Movements." *Annual Review of Sociology*, 35 (2009): 393–412.

——, ed., *Zouping in Transition: The Process of Reform in Rural North China*. Cambridge: Harvard University Press, 1998.

Walzer, Michael. *The Revolution of Saints: A Study in the Origins of Radical Politics*. Cambridge: Harvard University Press, 1965.

Wang, Ban. *The Sublime Figure of History: Aesthetics and Politics in Twentieth-Century China.* Stanford: Stanford University Press, 1997.

Wang, Dawen, ed. *Ke shu hui wang cheng gu xiang* [The temporary abode that we now call our hometown]. Beijing: Zhong guo gong ren chu ban she, 1998.

——. "Wo ai ni Beidahuang" [I love you, Beidahuang]. In *Ke shu hui wang cheng gu xiang* [The temporary abode that we now call our hometown], ed. Wang Dawen, 300. Beijing: Zhong guo gong ren chu ban she, 1998.

Wang, Youqin. "Student Attacks Against Teachers: The Revolution of 1966." *Issues and Studies* 37, no. 2 (2001): 29–79.

——. *Victims of the Cultural Revolution: An Investigative Account of Persecution, Imprisonment and Murder.* Hong Kong: Kaifang za zhi chu ban she, 2004.

Wang, Jing. *High Culture Fever: Politics, Aesthetics, and Ideology in Deng's China.* Berkeley: University of California Press, 1996.

Wang, Juntao. "Democracy Wall—the Roots of a Movement." *China Rights Forum* (Summer 1998): 28.

Wang, Rui. "Mao Zhu xi zui zhu yi zaofanpai bao zhi, ni men yao ba bao zhi ban hao" [Chairman Mao pays most attention to rebels' newspapers, you should run your paper well]. *Ji Yi* [Remembrance] 87, August 31, 2012.

Wang, Shaoguang. "'New Trends of Thought' on the Cultural Revolution." *Journal of Contemporary China* 8, no. 21 (1999): 197–217.

"Wang Li, Qi Benyu jie jian Chongqing shi zhong xue sheng hong wei bing bei shang gao zhuang tuan de jiang hua" [Speeches given by Wang Li and Qi Benyu at the meetings with the gao zhuang delegation of middle school students from Chongqing]. In *Hong wei bing zi liao xu bian* [Red Guard publications supplement], 4:2374. 8 vols. Washington, DC: Center for Chinese Research Materials, 1992.

Wang Xiaojian. "Qiu zhi qu shi [Anecdotes about knowledge seeking]." In *Qing ji huang tu di* [Emotional attachment to the yellow earth], ed. Lizhe Sun, 94–97. Beijing: Zhong guo guo ji guang bo chu ban she, 1996.

Wang Xizhe. "From Li Yizhe to Wang Xizhe." *Zhong guo zhi chun* [China spring] 158 (1996): 33–36.

Wasserstrom, Jeffrey N., and Elizabeth J. Perry, eds. *Popular Protests and Political Culture in Modern China: Learning from 1989.* Boulder: Westview, 1992.

Weber, Max. *Economy and Society: An Outline of Interpretive Sociology.* 2 vols. Ed. Guenther Roth and Claus Wittich. Berkeley: University of California Press, 1978.

——. *The Theory of Social and Economic Organization.* New York: Free Press, 1964.

Wei Dong. "Ren Baige ji qi tong huo shi zen yang zhen ya shan cheng wen hua da ge ming de" [How Ren Baige and his followers suppressed the Cultural Revolution in the mountain city]. *Shan cheng hong qi*, June 7, 1967, 4. In *Xin bian hong wei bing zi liao III*, ed. Yongyi Song, 16279. Oakton, VA: Center for Chinese Research Materials.

Whalen, Jack, and Richard Flacks. *Beyond the Barricades: The Sixties Generation Grows Up.* Philadelphia: Temple University Press, 1989.

White, Lynn T., III. *Policies of Chaos: The Organizational Causes of Violence in China's Cultural Revolution.* Princeton: Princeton University Press, 1989.

——. *Unstately Power:* vol. 1, *Local Causes of China's Economic Reforms.* Armonk, NY: M. E. Sharpe, 1998.

Whittier, Nancy. *Feminist Generations: The Persistence of the Radical Women's Movement.* Philadelphia: Temple University Press, 1995.

——. "Political Generations, Micro-Cohorts, and the Transformation of Social Movements." *American Sociological Review* 62, no. 5 (1997): 760–78.

"Why Is Chongqing So Red?" *Vista (Kan tian xia)* 2 (2011). Available online at www.vista story.com/index.php/Ebook/details/news_id/1719.

Widor, Claude, ed. *Documents on the Chinese Democratic Movement, 1978–1980,* vol. 2. Paris: Editions de l'Ecole des Hautes Etudes en Sciences Sociales, 1984.

Winter, Jay. "The Generation of Memory: Reflections on the 'Memory Boom' in Contemporary Historical Studies." *German Historical Institute Bulletin* 27 (Fall 2000). Available online at http://www.ghi-dc.org/bulletin27F00/b27winterframe.html (accessed December 5, 2005).

Wolin, Richard. *The Wind from the East: French Intellectuals, the Cultural Revolution, and the Legacy of the 1960s.* Princeton: Princeton University Press, 2010.

Wu, Yiching. *The Cultural Revolution at the Margins: Chinese Socialism in Crisis.* Cambridge: Harvard University Press, 2014.

Wu, Hung. *Remaking Beijing: Tiananmen Square and the Creation of a Political Space.* Chicago: University of Chicago Press, 2005.

Wu, Mi. *Wu Mi ri ji xu bian: 1967–1968* [Supplements to Wu Mi's diaries: 1967–1968]. Vol. 8. Beijing: San lian shu dian, 2006.

Xiao, Fuxing. *Chu mo wang shi* [Gently touching the past]. Jilin: Jilin ren min chu ban she, 1998.

Xiao Xiao. "Wen hua ge ming zhong de di xia du shu yun dong" [The underground reading movement in the Cultural Revolution]. *Beijing zhi cun* [Beijing spring] 9 (1997).

Xie, Quan. "Wo zai wen hua da ge ming zhong de jing li" [My experiences in the Cultural Revolution]. In *Wo men na yi dai de hui yi* [Our generation's memories], ed. Xu Youyu, 145–69. Beijing: Zhong guo wen lian chu ban she, 1998.

Xin Beida 1210 zhan dou dui. "Chan chu Yilin-Dixi de da du cao" [Uproot Yilin-Dixi's big poisonous weed]. *Xin Bei Da,* December 24, 1966, 3.

Xing, Qi. *Lao zhiqing liao zhai* [Tales of former educated youth]. Beijing: Gong ren chu ban she, 1994.

Xin, Qun, ed. *Sui yue liu hen—zhao pian, shi ci, ri ji, shu xin xuan* [Remains of the day: a collection of photos, poems, diaries, and letters]. Shenyang: Shenyang chu ban she, 1998.

——. *Wu hui nian hua—bai ming zhiqing hua dang nian* [Years of no regret: one hundred educated youth on their past]. Shenyang: Shenyang chu ban she, 1998.

Xin, Yizhi. "Chu bu jian cha" [Preliminary self-criticism]. March 1, 1967. Insert in *Xin Chongqing bao,* March 13, 1967.

Xi, Xuan and Jin Chunming. *"Wen hua da ge ming" jian shi* [A brief history of the "Cultural Revolution"]. Beijing: Zhong gong dang shi chu ban she, 1996.

Xu, Aijing. *Qinghua Kuai Dafu.* Hong Kong: Zhong guo wen ge li shi chu ban she, 2011.

Xu, Hailiang. "Wo de wen ge jian wen: Ling yi lei xue sheng yu wen ge" [What I saw and heard in the Cultural Revolution: another type of student and their Cultural Revolution]. *China News Digest Supplement* 522, August 23, 2006. Available online at http://www.cnd.org/CR/ZK06/cr356.gb.html (accessed December 26, 2014).

Xu, Jilin. "Qi meng de zi wo wa jie" [The self-disintegration of enlightenment]. *Er shi yi shi ji* [Twenty-First Century] 4 (2005): 4–16.

Xu, Jing. *Da yue jin yun dong zhong de zheng zhi chuan bo* [Political communication in the Great Leap Forward campaign]. Hong Kong: Hong Kong Social Sciences Press, 2004.

Xu, Xiao. *Ban sheng wei ren* [Half of my life]. Beijing: Tong xin chu ban she, 2005.

——, ed. *Min jian shu xin: zhong guo min jian si xiang shi lu* [Letters from the ground: true records of unofficial thinking in China]. Hefei: Anhui wen yi chu ban she, 2000.

Xu, Xiao, Ding Dong, and Xu Youyu, eds. *Yu Luoke: Yi zuo yu hui yi* [Yu Luoke: Posthumous writings and recollections]. Beijing: Zhong guo wen lian chu ban she, 1999.

Xu, Youyu. *Xing xing se se de zao fan: Hong wei bing jing shen su zhi de xing cheng ji yan bian* [Rebels of all stripes: a study of Red Guard mentalities]. Hong Kong: Chinese University Press, 1999.

——. "Yi duan si chao he hong wei bing de si xiang zhuan xiang" [Heterodox thoughts and changes in the thinking of Red Guards]. *Er shi yi shi ji* [Twenty-first century], no. 10 (1996): 52–64.

Yan, Mei. "Ta zai shen qing de re tu shang" [Stepping onto the heart-warming land]. In *Qing ji huang tu di: Beijing zhiqing yu Shanbei* [Emotional attachment to the yellow earth: educated youth of Beijing in northern Shaanxi], ed. Lizhe Sun, 225–30. Beijing: Zhong guo guo ji guang bo chu ban she, 1996.

Yang, Bin. "'We want to go home!': The Great Petition of the Zhiqing, Xishuangbanna, Yunnan: 1978–1979." *China Quarterly* 198 (2009): 401–21.

Yang, Fenggang. *Religion in China: Survival and Revival Under Communist Rule.* Oxford: Oxford University Press, 2012.

Yang, Guobin. "China's Zhiqing Generation: Nostalgia, Identity, and Cultural Resistance in the 1990s." *Modern China* 29, no. 3 (July 2003): 267–96.

——. "From Nostalgia to Rights Defense: Changes in the Zhiqing Narratives Since the 1990s." Paper presented at the International Conference on History and Memory of China's Zhiqing Generation: Multidisciplinary Perspectives. December 13–14, 2013, Fudan University, Shanghai.

——. "The Liminal Effects of Social Movements: Red Guards and the Transformation of Identity." *Sociological Forum* 15, no. 2 (2000): 379–406.

——. "Mao Quotations in Factional Battles and Their Afterlives: Episodes from Chongqing." In *Mao's Little Red Book: A Global History*, ed. Alexander C. Cook, 61–75. Cambridge: Cambridge University Press, 2014.

——. "'A Portrait of Martyr Jiang Qing': The Chinese Cultural Revolution on the Internet." In *Re-envisioning the Chinese Revolution: The Politics and Poetics of Collective Memories in Reform China*, ed. Ching Kwan Lee and Guobin Yang, 287–316. Stanford: Stanford University Press, 2007.

——. "The Routinization of Liminality: The Persistence of Activism Among China's Red Guard Generation." In *East Asian Social Movements: Power, Protest, and Change in a Dynamic Region*, ed. Jeffrey Broadbent and Vicky Brockman, 437–55. New York: Springer, 2011.

———. *The Power of the Internet in China: Citizen Activism Online.* New York: Columbia University Press, 2009.

Yang, Dongping. *Jian nan de ri chu: Zhong guo xian dai jiao yu de 20 shi ji* [The difficult sunrise: modern Chinese education in the twentieth century]. Shanghai: Wei hui chu ban she, 2003.

Yang, Jian. *Wen hua da ge ming zhong de di xia wen xue* [Underground literature during the Cultural Revolution]. Beijing: Zhao hua chu ban she, 1993.

———. *Zhong guo zhi qing wen xue shi* [A history of sent-down youth literature in China]. Beijing: Zhong guo gong ren chu ban she, 2002.

Yang, Xiguang. *Captive Spirits: Prisoners of the Cultural Revolution.* New York: Oxford University Press, 1997.

———. "Where Is China Heading?" *Contemporary Chinese Thought* 32, no. 4 (Summer 2001): 56–80.

———. "Whither China?" In *The Revolution Is Dead. Long Live the Revolution: Readings from the Great Proletariat Cultural Revolution from an Ultra-Left Perspective*, 180–200. Hong Kong: The 70s, 1976.

———. "'Zhong guo xiang he chu qu?' da zi bao shi mo" [The story behind 'Whither China?']. *China Spring* 12 (1990).

Ya Yi. "Out of the Conscience of an Intellectual: An Interview with Dr. Mu Zhijing." *Beijing Spring* 37 (1996): 68–75.

———. "Ren quan yi shi zai Zhong guo de jue xing: Fang lai zi Shanghai de ren quan wei shi Yang Zhou [The awakening of human rights consciousness in China: an interview with the Shanghai human rights guardian Yang Zhou]." *Beijing zhi chun* [Beijing spring] 30 (November 1996).

Yin, Hongbiao. *Shi zong zhe de zu ji: Wen hua da ge ming qi jian de qing nian si chao* [Footprints of the missing: thoughts of the youth during the Cultural Revolution]. Hong Kong: Chinese University of Hong Kong Press, 2009.

Yu, Xiguang. *Wei bei wei gan wang you guo* [Dare not to forget worrying about the country even in a low position]. Changsha: Hunan People's Press, 1989.

Zarrow, Peter. "Meanings of China's Cultural Revolution: Memoirs of Exile." *positions: east asia cultures critique* 7, no. 1 (1999): 165–91.

Zelizer, Barbie. *About to Die: How News Images Move the Public.* New York: Oxford University Press, 2010.

———. *Remembering to Forget: Holocaust Memory Through the Camera's Eye.* Chicago: University of Chicago Press, 1998.

Zhang, Fusheng. "Wo liao jie de 'huang pi shu' chu ban shi mo" [What I know about the beginning and end of the publishing of "yellow-cover books"]. *Zhong hua du shu bao*, August 23, 2006, 10.

Zhang, Xudong. *Chinese Modernism in the Era of Reforms: Cultural Fever, Avant-garde Fiction, and the New Chinese Cinema.* Duke: Duke University Press, 1997.

———. "National Trauma, Global Allegory: Reconstruction of Collective Memory in Tian Zhuangzhuang's *The Blue Kite*." *Journal of Contemporary China* 12, no. 37 (2003): 623–38.

Zhang, Yangong. "Beijing–Yan'an tu bu chang zheng ri ji [Diary on a walking journey from Beijing to Yan'an]." In *Da chuan lian* [The great linkup], ed. Liu Tao, 265–343. Beijing: Zhi shi chu ban she, 1993.

Zhang, Zhilu. *Zhong guo shao nian er tong dian ying shi lun* [A historical study of children's films in China]. Beijing: Zhong guo dian ying chu ban she, 2005.

Zhao, Suisheng. "Deng Xiaoping's Southern Tour: Elite Politics in Post-Tiananmen China." *Asian Survey* 33, no. 8 (August 1993): 739–56.

Zhao, Zhenkai. "Zou jin bao feng yu" [Walking into the storm]. In *Bao feng yu de ji yi: 1965–1970 nian de Beijing si zhong* [Memories of the storm: Beijing's No. 4 Middle School, 1965–1970], ed. Bei Dao, Cao Yifan, and Wei Yi, 236–66. Beijing: San lian shu dian, 2012.

Zheng, Qian. "'Wen hua da ge ming' de bali gong she qing jie" [The Paris Commune Complex in the 'Great Cultural Revolution]. *Zhong gong dang shi yan jiu*, no. 2 (2010): 5–16.

Zhi Qing (Pseudonym), ed. *Lao cha hua dang nian: Shanxi zhiqing sheng huo lu* [Sent-down youth talk about their past: lives of youth sent down to Shanxi]. Beijing: Da zhong wen yi chu ban she, 1994.

Zhong, Xueping. "'Long Live Youth' and the Ironies of Youth and Gender in Chinese Film of the 1950s and '60s." *Modern Chinese Literature and Culture* 11, no. 2 (Fall 1999): 150–85.

Zhong gong zhong yang guan yu bao zhi wen ti de tong zhi (Zhongfa 67, no. 9), January 3, 1967. In Yongyi Song, ed., *Chinese Cultural Revolution Database*. Hong Kong: Universities Service Centre for China Studies, the Chinese University of Hong Kong, 2002.

Zhong guo bai ke nian jian. Beijing: Zhong guo da bai ke quan shu chu ban she, 1980.

Zhong hua ban ben tu shu guan, ed. *Quan guo nei bu fa xing tu shu zong mu: 1949–1986* [All-China complete catalogue of books published for internal distribution, 1949–1986]. Beijing: Zhong hua shu ju, 1988.

Zhou, Lijing. "Zhang zai chuang ba shang de shu: Dui 'wen ge' shou chao ben de yi ci zong jie yu biao da: dai xu" [Trees growing out of scars: a summary and an expression of the hand-copied fiction of the Cultural Revolution: In lieu of a preface]. In *An Liu: Lu se shi ti* [Undercurrents: green dead bodies], ed. Bai Shihong, 12–29. Beijing: Wen hua yi shu chu ban she, 2002.

Zhou, Lunzuo. *Wen ge zao fan pai zhen xiang* [The historical truth about rebels during the Cultural Revolution]. Hong Kong: Tian yuan shu wu, 2006.

Zhou, Yong. "Chongqing de 'chang, du, jiang, chuan' yu guo jia wen hua ruan shi li" [Song, reading, storytelling, and disseminating red culture in Chongqing and national soft power]. *Chong Social Sciences*, no. 5 (2011): 92.

Zhou, Yuan, ed. *Xin bian hong wei bing zi liao* [A new collection of Red Guard publications. Part 1, Newspapers]. 20 vols. Oakton, VA: Center for Chinese Research Materials, 1999.

Zhou, Ziren. *Hong wei bing xiao bao zhu bian zi shu* [Personal story of an editor of a Red Guard newspaper]. Fort Worth: Fellows Press of America, 2006.

Zhu, Dandan. *1956: Mao's China and the Hungarian Crisis.* Ithaca, NY: Cornell University Press, 2013.

Zhu, Qingfang. "On the Evolution and Changes of the Individual Economy and Counter-measures." *Chinese Economic Studies* 21, no. 2 (1988): 100–76.

Zhu, Wenjie. *Lao san jie cai fang shou ji* [Notes on interviews with the old three classes]. Xian: Tai bai wen yi chu ban she, 1998.

Zhu, Xueqin. "Si xiang shi shang de shi zong zhe" [The missing thinkers in intellectual history]. *Du Shu* [Reading] 10 (1996): 55–63.

Zweig, David S. "The Peida Debate on Education and the Fall of Teng Hsiao-p'ing." *China Quarterly* 73 (1978): 140–58.

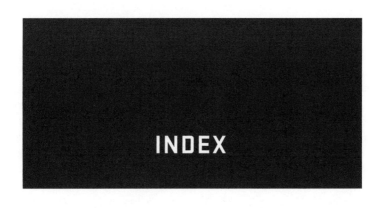

INDEX

STUDIES OF THE WEATHERHEAD EAST ASIAN INSTITUTE

COLUMBIA UNIVERSITY

Selected Titles (Complete list at
http://www.columbia.edu/cu/weai/weatherhead-studies.html)

The Age of Irreverence: A New History of Laughter in China, by Christopher Rea. University of California Press, 2015.

The Nature of Knowledge and the Knowledge of Nature in Early Modern Japan, by Federico Marcon. University of Chicago Press, 2015.

The Fascist Effect: Japan and Italy, 1915-1952, by Reto Hoffman. Cornell University Press, 2015.

The International Minimum: Creativity and Contradiction in Japan's Global Engagement, 1933-1964, by Jessamyn R. Abel. University of Hawai'i Press, 2015.

Empires of Coal: Fueling China's Entry Into the Modern World Order, 1860-1920, by Shellen Xiao Wu. Stanford University Press, 2015.

Casualties of History: Wounded Japanese Servicemen and the Second World War, by Lee K. Pennington. Cornell University Press, 2015.

City of Virtues: Nanjing in an Age of Utopian Visions, by Chuck Wooldridge. University of Washington Press, 2015.

The Proletarian Wave: Literature and Leftist Culture in Colonial Korea, 1910-1945, by Sunyoung Park. Harvard University Asia Center, 2015.

Neither Donkey Nor Horse: Medicine in the Struggle Over China's Modernity, by Sean Hsiang-lin Lei. University of Chicago Press, 2014.

When the Future Disappears: The Modernist Imagination in Late Colonial Korea, by Janet Poole. Columbia University Press, 2014.

Bad Water: Nature, Pollution, and Politics in Japan, 1870-1950, by Robert Stolz. Duke University Press, 2014.

Rise of a Japanese Chinatown: Yokohama, 1894-1972, by Eric C. Han. Harvard University Asia Center, 2014.

Beyond the Metropolis: Second Cities and Modern Life in Interwar Japan, by Louise Young. University of California Press, 2013.

From Cultures of War to Cultures of Peace: War and Peace Museums in Japan, China, and South Korea, by Takashi Yoshida. MerwinAsia, 2013.

Imperial Eclipse: Japan's Strategic Thinking About Continental Asia Before August 1945, by Yukiko Koshiro. Cornell University Press, 2013.

The Nature of the Beasts: Empire and Exhibition at the Tokyo Imperial Zoo, by Ian J. Miller. University of California Press, 2013.

Public Properties: Museums in Imperial Japan, by Noriko Aso. Duke University Press, 2013.

Reconstructing Bodies: Biomedicine, Health, and Nation-Building in South Korea Since 1945, by John P. DiMoia. Stanford University Press, 2013.

Taming Tibet: Landscape Transformation and the Gift of Chinese Development, by Emily T. Yeh. Cornell University Press, 2013.

Tyranny of the Weak: North Korea and the World, 1950–1992, by Charles K. Armstrong. Cornell University Press, 2013.

The Art of Censorship in Postwar Japan, by Kirsten Cather. University of Hawai'i Press, 2012.

Asia for the Asians: China in the Lives of Five Meiji Japanese, by Paula Harrell. MerwinAsia, 2012.

Lin Shu, Inc.: Translation and the Making of Modern Chinese Culture, by Michael Gibbs Hill. Oxford University Press, 2012.

Occupying Power: Sex Workers and Servicemen in Postwar Japan, by Sarah Kovner. Stanford University Press, 2012.

Redacted: The Archives of Censorship in Postwar Japan, by Jonathan E. Abel. University of California Press, 2012.

Empire of Dogs: Canines, Japan, and the Making of the Modern Imperial World, by Aaron Herald Skabelund. Cornell University Press, 2011.

Planning for Empire: Reform Bureaucrats and the Japanese Wartime State, by Janis Mimura. Cornell University Press, 2011.

Realms of Literacy: Early Japan and the History of Writing, by David Lurie. Harvard University Asia Center, 2011.

Russo-Japanese Relations, 1905–17: From Enemies to Allies, by Peter Berton. Routledge, 2011.

Behind the Gate: Inventing Students in Beijing, by Fabio Lanza. Columbia University Press, 2010.

Imperial Japan at Its Zenith: The Wartime Celebration of the Empire's 2,600th Anniversary, by Kenneth J. Ruoff. Cornell University Press, 2010.